KEVIN QUIRK

# Not Now, Honey, I'm Watching the Game

*What to Do*
*When Sports Come*
*Between You and Your Mate*

FIRESIDE BOOKS
Simon & Schuster Inc.

FIRESIDE
Rockefeller Center
1230 Avenue of the Americas
New York, NY 10020

FIRESIDE and colophon are registered trademarks
of Simon & Schuster Inc.

Designed by Kathryn Parise

Manufactured in the United States of America

1   3   5   7   9   10   8   6   4   2

LIBRARY OF CONGRESS CATALOGING-IN-PUBLICATION DATA
Quirk, Kevin.
Not now, honey, I'm watching the game / Kevin Quirk.
p.   cm.
Includes bibliographical references (p.     ) and index.
1. Sports spectators—United States—Family relationships.
2. Sports spectators—United States—Psychology.   3. Compulsive
behavior—United States.   I. Title.
GV715.Q57   1997
362.2—dc21                    97-19429   CIP
ISBN 0-684-83447-2

# AUTHOR'S NOTE

For twenty-five years, I was a "sportsaholic." I lived for sports, first as a passionate sports fan and then as a professional sportswriter. By most sports-lover standards, I had it pretty good. Growing up near Boston, I was standing in Fenway Park when Carlton Fisk's twelfth-inning home run ended Game Six of the 1975 World Series between the Red Sox and Cincinnati—what some still call the greatest World Series game ever played. As a sportswriter for the *Charlotte Observer* in 1982, I chronicled the early basketball career of Michael Jordan. Sports consumed my days and nights, my energy and attention, my thoughts and feelings.

But about ten years ago, I sensed that something was missing in my life, and I set out to discover what it was. I left sports behind completely. Looking back at my years absorbed in sports, I began to recognize how sports-watching functioned as an addiction and held me back in life. Looking further, I understood how "sports-aholism" impacted my first marriage, which ended in divorce. Today, many discoveries later, I counsel men and women who are grappling with major life transitions, and I teach classes on the differences between men and women and how we can better relate to one another.

Knowing that sports today exert an even greater influence on the lives of individual sports fans and our entire culture, I decided to check in on the sports world I left behind. A year ago, I launched a national survey of sportsaholics and the women who love them. I've heard from hundreds of men, women, and couples eager to share their experiences and attitudes toward sports. From the start, it became clear that "sportsaholism" triggered the most problems in the realm of male-female relationships, and that those old jokes about "football widows" weren't so funny anymore —especially to women.

So this book addresses what to do when sports come between you and your mate. It offers new ideas and new directions for couples struggling with the role of spectator sports in their relationships. Along the way, it explores how and why men get hooked on sports, and describes how sportsaholism looks as it's acted out in living rooms, family rooms, and bedrooms from Seattle to Miami. The insights, exercises, and teachings are as useful to individual men and women as they are to couples.

Throughout the book, I draw upon real-life examples of men and women who participated in the national survey. I have changed their first names to protect their confidentiality, but all other references to them—including age, hometown, job, marital status, and all their stories about living with sports—are true and unaltered.

A note about sports metaphors: Now ten years into my "recovery" from sportsaholism, I have, of course, flushed all sports talk out of my system (well, almost all). However, in the interest of the sportsaholics among us, I will call upon a sports metaphor in this book about as often as a good knuckleball pitcher sprinkles in a fastball. Bear with me. You may not even notice them anymore by the time we hit the seventh-inning stretch!

*Kevin Quirk*
*Charlottesville, Virginia*
*September 1997*

# ACKNOWLEDGMENTS

The vision for this book emerged from my year of personal and spiritual exploration at the former Institute in Culture and Creation Spirituality in Oakland, California. I appreciate my fellow students and journey-takers for reminding me of the power and value of sharing our stories. Special thanks to Matthew Fox for modeling how to challenge entrenched beliefs, and to Jim Conlon for teaching what it means to be a cultural worker.

Many friends, teachers, and colleagues at the Omega Institute in Rhineback, New York, provided invaluable support, encouragement, and guidance. Jacquelyn Small's 1995 class "Coming Alive with Meaning and Purpose" was especially inspiring in recognizing the potential for this project. Chicago Bulls coach Phil Jackson graciously permitted me to invite members of his Omega class "Beyond Basketball" to join in my national survey. Linda Woznicki opened her little black book and shared the names of all those many sportsaholic candidates she knew. Elizabeth Lesser helped plant seeds for this book years ago, and welcomed me back to the writer's world where I would bring it to fruition. Omega's staff has been consistently supportive.

Barbara Branagan lent solid marketing advice when I needed a bridge back to my media roots. Joan Goldstein of Conscious Singles Connection helped me broaden my vision and urged me to go for it with courage and conviction. Si Lewis offered wisdom and cheerful support.

Conducting a national study of the habits and passions of sports fans requires a great deal of assistance and cooperation, and I was blessed with plenty of both. In the academic community, Lawrence Wenner and Walter Gantz generously shared the findings of their own studies into TV sports and relationships. Michael Messner and Daniel Wann pointed me toward their useful research and told me about their own experiences and perspectives in the sports world. Dr. Richard Lister, Arnie Scher, and Pat Fitzgerald shared professional insights regarding addictions, sports, and relationships.

ABC, CBS, NBC, ESPN, Fox, DIRECTV, Primestar, TBS, and WGN were all part of my television lineup of critical research aides. League officials in the NFL, NBA, and Major League Baseball all cooperated when asked for specific information, and many individual pro teams spent time gathering comparison numbers of TV schedules and contracts through the years. Administrators at many universities also helped, particularly Rena Vicini at Kentucky. Team Licensing Business and Collegiate Licensing Co. helped me track the growth of sports merchandise. Dave Lang, Rick Scott, Rich Bonn, and Ron Barr were instrumental in painting the picture of sports-talk radio.

I gleaned evidence of the impact of sports on the culture from Lieberman Research, Inc. Numerous booster club and fan club members responded to my requests for survey volunteers themselves, and led me toward other possible candidates. Sports-loving internet users also pitched in.

As a former professional journalist, I am especially grateful for all the newspapers, magazines, and radio stations that publicized my national survey of sportsaholism and made it possible for readers and listeners to contact me to join in. A special wave of the championship banner goes to *Dallas Cowboys Weekly* and *Nebraska Sports America* for opening the door to the loyal and enthusiastic followers of the Cowboys and Cornhuskers.

Penny Fleming, producer of ABC's *20/20*, demonstrated keen insight into the impact of sports and relationships in bringing this story to national TV, prompting me to make new discoveries about myself and the book along the way. I am indebted to the following brave couples for appearing with me to tell their marital stories: Kathy and Michael Lewis, Bill and Jean Zeman; and Stacy and

Dan Schochler. Thanks also to all the other couples who were willing to wait in the on-deck circle for that TV segment.

Closer to home in Charlottesville, Jim Barns and Sharon Petro helped with contacts and research tips. Mary Mapel, Leslie Middleton, Pat Punch, and Karen Milnick were among many friends offering support, encouragement, inspiration, and treasured listening. From the beginning, Daniel Mapel understood this project better than almost any man could and provided valuable feedback in reading early versions of the manuscript.

Jim Hornfischer proved a bold and prophetic agent and was totally dedicated to the cause, even when he was fantasizing of playing first base for the Red Sox. I am especially appreciative of the work of two gifted editors. Laureen Connelly Rowland contributed enthusiasm, vision, and insight to the project, and Sarah Baker was an enjoyable partner in the co-creation of many of the final pieces.

And Krista was there for it all. She literally helped lay the foundation for the writing of the book and was a source of loving support throughout. A writer of matters relating to sports couldn't ask for a more loyal rooter.

*To the women and men who boldly told their sports stories
through the national survey of sportsaholism.
You are our teachers.*

# CONTENTS

## PART THREE
## Men in Hiding: The Safe Haven of Sports

## PART FOUR
## Mapping Out a New Game Plan

# Introduction

On Super Bowl Sunday 1996, our phone began ringing in the early morning, hours before the Dallas-Pittsburgh kickoff. The volume of calls tapered off as the game began. Then, as the Cowboys finished off their championship business, the floodgates opened. The deluge lasted past the TV-orchestrated celebrations and didn't let up until after midnight, long after Krista and I had begun trying to get some sleep.

No, I'm not a bookie. Nor were we hosting the neighborhood's hot Super Bowl party. Those weren't my former sports buddies eager to share their expert opinions on how the Steelers could have pulled it off. Nor were they Krista's women friends calling to commiserate over another seemingly endless Super Bowl day and night. But if you guessed that, you're getting warmer.

My phone line was buzzing with response to my national survey of "sportsaholism." Men who love sports wanted to test themselves to see if they would be classified as "sportsaholics." Most of the women who called *knew* they were living with a sportsaholic, and on that day above any other they wanted to do something—*anything*—about it. I heard the urgency in their voices. In the background, I detected the blaring of a TV, loud male voices, and here and there a baby crying. As I played back a few of these calls, I could hear a woman's own sobs punctuating the message, which included her name, address, and phone number.

Over the next two weeks, I mailed off more than a hundred copies of my "Sportsaholism Questionnaire" to men (or women)

1

who wondered if they were prime sportsaholic candidates. I sent out as many copies of the "Women Who Know a Sportsaholic" Survey to those women in a current or past relationship with a passionate sports fan. From Boston to San Francisco, sports fans were drawn to take the questionnaire to assess their unique sports habits.

By answering the questions, a respondent could begin to explore whether he was really a sportsaholic—that is, someone who lives life *through* sports or *for* sports. If he determined that he was a sportsaholic, he then would wonder: Just how much pride do I take in my sportsaholic identity? Do I wear it as a badge of honor and display it to my friends and family along with my official Dallas Cowboys jersey, Dallas Cowboys jacket, Dallas Cowboys cap, Dallas Cowboys belt buckle, Dallas Cowboys socks?

Or, after completing the questionnaire, he might figure that he couldn't possibly be a sportsaholic. He may believe that he's not nearly as bad as he imagines a "true" sportsaholic must be— a guy who knows the answer to every sports-trivia question, competes in three Fantasy-Baseball Leagues, listens to sports-talk radio, and watches four games at once. After all, he may say to himself, the most *I* ever watch is two games at once—and only during basketball playoffs.

Relieved, he may very well take this passing of the test as cause to celebrate, an opportunity to pop open his Yankees' World Series highlights video or sit down for one of those gloriously slow mornings of back-to-back showings of ESPN's *SportsCenter.* Now, if anyone in his life still has a problem with his sports habits, then it's just *their* problem.

But that's not how the women calling me that day saw the picture. Through the Women Who Know a Sportsaholic Survey, they made it quite clear that the men in their lives were sportsaholics, and though it was obviously *his* problem, it made *her* feel angry, frustrated, resentful, confused, and alienated. For these women, Super Bowl Sunday represented the culmination of five grueling months, a full season enduring life with him wedged solidly behind the great wall of football.

She hardly saw him on the other side of that wall, what with Sunday tripleheaders, Monday-night games that lingered past midnight, and that full month of playoffs that begin around Christmas (you remember, America's once-favorite holiday, pre–Super Bowl XX or so). And when she did catch a glimpse of him, she didn't much like what she saw: the man in her life intently focused, emotionally expressive, utterly involved, totally alive, deeply caring, wildly passionate, and displaying every other sign of a rich and rewarding intimate relationship . . . *but not with her!*

If only he would give me *half* the time, attention, and energy he devotes to sports, she reasoned, we could be so much happier. Why, she wondered, do men get so hooked on sports in the first place? Why would any man rush home to spend most of his free time tuning in to his beloved sports teams and tuning out the people, events, and drama in his own life? More important, she worried, was she doomed to run a distant second to sports forever?

Many women taking the survey complained of being stuck in a home where sports dictated all family planning (that is to say, the few plans they were able to make as a couple or family that didn't conflict with a big game). Sports also dominated any serious conversation around the house at any time of year, any season of the sports calendar.

Not every woman who called was down on sports. Some argued that a woman can love sports just as passionately as any man. Other women told of becoming recent converts, scoring big points with their sportsaholics by playing the willing sports pupil. "He taught me how to keep score in baseball, and I learned enough about basketball to enjoy watching that on TV sometimes," she might say. "I still don't get football, but I'm working on it." But those who reported peace and harmony over sports often added a disclaimer: "I'm probably not like most of the women in your survey . . ." All things considered, they'd be right.

From the kickoff of the survey at the start of the '95 football season, women rushed to it as an opportunity to vent their feelings about men and sports. A composite comment might read: "It's about time someone took this seriously! Yes, he really is addicted to sports, and while he's eating, breathing, and dreaming about how the Cowboys can build a greater dynasty, I'm sitting here wondering how we can build any real intimacy. I can't get through to him. When I bring up how I feel, he gets defensive or angry, tells me to leave him alone and deal with my own problems. I just wish he could understand what this sports habit looks like from my side."

I'm a man, but I understand such frustrations. As a former sportswriter for the *Charlotte Observer* and correspondent for *Sports Illustrated*, I've witnessed the sports world from locker room to living room. In our culture, there's no doubt that sports have taken on an exalted status, and in questioning the merits of sports you may feel that you don't have a leg to stand on. Sports saturate TV coverage on weekends and most weeknights. They dominate space in major newspapers such as *USA Today*. They infiltrate everyday language at work, in politics, and in most social gatherings.

And though the number of women sports fans may be growing, it's still very much a man's world. A man's right. In the eyes of many, to be a man is to love sports.

Men grow up learning to play sports and to watch sports, and over the years the watching usually overtakes the playing. Organized sports weed out all but the elite few Michael Jordans and Jerry Rices, so the rest of us become fans who follow them. Millions of sports lovers continue playing basketball at the Y, softball in the city recreation league, or golf into their thirties, forties, and beyond. But those are just hobbies. Watching sports can become a job. And many take this job very seriously, fully encouraged by the powerful sports media.

So almost any time a woman dares ask why, or deigns to suggest that her husband's sports devotion just might be interfering with their marriage, she gets tackled for a loss. It's just what men do, she hears in response. It's in their genes. It's the way their fathers were, even in those prehistoric days before ESPN and satellite dishes. Take it or leave it. Love 'em or leave 'em. And many women do leave.

When women who question the dominance of sports are mentioned at all in our society, it's usually as the butt of a bad joke about being a football widow (or the baseball or basketball equivalent). One common joke recycled now and then goes like this:

*She* says, "You love football more than you love me." *He* says, "Yeah, but I love you more than I love baseball."

Like many jokes that encourage us to laugh away problems, this one is dead-on in many households today, although the second part requires updating. While football remains the number-one spectator sport among men, basketball has replaced baseball as the second choice. So how does a woman fare when pitted against her man's current number-two sport? Best not to ask during the NBA Finals, especially if Michael Jordan's playing.

Even women's groups offer little support for women in a sports-aholic household. Organizations such as NOW focus their sports-related energy on equal rights and funding for women to *play* organized sports in schools and universities. Occasionally, women's groups speak out against the many incidents reported in the media of male athletes charged with rape and physical abuse of women. Those are real problems, worthy of everyone's attention. But so are the equally real problems, concerns, and baffling questions of women living with a sportsaholic.

More and more, women are burdened by such questions as: Why can't I ever schedule a wedding, party, vacation, or simple family outing without consulting his sports calendar? How can we carry on a simple dinner conversation with two or more males in the house without the subject turning to sports after the first few minutes? How can I share my deepest feelings with him when he's still angry and depressed about the game—not only the one that just ended, but that playoff game his team lost a month ago? How can I engage him in planning our future when the furthest he can see is the start of football season next month? Do I even have a future with him—and if not with him, are there *any* guys out there who are not obsessed with sports?

For too long, women have found these kinds of questions almost too painful to ask. Who's going to listen, anyway? they wonder. In frustration, they're sometimes tempted to conclude that they should just go on and accept how it is with sports and men in America. But those burning questions persist and fester. To hide forever what you know to be true is seldom possible, especially in matters of the heart.

Finally given a forum to express their true feelings about men and sports, women across the country responded enthusiastically to my survey. For the most part, they faithfully answered all questions in great detail and often colorful images. Many added lengthy notes, comments, and letters. Whether a husband or boyfriend, a boss, a father, brother, or son (or all of the above), some man's sports addiction inspired these women to share their stories with passion, conviction—and often great relief. You'll hear many of their stories in the following pages. And, whether you're a woman or a man, I'll bet you see yourself in at least some, if not many of these stories.

## Finding Signs of Hope

If you believe that men don't have a clue about how addicted they've become to sports and how much their addiction impacts their relationships, you may be surprised to see some evidence to the contrary. Here's a sneak preview:

One fine spring weekday afternoon, when sports addictions are fed only by such things as all-sports-talk radio, I was giving an interview about sportsaholism . . . on all-sports-talk radio. The station was WTEM in Washington, D.C., which goes by the promotional nickname "The Team." (Most sports-talk radio stations market themselves with similar sports nicknames—"The Fan" for WFAN in New York, "The Ticket" for KTCK in Dallas.)

When I enter the territory of sports-talk radio with my message about sports addiction, I come prepared for heated denials, or at least some good-natured kidding. So what happened on that WTEM show caught me off guard. As callers phoned in to respond to my comments, the conversations began something like this:

*"Hi, I'm David and I'm a sportsaholic. Let me tell you how sports have messed up my relationship."*

Five or six callers in a row introduced themselves this way, mimicking the well-known introductions common to AA meetings. They spoke of sports-triggered divorces, family reunions missed because of a Redskins game, and supposedly romantic vacations with detours to new sports sites. Often these guys would swear that the story really related to a "good friend" who had gone through two divorces that "could have been caused by sports." Perhaps they really were talking about their friends, but I couldn't help comparing this to someone first approaching AA or another twelve-step program for assistance. It's common to tell a story about a problem "a friend has." The friend usually turns out to be the person calling for help.

These few brave men also talked about compromises they had made for the women in their lives. Maybe he skipped the second NFL game one Sunday afternoon to go to the mall with her. Perhaps he went to bed three straight nights without hearing the results from the West Coast games, not knowing their impact on his Fantasy-League baseball team. One man even reported making the supreme sacrifice: no basic cable TV, which means no ESPN!

Right there on all-sports-talk radio, an exciting dialogue had begun. Men were actually admitting that their sports obsessions sabotaged their relationships with women. And they weren't even blaming women for the problem. Instead, these men were willing to look at their own sports habits, listen to the input of women, and seek out the best possible choices in a spirit of balance and fairness.

All across the country, dozens of other radio interviews, newspaper articles, and magazine accounts of my survey inspired similar conversations about sportsaholism. ABC-TV's *20/20* program devoted a full segment to "TV Sports Junkies," focusing on the findings of my national survey. The dialogue is spreading. Women are talking about their frustrations in living with a sportsaholic. Men are revealing all the fascinating details of their sports habits and passions, offering an inside look at what often stands as their most intimate relationship in life.

Couples in the survey have explored their feelings, attitudes, and opinions about how sports impact their lives and their relationships together. Many found that simply by taking the survey, they opened lines of communication that had been shut for months of sports Sundays and seasons of discontent. Women have admitted their surprise when, upon reading their survey answers to their husband or boyfriend, he suddenly sacrificed an important game to spend time with her! ("She scared me," he often explains.) Other couples have discovered just how wide a gender gap they have over sports—including widely conflicting reports from the same household of just how many hours each week he spends with sports.

This book gives you the opportunity to join in, to talk about and explore men's addiction to sports and what it's doing to relationships today. If you're a woman aching to figure out why men get hooked on sports and what to do with the sportsaholic in your life, you'll likely hear yourself in many women's stories. Others may present a totally different perspective that may challenge your beliefs about sportsaholism, or provide a glimmer of hope for change. You'll also hear dozens of men's voices that may anger you, annoy you, amuse you, or even give you insight and inspiration.

If you're a man, you'll take the challenge and decide for yourself how sportsaholism may be affecting *your* life. You'll get to check out how you compare with other sports fans. You'll hear how other men feel about their sports devotion. And yes, you'll also get an earful from women about how they see you.

If you're a couple reading this book together, congratulations! You have taken a bold first step toward improving your communication and enhancing your relationship. You'll have much to discuss from the findings of the survey and the folks like you featured in the ensuing chapters, and I can assure you that this will lead you toward a clearer understanding of your own feelings, beliefs, and attitudes. And whether you step on this playing field as a couple united in sports or divided as sports lover and sports avoider—or somewhere in between—the experience is bound to be a lot of fun!

As you enter the national dialogue on sports and relationships, you will have the opportunity to take the questionnaires for yourselves. The Sportsaholism Questionnaire and the Women Who Know a Sportsaholic Survey appear in Chapter 2. I'll guide you through them, and we'll discuss what your answers may mean for you. I'll share some of my own experiences with sports, including a long-ago Super Bowl Sunday spat with my ex-wife that triggered marital counseling and ultimately our divorce.

If you believe you already understand the full picture of sports in your household and want some ideas about what to *do* about sportsaholism in your relationship, you'll find several exercises for you to follow individually and as a couple in what will become your Sportsaholism Recovery Playbook. These activities will offer you many new insights, approaches, and directions.

Men, don't be alarmed—I'm not out to scramble anyone's satellite dish. I never recommend that anyone go cold turkey from sports. Unlike alcoholism or chemical dependency, sportsaholism does not require you to abstain from sports forever to make healthy changes. Rather, these discussions and exercises can help you map out your own revised game plan—one that allows you to continue enjoying the drama and excitement of sports, while creating winning relationships and a more fulfilling life outside of sports.

With sportsaholism, there may be scant few answers we all can agree on, no surefire solution to the differences between women and men regarding sports. Every person and every couple's situation is different, and only you know what changes may be right for you. Think of this exploration into sportsaholism as a process of discovery, and open your mind to where your personal discoveries take you.

## PART ONE

# The Makings of a Sportsaholic

# ONE

# Sports Glut USA!

*What we're creating here is a network for sports junkies.*
—ESPN vice president Scott Rasmussen
(*Sports Illustrated,* July 23, 1979)

It's autumn in America. A Sunday afternoon. Good weather, maybe the last nice weekend day before it begins to turn cold and gray.

She wants to get outdoors and enjoy it together with him. Go for a walk. Eat a picnic lunch in the park. Take a drive to see the bright colors and beautiful scenery. Maybe stop for dinner on the way home.

He's got a different idea. The Redskins are playing the Raiders in the early football game, and right after that the Cowboys and 49ers meet in the big showdown. The bright, sunny weather? Not a problem, he'll just close the drapes to cut off any glare on the screen. Food? There's time for a quick pizza before the evening's World Series game starts.

Between innings, he'll be checking in on the Sunday-night football game on cable. And when the games are over, he'll want to catch up on all the highlights of the day on *SportsCenter* or one of those all-sports-news networks. For him, this would be a day well spent.

The picture doesn't change much after the weekend sports-o-rama. The new week kicks off with *Monday Night Football*. Tuesday night the World Series resumes. When the series ends, pro basketball arrives to keep his weeknights lively. Come Saturday, college football blankets the day and night. Sunday, it's back to the NFL, which maintains its firm grip right on through to the Super Bowl in late January.

Will February snap him out of his sports trance? Not likely. The winter of basketball and hockey peaks with the NCAA basketball tournament, known in offices everywhere as March Madness. April ushers in the new baseball season. In May, the NBA playoffs arrive, with every game on TV, and the finals linger until late June. And on and on it goes.

We're living in Sports Glut USA, and there's no escaping it. In the last twenty-five years we've entered an era of saturation in which a sports fan almost can't help getting hooked. We've unwittingly created a society of sportsaholics, fans who live their lives *for* sports or *through* sports. They're hooked on the vicarious pleasures of spectator sports, and they're having too much fun riding the emotional roller coaster of sports fandom to think about coming down.

Too much sports? No way, a man who loves sports would contend. He could handle at least another month or two of football, and why can't they sprinkle in an NFL game every night of the week? There's no such thing as too much sports excitement and drama, he reasons. And how would he get through the week without some big game to anticipate?

He calls sports the water of life—he could die without them but he can never drown. He craves each new season and suffers withdrawal when it ends. He watches sports, talks sports, thinks sports, dreams sports. He cultivates a rich and full relationship with his favorite team.

But if you're a woman in a relationship with a sportsaholic, you may find yourself cringing at the force of Sports Glut USA. You may be asking: Why can't we ever do anything fun together on the weekend anymore? How can I compete against all these twenty-four-hour sports channels? Why do even the commercials mock real life, with Keith Jackson doing the play-by-play of a wedding? Why does the sports year seem to get longer and longer, with each season dragging into weeks of playoffs and championships? When can I get to know this guy in my house without having to share him with John Madden, Bob Costas, and Chris Berman?

You watch how intense men get watching sports and call it strange, even pathetic. You can't imagine how they could get so worked up over a game. You can *never* get his attention during the game, and you can hardly ever find a time when there isn't *some* game on. You call sports a waste, an excuse for men to avoid real life—and you!

So you hide the remote, you argue, you compromise, you keep searching for something else to do, or maybe you watch a little with him. Maybe you fantasize of some new law that would ban sports from TV. But then you remember, *there's more!* There's much more to this glut than the steady bombardment of TV sports. Everywhere we turn, we see the signs of a sports world bulging out on all sides.

All-sports-talk radio has emerged as one of the fastest-growing formats of the industry. Sports magazines are flourishing. Sports bars dazzle the senses with games on wall-to-wall rows of huge screens. Fantasy leagues have evolved from an obscure outlet for statistic-obsessed baseball followers to a popular all-sports immersion. The internet serves up instant sports news, live play-by-play accounts, and fan-club link-ups. Sports computer games have become as sophisticated as the games on the field. Authentic team apparel is for sale everywhere and worn almost every day, not only in our homes but in our offices and schools (dress codes permitting).

What was once a tiny subculture has become a dominant force in our mainstream culture. Sports are bigger in every way. The money is bigger. The hype is bigger. TV coverage is bigger. The advertising push for sports merchandise is bigger. Even business and politics have been overrun by sports talk. Whether a true sportsaholic, casual fan, or frustrated sideline observer of all this hoopla over sports, one can hardly go through a single day without feeling its pervasive influence.

Are you old enough to remember the simpler days, when the baseball *Game of the Week* on Saturday afternoons stood as one brief diversion from an otherwise enriching life, full of things like reading and enjoying the outdoors? Long gone, even before ESPN showed us the way.

The spectator-sports craze is having an unprecedented growth, which, despite an influx of women fans, remains dominated by a solid male majority. For every big-time college and pro sports team with its roster of ten to fifty players, there may be millions of fans watching them play. According to a 1991 national survey conducted by Lieberman Research, Inc., in New York, and commissioned by *Sports Illustrated*, 30 percent of all Americans say they are *very* interested in sports. Another 43 percent of those polled said they were at least *fairly* interested in sports. That's 73 percent of the population who call themselves sports fans to at least some degree!

But other than exuberant TV-sports advertisers and happy sports retailers, who pays much attention to the life of the sports fan? Even the emerging academic field of the sociology of sports seldom delves into a fan's world. Sports fans outnumber players by millions, but they don't get any press, except during a baseball strike or when that twelve-year-old boy leaned over the wall to catch a fly ball at Yankee Stadium and influenced the outcome of a playoff game. While the media tells us all about the impact of big money on players and owners, it offers little insight into what this sports boom has triggered in the living rooms and bedrooms across America.

Well, now we're going into those living rooms—*your* living rooms. In the next chapter, you'll have the chance to take the Sportsaholism Questionnaire and its companion Women Who Know a Sportsaholic Survey to explore the sports world's personal impact on *your* life and relationship. Before you do that, let's pause to look more closely at the sports smorgasbord that hooks a sportsaholic and frustrates the woman in his life.

I know, you get the picture already. Sports are EVERYWHERE! Every year we find more games, more teams, more drama. But you might find some developments you missed, or others whose full impact hasn't yet hit your home but could be coming soon. The first step in changing anything is understanding it. To understand sportsaholism, we need to go back, back, back to the origins of Sports Glut USA. First stop . . .

## ESPN

When it began in 1979, we all laughed. Sure, men loved sports. They might watch a game on a weekend afternoon, but rarely both Saturday and Sunday on the same weekend. They'd tune in on Monday night, but only during football season. They might check in on their hometown baseball or basketball team on a weekday evening, and settle in for the World Series in October.

But seven days a week, twenty-four hours a day of sports? What could a network possibly find to fill up all that airtime? There are only so many sports and so many teams to go around, we reasoned, and then you're stuck with repeats of box lacrosse. And this *SportsCenter,* a half-hour program devoted exclusively to *sports* news? What are they trying to tell us—that sports deserve the same attention as *World News Tonight?*

ESPN would be dead in six months, we predicted. TV sports already seemed to be reaching its saturation point, and what kind of wife would stand for her husband watching sports at two A.M., anyway? No, there just couldn't be that many sports addicts to make something like this fly, could there?

There could. And they did.

Here we are almost twenty years later, and ESPN is still going and going . . . and still showing sports twenty-four hours per day, 168 hours per week, every week of the year. Propelled forward by the dramatic expansion of cable access, ESPN now reaches more than seventy million households, some 70 percent of all homes with televisions. Women looking to name the chief culprit for today's sports onslaught have learned one safe motto:

*Blame it on ESPN!*

The wonder is, ESPN helped fashion a life built around TV sports not with box lacrosse but with ever-expanding doses of meat-and-potato sports like football, basketball, and baseball. Sprinkle in some hockey, a bit of golf and tennis, add regular doses of sports news, highlights, and commentary, and a sports-aholic's head is constantly buzzing with all the sights and sounds of sports around the clock.

Not enough real sports to go around, indeed! With only occasional fill-ins of unconventional events like the Extreme Games, ESPN has not only earned a major place in the evolution of sportsaholism in America, it grew up and had babies. In 1993, we witnessed the birth of ESPN2, another twenty-four-hours-a-day sports network offering more games, more sports, more highlights. And the latest creation . . .

## ESPNEWS

This network's 1996 debut was followed closely by the launching of CNN/SI, the offspring of a union between CNN and *Sports Illustrated*. Each devotes its full twenty-four hours of daily programming to sports news. It made sense, at least to network officials, that if CNN's Headline News succeeded as an all-news operation, then all-sports-news networks would soar.

After all, millions of men regard sports news as the *real* news of the world. For years, they've treated ESPN's *SportsCenter* as their equivalent of NBC's *Nightly News,* ABC's *Nightline,* and CBS's *This Morning* rolled into one. They turn to *SportsCenter* last thing before bed to catch every highlight of every game that day, then flip it on as they awake to see what happened in the late games on the West Coast. But would fans really go for sports news all day and all night? In Sports Glut USA, few would dare to predict failure for all-sports news or for sports-dominated . . .

### Digital Satellite Systems

Primestar and DIRECTV are the main players so far, and while neither offers sports *exclusively,* you might have thought as much from their marketing strategy. "The appeal of sports has gone beyond the die-hard sports fan and become a social thing," says

Bob Marsocci, DIRECTV's senior manager for public relations. "It's something we seek to capitalize on."

So both Primestar and DIRECTV stacked their hundred-or-more-cable-channels lineup with plenty of heavy hitters among the leading sports offerings, including the ESPN family, TBS and TNT from Turner Broadcasting, and such off-the-bench talent as The Golf Channel. They also tossed in several movie channels and other standard cable fare, but they're clearly targeting sports-aholics, especially with such new twists as . . .

## Out-of-Market Games

After consuming all the pro and major-college sports on the regular commercial networks and primary-cable outlets, there's still more if you want it. For $159 per season (beyond your fees for basic cable service) you can buy NFL Sunday Ticket. This taps you into the live broadcasts of pro football games in other cities, beyond the Sunday offerings on the networks, which are restricted by tight league rules.

So if you live in Washington but grew up in Detroit, you can select the Detroit–Green Bay game instead of the local Redskins–Saints telecast. Or if you simply can't get enough football via traditional channels, you can spend Sunday doing the satellite surf in your personal four-TV sports control room. Similar expanded offerings are available in baseball and basketball. Out-of-market games are a big hit in sports bars, but NFL officials are banking on individual fans choosing this pay-per-season option for their own homes. They're optimistic because of . . .

## NFL Ratings

We all know that football is America's most-watched sport, but by how many? The audience for Super Bowl XXX in January 1996 was 135 million people. The Super Bowl, though, has become more of a national holiday than a mere football game. One study during a typical Sunday-Monday period in November found that

113 million people watched at least part of an NFL game, according to Joe Ferreira, NFL director of broadcasting research. That's on top of the 800,000 to 900,000 attending NFL games each weekend in person. Pro football is as much a part of American life as pizza and beer.

Of course, if you're counted among those 113 million, it doesn't mean you're watching every minute of every game. With longer pregame and postgame shows and the Sunday-night game, football Sundays now run from late morning to late night. How much football to watch? When will that last game finally end? Why do we have to watch the highlights at night when we already saw them in late afternoon? Questions, decisions, compromises, arguments. They're part of our Sunday cultural heritage of the '90s, replacing discussions of the morning sermon, walks through the woods, and family dinners.

Sunday's tripleheader does include a courtesy dinner break before the night game, but most football families don't expect to tackle any subject beyond the makings of the latest 49ers' fourth-quarter rally. Football Sundays tax every coping strategy employed by women, who may hit their limit by halftime of the first game. And just when the sportsaholic household has begun to recover from the Sunday football marathon, here comes the old familiar . . .

## Monday Night Football

Though the birth of ESPN in 1979 clearly intensified the explosion of TV sports, the dawn of *Monday Night Football* set off the initial fireworks nine years earlier. Sports invaded prime time, a move previously considered foolhardy. During the 1960s, the reasoning was that sports were fine for the weekend, especially since the dominant male viewership draws advertisers for beer, cars, shaving products, insurance, etc. But prime time? That was the domain of sitcoms and variety shows. On Monday night, network executives reasoned, viewers prefer *Laugh-In*. And, they figured, women would never stand for football on a weeknight.

Back to the '90s. As we close in on three decades of *Monday*

*Night Football,* the tardy rates at work and school on Tuesday morning stand among many enduring symbols of this entrenched ritual. When *Monday Night Football* became an instant smash in 1970, word quickly spread that when it came to sports programming, any time was fair game. In '71, the World Series featured its first night games, and by '85 the entire World Series was shifted to prime-time telecasts. And thus ended an October tradition of boys sneaking radios into school to hear the daytime games.

The influence of TV on sports and sports on TV once stirred great debates. Now, it's all taken for granted. We recognize that sports created ESPN, that TV saved the NFL in the '60s, that TV pumps millions into university budgets for the rights to college football and basketball, that the needs of TV dictate game starting times, interleague matchups, and those long TV timeouts. TV sports even pried open the door to a fourth major network in the form of . . .

## Fox Network

When Fox became a seven-day programming network in 1993, it drew titters with bold suggestions that it could compete with the big three: NBC, CBS, and ABC. Then Fox bought a slice of NFL football on Sunday. As football commentator John Madden might say, "That Fox just rushed right in there through that hole and, boom! Before you know it, they've got themselves a real network." Soon, pro hockey and even Major League Baseball followed, with the 1996 World Series lined up not on CBS, NBC, or ABC, but Fox.

Fox couldn't stop the slide of baseball's TV ratings, a dip attributed not only to baseball strikes but also to football's dominance and pro basketball's surge of interest. But maybe baseball's own TV saturation had something to do with it. Baseball on Saturday was once a weekly treat, like going to the ice-cream stand for a hot-fudge sundae on a hot July evening. Today, many baseball fans have had their fill by the end of June, what with ESPN's Sunday-night baseball and Wednesday-night doubleheaders. And fans can see their local baseball team any old time, thanks to . . .

## Regional Sports Cable

This new twist snuck up on us during the '80s, providing an easy excuse to curl up with your hometown baseball team summer night after summer night. Let's say you live in Cleveland and love the Indians. In the '96 season, commercial TV outlet WUAB telecast seventy games, not nearly enough for a true fan. SportsChannel Ohio, to the rescue! This regional cable outlet covered sixty-five more Indians games, giving hungry fans the vast majority of their games on TV. New York Yankees followers were blessed with the opportunity to see *every* Yankees game on some TV outlet, from April through the '96 World Series championship in October.

In Sports Glut USA, we simply expect most of our own team's games and any major national event to be televised. And we're seldom disappointed. In pro basketball, SportsChannel Chicago's involvement helped ensure that every game of the Chicago Bulls' record-setting, 1995–96 season made the tube. In the NBA play-offs, every game of *every* series is televised on some national network—a far cry from the early 1980s, when the NBA championship series was shown on tape delay after the eleven-P.M. news. It's not your imagination. There are more pro sports events on TV: yearly, weekly, daily. And there are lots more college sports, thanks to . . .

## ESPN (College Style)

College football used to be strictly a Saturday tradition, but ESPN has nudged into Thursdays. College football might have spread to Sundays long ago, except that would have meant infringing on NFL turf. Even in TV sports, some traditions are still sacred. Major-college powers were once limited to a handful of network telecasts each season to give more schools a chance to be seen (and profit). Now, every Notre Dame football game turns up on some TV network. College-football Saturdays now last as long as NFL Sundays, from noon to late night.

In college basketball, CBS brings us every game of March Madness, with live updates beaming viewers to two or three sites at once. With ESPN's two hundred telecasts per season adding to other national and regional networks, wall-to-wall weekend coverage and weeknight doubleheaders are routine. Ratings dropped a few notches in the '90s, leading critics to wonder if fans have gone bug-eyed over Boise State at midnight. Will that mean fewer telecasts? Dream on, frustrated women. And even when he's not watching a college or pro game, a sportsaholic can stick close to his Michigan Wolverines or Buffalo Bills by turning to . . .

## Sports-Talk Radio

When your team is not playing but your thoughts and feelings are still fixated on them, here's the perfect outlet. Through sports-talk radio, you can share the joys and sorrows of your beloved hometown team with your fellow fans. Individual sports-talk shows have been around for decades, but WFAN in New York broke new ground in 1987 when it became the first essentially all-sports-talk radio station. More than a hundred other stations have joined the all-sports-talk movement, and dozens more offer large chunks of sports-talk programming.

Sports-talk-radio executives have more than touchdowns on their minds. Like many speculators of Sports Glut USA, they're thinking money. "The format is ideal for advertisers targeting males twenty-five to fifty-four," says Rich Bonn, vice president of programming for One-On-One Sports Network. "Advertisers aren't wasting a dime—not many kids or old folks, very few women."

As a sportsaholic, you're not listening for the stereo ads. You want to talk about the Cowboys' latest trade rumors on KTCK in Dallas or the Indians' pennant chances on WKNR in Cleveland. Or you call WFAN to tell the Jets about the coach they need to hire. You can take sports-talk radio with you almost anywhere, and with headphones you can conceal from your mate this extra time with your team. But you can't hide your love and allegiance when you wear it on your sleeve (and everywhere else) through your growing collection of . . .

## Sports Merchandise

*Team Licensing Business* magazine, which follows the business of sports merchandise in major pro and college sports, reported that sports merchandise rang up about $12 billion in retail sales worldwide in 1995. How fast is the business of sports stuff growing? NBA retail sales in the U.S. rose from $173 million in 1987 to $2.6 billion in '95. Now you never have to worry about a Christmas or birthday idea for the sportsaholic on your gift list. Don't expect any bargains, though. *The Indiana Pacers Home Court Gift Shop* '96 catalog lists jerseys for $40 and jackets starting at $100, though you can snag a Pacers dog leash for under $16.

Fans of any team can count on such official merchandise as: wristbands, ties, glasses, mugs, clocks, rugs, blankets, lamps, watches, key chains, pennants, towels, telephones, pins, lapels, pompons, cards, balls, plaques, flags, stools, stationery, license plates, videos, stuffed animals, wastebaskets, calendars, yearbooks, chairs, shower curtains, and ponytail-holders. When old stadiums get torn down, fans even buy the seats and put them in their patios.

Decades ago, we looked upon such "souvenirs" as frivolous. We just collected baseball cards, which were like gold to us long before they became worth thousands as "collectibles." If you have a son today, you know that a Penny Hardaway jersey is considered a necessity, and possession of a Los Angeles Raiders jacket has been known to incite gang wars. Adults feel their own peer pressure. To be a Nebraska football fan and dare to enter Memorial Stadium dressed in anything but official red team clothing would be uncivilized. Wearing team colors helps fans feel part of their favorite team. Now you can even become owner of a team through . . .

## Fantasy Leagues

Far from a fantasy to participants, this is as close to the real thing as you can get without being George Steinbrenner. Fantasy Leagues first sprouted up in baseball, often referred to as Rotisserie Leagues. It was so much fun, the idea quickly spread to football and basketball, and just about any other sport that keeps vital statistics.

For those who haven't caught the Fantasy League wave, it works like this: A group of four or more fans form a league, and each owner names his team. One funeral director named his team Digger's Deadbeats. Just before the start of the real baseball season, owners plunk down an entry fee of $50 or so and gather for a player draft. They go around the tension-packed room picking the twenty-five or thirty players from major-league baseball rosters who perform for their Fantasy League owners through actual statistics in selected categories in batting and pitching. The owner with the highest point total becomes Fantasy-League champion, as wives and girlfriends endure his late-night trade talks on the phone and his mornings devouring box scores.

With Fantasy Leagues, a sportsaholic need never sit out a sports season just because he doesn't like the sport. A football fan who doesn't much care for basketball may be lured into a Fantasy Basketball League by his football buddies. Suddenly, he's an expert on Reggie Miller's jump shot. As a Fantasy-League owner, you have a stake in every game. The woman in your life may be bewildered by your sudden interest in the eleven-P.M. Pittsburgh–San Diego telecast, but when the Pirates pitcher and three Padres hitters play for you, you're invested.

## The New Technology

Many longtime sportsaholics still swear by those old sports games with cards and dice, but technology marches on. While watching the '96 Nebraska-Florida national football championship at a sports bar (research purposes only!), I stumbled upon a live interactive computer game that engaged you in the real game on TV. Before each play, you could predict what Nebraska or Florida would do with the ball: a fullback run up the middle, a short pass to the tight end, etc. Other contestants enter their predictions, and after the play you're instantly awarded points based on the accuracy of your prediction. As I marveled at this latest wizardry at vicarious sports involvement, I felt like George Bush taking in his first grocery-store price scanner.

What will sports technology come up with next? How about SportsTrax, a portable beeper that can give you a complete update of all the current scores in about fifteen seconds? It attaches to your belt buckle, so you can carry it with you when you're out to dinner with your wife—and presumably taking a break from sports. And when you agree to take the family on a Florida vacation, keep this in mind—the ESPN Club at Disney World offers a sports bar with TV monitors in the restrooms, so you don't have to miss the game action when you need to take a personal timeout. Of course, if you're living with a sportsaholic, you're likely to know all about the popular vacation plan of a . . .

## Sports Road Trip

Baseball parks and football stadiums are like shrines to a sports fan, and a vacation designed to take in games in five ballparks in five cities is heaven. It's a bit like taking a national map of sports sites and playing connect-the-dots. Under this plan, a sports fan from Iowa might blaze a trail east, weaving in stops at Camden Yards in Baltimore, Yankee Stadium in New York, the Baseball Hall of Fame in Cooperstown, and Pittsburgh's Three Rivers Stadium on the way home. Sportsaholics brag about how many parks they've seen and keep updated lists of the ones still to visit. If you're a woman along on these trips, you may dream of that California vacation where you don't have to leave the coast just to hop a freeway to Dodgers Stadium.

## What to Do?

In frustration, it's easy to blame the makers of Sports Glut USA for getting men hooked. Bringing in new waves of TV games and this other sports stuff is like spiking cigarettes with extra nicotine, you might say. And once they're hooked on sports, sportsaholics may find it unthinkable ever to give it up. But what if this sports bombardment never happened? Would men be content to relate to sports as a distant cousin rather than the love of their life? Is there any way to go back to those simpler days, when a boy listened to Red Barber on the radio while doing his homework and used his imagination to visualize his heroes?

Or have sports fans always wanted more and more sports, more and more often, with team owners and network bosses scurrying to keep up? That's how Ron Barr looks at it. His late-night syndicated sports-talk radio show, *Sports Byline USA,* started small, but with its expansion to three hundred outlets, Barr sees himself as the Ted Koppel of sports. "There is," says Barr, "an insatiable appetite for sports in this country."

It's like the debate about violence on TV. Are we more violent today because of the prevalence of violence on TV, or is there more violence on TV because we're a violent society and that's what we want to see? Probably some of both are true. And with sports, no protest groups are banging down the doors to ESPN demanding they balance football and basketball with reruns of *Leave It to Beaver.* Sports are fun, exciting, dramatic . . . and they're not going anywhere. Sports Glut USA has a firm grip on our society. Love it, tolerate it, or hate it—it's not changing.

But *you* can make changes in your relationship to this sports smorgasbord, if you choose. That's what we'll be looking at in the next chapters, beginning with the Sportsaholism Questionnaire and the Women Who Know a Sportsaholic Survey in Chapter 2.

Now you can answer questions about your place in the sports world. You can take what you learn from the questionnaires and compare it to the stories of others like you in the pages that follow, as we explore sportsaholism and its impact on life and relationships. As we proceed, you'll also be keeping a Sportsaholism Recovery Playbook, with exercises that will give you ideas and inspiration to help you take on a new or revised role in the sports world.

A final word about change: For some of you, your only change after taking the questionnaire and reading the exercises may be to understand the full brunt of sports in your daily life a bit better, nod your head, and go on about your sports business. If that's right for you, great. Or maybe you'll be able to talk about the influence of sports on your life more openly with friends, spouse, or family. That's fine, too.

And if you're looking for bigger changes, now's the time to begin. As a woman, reading about the rise of Sports Glut USA may have left you even more frustrated with sports and the men who get swept away by them. You want more than ever to learn how to deal with it in your relationship. Perhaps you're a couple noticing that the issues emerging in this chapter are creeping into your relationship more often these days. Or maybe these problems have been gnawing at you for years and you just feel stuck.

Take out your pens or pencils and prepare to take a very different kind of sports quiz.

# Two

# Is He a Sportsaholic?

*My wife thinks I'm a sportsaholic, but I don't believe that
I am. I guess it's all in the definition.*
—Ned, an advertising manager from Huntsburg, Ohio

So are you a sportsaholic? Is someone in your life a sportsaholic?
Let's find out. A few points before you begin:

## 1. Scores

You won't get any here. This isn't one of those multiple-choice
quizzes where you rate yourself somewhere on a scale of one-to-
five on every question, then add up your total points to see which
predetermined category fits you. The last thing a sportsaholic
needs is another score! And if the survey did result in a score and
rating, *some* sportsaholics might be tempted to rig it. Let's say a
score of 80 qualifies you as a serious sportsaholic, and you don't
want to end up with that label. You'd find a way for your final
score to come in at, say, 79.

Then you might leap from your seat, imagining the score
flashed on the scoreboard as you announce: "Yesss! I beat the test.
I'm not that bad. I'm only a *moderate* sportsaholic, so no one can
complain about what I do. It all came down to the final question,
and I nailed it—a three-pointer from midcourt!"

Other respondents in a score-oriented test might adopt the

opposite strategy of going for the highest possible score. Sports get the competitive juices flowing, even for fans who love to compete with one another in expertise and degree of fandom. One respondent to my survey, who considered himself the biggest fan of the University of Michigan, told me about the day he was challenged in that distinction by a fellow Wolverines fan in a bar.

The two contestants studied each other's clothing to see who had the most complete Michigan wardrobe. Jersey, pants, jacket, belt buckle, socks—they appeared to be headed for a Wolverines draw. For the tiebreaker, they went to the next layer: The challenger was wearing regular white boxers, but my survey respondent proudly revealed his official gold-and-white Michigan Wolverines undershorts. Victory!

With a number-rated test, you might want to rack up a score that goes off the charts and proclaim yourself "America's Biggest Sportsaholic," or the "Woman Who Put Up with the Worst Sportsaholic." You can still give yourself those titles, or any other ranking or category of your own choosing. But the evaluations come from you. Those scored tests can be a lot of fun and may even teach us something, but I know from my own experience they're usually forgotten five minutes later. It's sort of like eating Chinese food. As a vehicle for discovery, I hope these questionnaires will stick with you for a while—at least until the newspaper's sports section arrives with tomorrow's breakfast.

You'll find many of the questions fun to answer, like the one that asks you to describe how you'd live your life if you were a millionaire sports superstar. And for numbers-lovers, the tabulations from many of the individual questions in the national survey will be sprinkled throughout the chapters. Here's a sneak preview: One of the hottest races was the most disliked sportscaster, with Dick Vitale, Dan Dierdorf, and Brent Musburger contending. Who do you think won? You'll find out in Chapter 10.

## 2. Taking the questionnaire alone

I'm not one to suggest that you lock yourself in a quiet, secluded room or wing of your house with a DO NOT DISTURB sign on your door for an hour of quiet reflection. If that works for you, great. But if the best way for you to concentrate on the role of sports in your life or relationship is to fill this out at halftime of *Monday Night Football,* go for it! Or if the sight of your husband's Pittsburgh Steelers banners and posters on the nearest wall will most help you to focus on how his sports habits impact your relationship, that's where you should be.

### 3. Taking the questionnaires as a couple

Again, I urge you to fill in your answers in the most comfortable place for you both, wherever that is. But if you're a couple participating together, I would recommend that you avoid taking the questionnaires in the same room at the same time. Experience has shown that you may find yourself censoring your answers when you know he or she is watching. Also, you might feel compelled to blurt out your answers to your loved one as you write them down, in order to get the first word in on any potential argument. Or you may even fall victim to the warm fuzzies toward the guy across the room and forget the time he blew off your Valentine's Day dinner to watch the big basketball game.

So the man taking the Sportsaholism Questionnaire and the woman filling out the Women Who Know a Sportsaholic Survey should work in different places or at different times. You'll have ample opportunity later to make sure he or she knows exactly what you are feeling and writing. If you do insist on taking the surveys in the same location together, at least agree to refrain from making loud verbal comments or expressions while filling in your answers. Save that for later.

### 4. Sharing your answers

Whether you take the questionnaire alone or as a couple, you'll get more from the exercise by talking it over with someone later. Of course, couples participating together should *plan* to sit down together and share answers. (This time, a quiet place is a good idea.) Even if you believe he or she will be bothered by your responses, be brave and share them anyway. You might be surprised at the other person's receptivity. Also, while conflicts certainly may emerge through your different versions of the same story, don't be too surprised if some of your partner's answers paint you in a more favorable light than you might have expected. This is the kind of exercise that can bring all sorts of feelings and impressions to the surface, even favorable ones.

If you take the questionnaire alone but you're in a relationship where spectator sports are an issue, try sharing your answers with your spouse or partner even if they initially scoff at the idea. By relating your own experience and discoveries, you can often engage in constructive and helpful conversation with your mate. As a bonus, he or she may even decide to take the questionnaire.

If you're no longer in an active relationship where sports are a hot topic, you may find a friend willing and interested to act as your ear in reading your answers and listening to your views about sportsaholism. Your best friend or ally also may emerge from the stories of survey respondents in the following chapters. Hearing your feelings echoed in another person's voice, or relating someone else's perspective to your own experience, will remind you that sportsaholism is a major national phenomenon. We all have much to learn from one another.

### 5. Who's the fan in the house?

Living in Sports Glut USA has drawn more women into the sportsaholic fold. If you're one of them and you feel you're every bit the fan the most sports-possessed guy is, feel free to take the Sportsaholism Questionnaire. Likewise, if you're living with a man who doesn't like sports much and considers you the real sportsaholic in the household, it might be fun for him to take the women's survey. Some men in my survey did that. Just change the gender references around to fit your situation.

### 6. Time limits for the questionnaire

Allow yourself whatever time you need for the questionnaire. Sixty-four questions are a lot, but that's the number of teams that compete in the NCAA basketball tournament every March, and that was my favorite event. I couldn't help it. The women's survey (on page 37) has twenty-five questions to match the format of national college football and basketball polls and . . . You see, sportsaholism still surfaces in my life.

Give yourself some time to consider the more challenging questions before rushing to grab the first one-word answer that comes to mind. The more you put into it, the more you'll get out of it. Give yourself lots of room to laugh, snarl, remember, fantasize. Have fun with it!

## PLAY #1:
## THE SPORTSAHOLISM RECOVERY PLAYBOOK

As you take these questionnaires, you'll begin work in your Sportsaholism Recovery Playbook, the exercises we'll call upon to dig deeper into the picture of sports in your life and help you learn to map out new directions. I'm using the term *playbook* for these exercises because sports metaphors fit our discussion, and following these exercises is very much like devising and implementing a game plan.

If you find the term a bit gimmicky or a concession to sports fans, consider the advantage of using a "playbook" because any playbook is at least partly about "play," and all these exercises will work best if you approach them with a light spirit. That doesn't mean you should take them less than seriously, or that you should laugh away any of your legitimate concerns about sportsaholism. Far from it. For a woman, these exercises should help support your conviction that his sports habits are no laughing matter. The idea that sports can be addictive and worthy of a recovery plan is foreign to most sports lovers. A light touch will help everyone ease into the idea gradually. As a couple, sharing a few laughs amid your verbal jousting may release some of the self-consciousness about what you're doing.

So take out a blank notebook or journal and label it your Sportsaholism Recovery Playbook. Dress up the cover any way you like. You'll be turning to your playbook for new exercises several times throughout the reading of this book, so you want it to look attractive and welcoming. If you're a couple reading this book together, deciding what to put on your playbook cover is an early opportunity to compromise! Break in your playbook by writing your answers to the questionnaire below that best fits your situation. I'll meet you in Chapter 3.

## SPORTSAHOLISM QUESTIONNAIRE

1. If sportsaholism was defined as living life *through* sports or living life *for* sports, would you consider yourself a sportsaholic? Why or why not? _____

2. How many total hours per week do you spend playing sports, watching sports at games or on TV, listening to sports, reading about sports, talking about sports? _____

3. How do you feel about the amount of time and attention you devote to sports? _____

4. How do sports enhance the quality of your life? _____

5. How can sports hurt your life in any way? _____

6. How does your spouse, friend, or family feel about all your attention to sports? _____

7. How do they express their feelings about it to you? _____

8. Which team or teams do you most closely follow? _____

9. How do you act when you're watching your special team play? _____

10. How is this different from your everyday personality? _____

11. How do you feel after your team wins? _____

12. How do you express those feelings? _____

13. How do you feel when your team loses? _____

14. How long after the game do those feelings stick with you? _____

15. What else other than sports grips you with the same interest and passion? _____

16. When you watch a game, how often do you drink an alcoholic beverage? _____

17. How many beers or drinks might you have during a game? _____

18. When you watch a game that does not involve your favorite team, how often do you still pick one team to root for? _____

19. How involved do you get with this game, compared to games with your main team? _____

20. What sports souvenirs, clothing, and merchandise do you own? _____

21. How often do you dress in the colors and clothing of your favorite team?
_____

22. Who are your favorite players? _____

23. What are their abilities or qualities that you admire most? _____

24. If you were a millionaire sports superstar, how would you live your life?
_____

25. How do you feel about today's player salaries? _____

26. How many hours per week do you spend actively playing sports, and which ones do you play most often? _____

27. Rank in order your favorite spectator sports and why you like them. _____

28. If you have friends who do not follow sports at all, how difficult is it for you to enjoy their company? _____

29. What else other than sports can you talk about with as much enthusiasm?
_____

30. How often and how much do you bet on sports? _____

31. What Fantasy Leagues or Rotisserie Leagues do you participate in? _____

32. How much money do you spend per year as a sports fan? _____

33. How often do you get into arguments or debates over sports? _____

34. How often do you tune in to sports-talk radio? _____

35. How often do you imagine yourself as coach or manager of a real pro or college team? _____

36. How well do you think your team would do? _____

37. What fan clubs, booster clubs, or internet sports groups do you belong to?
_____

38. Think back to when you attended your first pro or college sporting event. Describe when and where it was, whom you went with, your most memorable impressions of the scene, the game, and your feelings that day: _____
_____

39. How often do you attend games today, and how does your present experience compare with that first time? _____

40. What are your favorite sports movies, and why? _____
_____

41. Who are your favorite TV sportscasters or sportswriters? _____
_____

42. What do you like most about them? _____

43. Who are your *least* favorite TV sportscasters or sportswriters? _____
_____

44. What really bothers you about them? _____

45. Remember back to the last time one of your favorite teams won a major championship. Which team was it, when, how did you feel when it happened, and how did you celebrate? _____
_____

46. How long did your good feelings from the championship affect your everyday mood? _____

47. Remember back to the last time one of your favorite teams lost a major playoff or championship game. Which team was it, when, and how was that for you? _____

48. What details of those big games can you still vividly recall? _____

49. How often do you watch ESPN's *SportsCenter* or other sports-news programs? _____

50. How often do you watch regular TV news? _____
_____

51. When you read a newspaper, how much time do you spend with the sports section? _____

52. How much time do you spend with the rest of the paper? _____
_____

53. How much easier is it for you to relate to a woman if she cares about sports and knows something about them? _____

54. How do women show their lack of sports knowledge? _____
_____

55. How do you feel when relating to a woman who doesn't get sports at all? _____

56. How do you react when someone you know laughs at you or kids you about your sports habits? _____

57. What organized sports did you play growing up? _____

58. What fantasies have you ever had of proposing or getting married at a sports site? _____

59. If you didn't spend so much time and energy as a sports fan, how might you spend it? _____

60. If you did spend less time with sports, what might you gain? _____

61. If you spent less time with sports, what would you lose? _____

62. How would you define sportsaholism? _____

63. How closely does this definition fit you? _____

64. How do you feel about completing this questionnaire? _____

**Note**—Take a moment to jot down any additional comments or a longer answer to any of these questions in your Sportsaholism Recovery Playbook.

## WOMEN WHO KNOW A SPORTSAHOLIC SURVEY

1. If you know a man who is (or could be) a sportsaholic, what is his relationship to you and how long have you known him? _____

2. How many total hours per week would you say he spends playing sports, watching sports at games or on TV, listening to sports, reading about sports, talking about sports? _____

3. How do you feel about the amount of time and attention he devotes to sports? _____

4. How do you express those feelings to him, and how often? _____

5. How does he respond to you when you bring up the subject of his sports habits? _____

6. How do sports affect your relationship with him? _____

7. How does he act when he's watching his favorite team play? _____
_____

8. How is this different from his everyday personality? _____
_____

9. Describe one experience when he got really carried away by a game, and how you responded: _____

10. How often do *you* watch sports on TV, and which sports? _____
_____

11. When you watch sports with him, what percentage of the time are you doing it for your own enjoyment, and what percentage of the time to join him in his world? _____

12. How knowledgeable are you about sports? _____
_____

13. How does he respond to you when you show interest in sports? _____
_____

14. When he watches a game alone, how do you spend your time? _____
_____

15. How much do you enjoy these activities? _____
_____

16. What special interest of yours do you regard with the same passion he has for sports? _____

17. What do you most like about your special interest? _____
_____

18. How does the man in your life regard your special interest, and how much does he share in it? _____

19. What sports do you actively play yourself, and how often? _____
_____

20. What was the role of sports in your family when you were growing up?
_____

21. What is your overall attitude toward spectator sports? _____
_____

22. Why do you think men love sports so much? _____
_____

23. If he spent less time with sports, how might that change your relationship with him? _____

24. What is the one way that you would most clearly see the difference? _____
_____

25. How do you feel about completing this survey? _____
_____

**Note**—Take a moment to jot down any additional comments or a longer answer to any of these questions in your Sportsaholism Recovery Playbook.

# THREE

# Putting On His Game Face

*When his team is winning, he gets loud, excited, giddy.*
*When his team is losing, he gets depressed, takes it as*
*a personal blow. Away from sports, he's usually quiet,*
*uninvolved, apathetic, and goes with the flow.*
—Andrea, wife of a sportsaholic in a small city in Michigan

So now you've taken the sportsaholic questionnaires and have had a chance to get down on paper some of your thoughts and feelings about the role sports play in your lives and relationship. Maybe some of what came out surprised you, or perhaps it just confirmed what you've long known.

Either way, you're probably wondering how you compare to others around the country who've already taken the survey. If you filled out the questionnaires together as a couple, you may be struck by just how well you know (or don't know) each other when it comes to your feelings toward sports, and the sticking points between you.

It's time to figure out what to do with this information, to see what it all means for you. We'll be checking into many of your answers to the key questions throughout the rest of the book. In Chapter 4, for example, we'll see how many men called themselves sportsaholics and look at some of their own definitions of sportsaholism. For now, let's begin with the questions that sparked the hottest responses in the national survey: **"How does a sports-**

aholic act when he's watching his favorite team play? How is this different from his everyday personality?"

If you're a woman living with a sportsaholic, you can probably identify with the image described by Andrea at the start of this chapter. When a man sits down to watch a game on TV, he often transforms as dramatically as Clark Kent when he steps into a phone booth. If you've just met your man recently and you've only seen him put on his Game Face once or twice, you may be as much in the dark as Lois Lane. If you've lived with him awhile, you've probably seen this metamorphosis so often that you can probably guess what sport he's watching, which of his teams is playing, and how they're doing in the game—just by listening to him closely from the next room.

Men are different when they watch sports. They can be different in a funny way, a wild way, an endearing way, or a scary way. Or all of those ways combined. What does that sports fan Game Face look like in your household? Take a moment to look over your answers to Questions #7–9 from the Women Who Know a Sportsaholic Survey. See how your descriptions compare to comments from other women in the national survey:

*With each play, he becomes more active, yelling at the TV over both good and bad plays, yelling to the coach about his decisions, yelling to his team about how it's doing. Outside of sports, he does not raise his voice.*

—BETSY FROM CARROLLTON, TEXAS

*Honestly, he's like an animal watching the game. Normally, he's funny and enjoyable to be with. Away from sports, he never yells nor is he argumentative.*

—LESLIE FROM COLUMBUS, OHIO

*When things are going well for his team, he is jubilant and loud. When they go bad, he gets louder and has been known to throw things like his hat or the newspaper. When watching regular TV shows, he often does other things at the same time like read the paper or talk on the phone. This could never happen while the New York Mets are on.*

—BARBARA FROM KEARNY, NEW JERSEY

*With the game on, he's loud, aggressive, angry. Otherwise, he's low-key, quiet—a guy everyone loves.*

—DEBBIE FROM LAS VEGAS, NEVADA

### Praying for the Super Bowl

As any sportsaholic will tell you, the deeper his devotion to his team and the more intense the drama of the game, the greater his emotional display. Listen to Penny's experience with her boyfriend, Reggie, a twenty-eight-year-old Pittsburgh fanatic who was watching the Steelers-Colts January '96 playoff game on TV at his home:

"During those final crucial plays, Reggie was on his knees praying for the Steelers to win. He's not a religious person, yet here he was *really* praying for the Steelers to win and go to the Super Bowl. When they won on the last play, he was in tears! This is a man I've never seen cry over anything, including when our relationship was in turmoil and I threatened to leave him. I can't imagine what it's like to feel more emotion toward a game than another human being."

It's only a game, right? Well, don't dare tell a man that. In fact, when the game is on, it's wise not to tell him much of anything. If he's like most sportsaholics, he won't hear you anyway. And if you've had arguments over his sports habits before, criticizing him in the heat of the action will certainly trigger another one. When a man is watching his team, he doesn't want to be bothered. His focus is intense, his purpose single-minded. It's as if he's wearing a giant sign on his head that reads: GAME ON, DO NOT DISTURB!

"Usually, he can't sit still for five minutes," says Linda, wife of a sportsaholic in Goshen, Indiana, "but he can sit still and watch an entire *day* of football."

Adds Sandra of her sportsaholic husband in Alexandria, Virginia: "He's totally oblivious to everything else, even his children screaming."

Ellen lives with a sportsaholic in Omaha, prime fan territory of college-football powerhouse Nebraska. She says that when her man is keyed in to his beloved Cornhuskers "the house could burn down and he'd never know it."

Sound familiar? Is your sportsaholic the yeller, the kind prone to volcanic eruptions? Or is he the pacer, the quiet type who disappears into a deep, meditative sports trance? While every sportsaholic's Game Face is his unique creation, I've found that most men generally fall into one of two sports-watching styles. Here's how I describe them, in sports-friendly images:

## Deion Dancer

Deion Sanders, referred to by fans and sports media only by his first name, plays football for the Dallas Cowboys. He's a defensive back, meaning that it's his job to follow the game's best pass receivers, stop them from getting the ball, and intercept some passes that come his way. By personality, he's extroverted, flashy, brash, cocky, and demonstrative. He talks trash to his opponent to take his focus off his game, and speaks in rich and provocative images to the media, making sure he's always noticed. He's also immensely talented, almost always able to back up his bravado. When he scores a touchdown or makes a great defensive play, he often struts around the field in stylish dance moves. He's inspiring to his teammates, helping first the San Francisco 49ers, then the archrival Cowboys to Super Bowl championships.

So as a fan type, a "Deion Dancer" is a fan who acts out all his emotions with colorful, imaginative flair. Far from being a couch potato, he's all over the room when the game's on. He paces, hops, struts, crawls, dives, and kneels. Sometimes he'll get right up in the face of his TV. He talks incessantly—to his friends if he watches with them, to the players on TV, to the coaches, to the refs. He shouts instructions to his team, confidently offering advice based on his supreme sports knowledge and eye for the right strategy. If his team's coach should ever call him up and ask him for his advice, he'd be ready with the winning move every time. He shouts his approval, and screams his criticism. When his team scores a touchdown or makes any big play, he high-fives anyone around, raises both arms straight in the air in the touchdown signal, and bellows a joyful refrain.

When his team wins, he celebrates all-out. Dancing and prancing. Lots of food and drink. Bragging and recounting. He tells all his friends (and family if they'll listen) exactly how "we" did it. He'll make outrageous claims about how great his team is and how pitiful their opponents looked. He'll buy more team clothing and merchandise for his home, and when he goes to the game in person, he may even paint his face in team colors. If his team loses, he'll pound his fist and curse, maybe even cry. He'll forget about dinner and maybe breakfast the next morning. He'll skill-fully zero in on the one play, one player, or one bad call that cost his team the game. And he'll identify the one change they must make to win the next time, fully certain that he knows best.

## Cool Cal

Cal Ripken plays baseball for the Baltimore Orioles. As a short-stop or third baseman, he fields ground balls, makes smooth and accurate throws, and positions himself expertly for every individual batter. Offensively, he's a consistently solid hitter with good power and a penchant for delivering in the clutch. In 1995, he achieved baseball and sports immortality by breaking Lou Gehrig's record for the most consecutive games played, standing as a model in baseball and much of society for discipline, dedication, reliability, and perseverance. By personality, he's quiet but intensely focused, unassuming, humble, unwavering in his commitment to his team and his responsibilities to himself and to the public as a professional athlete. He seldom acts excited, does little to call attention to himself, looks you square in the eye with a stoic but intent gaze. His teammates depend on him as a day-to-day example of how to play and how to act.

So as a fan type, a "Cool Cal" is a more introverted sports-watcher. If he's nervous or excited, he doesn't show it. He sits steady and silent in his favorite seat, chosen for its proper distance or sight line to the TV, and perhaps a superstitious reason that he's not apt to share with others. He prepares for each game the same way, studying all the newspaper articles about the opponent and the matchup. He knows all the statistics going back several years. He keeps his eye on the little things and is quick to praise one of his players for a solid performance in fundamentals. When the game's on, he's able to block out completely everything else around him. He is not to be disturbed, interrupted, or tempted to leave his post until the job is done.

When his team wins, he gratefully acknowledges it, but quietly. Perhaps he shakes his fist and utters one sincere "Yes!" or "All right!" When his team loses, he may hurt deeply inside, especially if it's a big game, but his expression will hardly change. If one of "his" players clearly cost the game, he will note it in his calculating mind but say nothing out loud. He will immediately begin planning and preparation for the next game. He will never, ever consider missing one of his team's games on TV, and never break his allegiance to them, regardless of their standing from season to season.

So which fan type is the sportsaholic in your life (or you), a Cool Cal or a Deion Dancer? Perhaps it's a combination of both. Let's spend a moment checking out how the Game Face of the sportsaholic in the house looks in the mirror. This is the next exercise for your Sportsaholism Recovery Playbook.

## PLAY #2:
## DEION DANCER OR COOL CAL?

In your playbook, write down which fan type most closely resembles you or the sportsaholic in your life. Write down specific episodes pertaining to this personality in its fullest form, like the day he screamed and pounded the floor for half an hour after the Chiefs lost the playoff game. It's OK to embellish the story a little. If you're a couple reading together, each of you should offer input into the playbook profile.

If you find that the sportsaholic in question is some of both fan types, note how the blend looks and which type dominates under different game conditions. If neither type clicks for you, pick your own Game Face model from another sports character or any celebrity.

FOR THE WOMEN:

As a woman, you can add your own separate playbook entry. When you approach your sportsaholic to tell him about his habits and how you feel about them, which type are you? Are you a demonstrative complainer about how sports come between you, or do you just glare at him to show your displeasure? And which approach stands the best chance of having any impact on him?

Take a few minutes to record any other thoughts or ideas that come up from this exercise. Remember, have fun with it. We'll get to the more sticky points later.

## Without Sports, He's Almost Normal

No matter which fan type you outlined for the sportsaholic under study, chances are that he doesn't act that way outside the sports viewing area. In my national survey, three-quarters of women respondents reported significant differences between how their men behaved with the game on and when it's off. That doesn't mean the other 25 percent acted blasé and uninvolved while sitting in their sports-watching chairs. Far from it. Many sportsaholics in this group also yelled, screamed, wept, banged on chairs, and tuned out everything around them. Only the women in their lives simply believed they acted that way *all* the time, with or without sports.

So do the guys get it? Do they recognize in themselves the same kinds of personality transformations that women see so vividly? Or do they block out their sports-induced behavior and honestly believe that the Deion Dancer or Cool Cal in them is either their typical, everyday, taking-out-the-garbage self, or a gross exaggeration of how they appear when they sit down to watch the Raiders?

In the national survey, two-thirds of all respondents to the Sportsaholism Questionnaire said that yes, they do act differently during a game from how they do in their day-to-day lives. So most guys do recognize that sports turn them into a different person. Let's sample some of the answers to Questions #9 and 10 from the Sportsaholism Questionnaire, and see how they compare with your sportsaholic's self-evaluation:

*With the game on, I'm usually nervous, on the edge of my seat, pacing, yelling, cheering, clapping. Day to day, I'm usually calm and mellow.*
> —PAUL, A DALLAS COWBOYS FAN IN WEST HENRIETTA,
> NEW YORK

*I'm intense, can't sit still, emotionally hyper over all aspects of the game, including the score, the officiating, the reaction of fans at the game. Without sports, I'm calm and reserved.*
> —ANDY, A VIRGINIA TECH AND WASHINGTON REDSKINS FAN
> IN WILLIAMSBURG, VIRGINIA

*If the Steelers win a big game, I'm happy. I yell, give high-fives and hugs to everyone around me. If they lose and it's a crushing loss I get an empty feeling in my stomach and feel angry and depressed for a month or two. I don't usually experience that kind of emotional roller coaster in other areas of my life.*
> —RICKY, A STEELERS FAN IN MORGANTOWN, WEST VIRGINIA

Steve, a Houston Oilers fan, says that when he's watching the game he gets so nervous that he can't sit still, so he stands on one leg. His friends call him Stork. Many men perform elaborate pregame rituals, which may include fasting for hours before the game, putting on the right team clothing, calling the same friend at the same time, or sitting in the same spot. Fans probably follow more superstitions than players, and they give themselves full credit or blame for their team's fate, based on how diligently they followed their routine.

And how does a sportsaholic act after the game ends? How does he celebrate when his team wins a big one? How does he respond when his guys blow it? Let's see how he explains his behavior through his answers to Questions #11–14 in the Sportsaholism Questionnaire, **"How do you feel after your team wins, and how do you express those feelings? How do you feel when your team loses, and how long after the game do those feelings stick with you?"**

Think about some of his intense reactions to the outcome of a game—what he did and how long the fallout lasted. When his team wins, does he let out shrieks of joy, high-five the dog, and immediately order more official team clothing? When his team loses, does he grumble, groan, launch into a tirade against the officials or his team's coach, tear the newspaper into shreds, and crawl into an angry, depressed shell for minutes, hours, days, or weeks?

I'm always baffled when I read or listen to commentators on gender issues proclaim that men are not nearly as emotional as women, due to some inherent physical and biological differences. In fact, some say that men are simply incapable of expressing themselves emotionally or that if they have the ability to experience and share emotions at all, it's buried so deep that it will only come out in occasional dribs and drabs.

Such gender theorists obviously never spent much time around sportsaholics in action. Men are every bit as capable of feeling their full range of human emotions and expressing them openly as women. And they do so readily and often . . . over sports. Whether men can access and express the same emotions *without* sports is a question we'll address in Part III. As a woman who knows a sportsaholic, you may have some strong opinions about that.

But first, consider your guy's (or your own) reactions to the outcome of a game with one of his teams. Think about which feelings come up most. Sadness? Anger? Joy? Frustration? You may have touched upon some of these feelings while doing Play #2 a few minutes ago, so here's some more outside data for you to use as a point of reference. In a quick check of survey answers to Question #11—**"How do you feel after your team wins?"**—we see that men show a wide range of emotions: exhilarated, elated, satisfied, proud, smug, giddy, joyful, excited, horny, relieved, generous, loving, patient.

On the flip side, in answer to Question #13—**"How do you feel after your team loses?"**—men responded: crushed, grumpy, sullen, testy, disappointed, heartbroken, angry, depressed, embarrassed, sick, sad, argumentative, frustrated, vengeful, dejected, aggravated, helpless, and a few more profane descriptions.

In a graduate psychology class several years ago, my classmates and I were asked to draw our "family box." Inside this box, we were to write down all the emotions that were generally permitted to be expressed in our family environment growing up, without fear of repercussion or ridicule. Outside the box, we placed the emotions that were not allowed or encouraged in our families. For example, in a family where everyone was supposed to put on a happy face no matter what, anger would be outside the box. Or elation might be outside the box, if you believed as a child that your parents would immediately bring you down to earth by telling you that life was going to be rough—that if you got too excited, something bad would surely come along to knock you down.

Similarly, any sportsaholic constructing a "sports emotion box" would find that just about every feeling he could think of would be placed *inside* his box. As a response to the intense excitement and drama of a big sporting event, anything goes. Put a group of men together watching an important game at a sports bar and you'll quickly see that no one will ever be criticized for acting out his feelings. You can yell, scream, cry, pound your fists on the table, or tear your napkin to shreds and chew on the pieces. The thrill of victory and the agony of defeat is not just a cliché among passionate sports fans. It's a very deep reality. During and after a close game for high stakes involving his favorite team, emotional extremes are commonplace.

Let's look next at answers to Question #12, **"How do you express those feelings after your team wins?"** In the national survey, men answered with some of the images we've already mentioned, such as high-fiving friends, shouting, jumping around, snapping their Pittsburgh Steelers Terrible Towels, etc. But male sportsaholics also like to take concrete action to celebrate their team's triumph.

If you're a Cleveland Indians fan and the Indians just clinched their divisional championship, you naturally want to talk about this achievement with all your friends and brag about "your" superiority to anyone who might root for some lesser team, like the Chicago White Sox. Women complain that after the game is long over, he's still incessantly talking about every last play, every detail, every member of his team, and what's going to happen to them in the next game, the next playoff series, the next season.

In the first day or two after a major win, a sportsaholic may also keep the good feelings alive by replaying the game via tape he made while watching it live, reading every newspaper account he can find, listening to his fellow fans relive the game on his local sports-talk radio program; buying more of his team's sports merchandise. He needs to prolong the moment, drink it in, consume it, and live it again.

## Streaking on a Frosty Nebraska Night

The bigger the win, the bigger the emotional display, so it stands to reason that championships naturally trigger the wildest outbursts in sportsaholics. The night the University of Nebraska won its first of two national college football titles of the '90s, Dave, a graduate student in the university's mechanical engineering program, was celebrating near the campus in Lincoln. His friend dared him to run around the block dressed in nothing but a Nebraska flag. As a former decathlon athlete and a fan in Cornhusker euphoria, Dave naturally said yes.

"We set up a little relay carrying the flag," he remembers. "When I got it, all the people in my neighborhood were out gawking from their balconies. The folks next door took a picture of me. I did have shoes on, but there was ice on the street and it was about zero degrees. I had a cold for a week."

Championship euphoria lasts weeks, months, even years. Those living with this condition pray only that no remedy is found, and even nonfans can get swept up in the fun. But what about passionate fans whose team loses the big one? How long do those painful emotions linger? Let's check your sportsaholic's answer to Question #14, **"How long after the game do those feelings stick with you?"**

Most likely, his first response is a qualifier: It depends on the game. For an average game, he might say he's out of his losing funk after thirty minutes, an hour tops. For a more important game that he believes his team should have won, it might be a day or two before he can let it go. During football season, the painful emotions could stick until the following Saturday or Sunday, when his Miami Dolphins get to play again and erase the bad memories. And what about the recovery period for a playoff defeat or championship loss? It could be a week, two weeks, a month, until the start of the next season, forever and a day.

Long-suffering Boston Red Sox fans tumbled into winter-long doldrums after watching their team blow the 1986 World Series against the New York Mets. Cowboys fans in my survey, still gloating months after their '96 Super Bowl triumph, wouldn't talk about their playoff loss to San Francisco the previous season. But the sting can last much longer than a year. An old-time Dodgers fan who took the survey said that you still can't bring up Bobby Thomson's home run that cost the Brooklyn Dodgers the National League pennant to the New York Giants . . . in 1951.

Sports followers love to tease their rival fans by bringing up those touchstone moments of their team's past. Chicago Cubs fans will forever wince at references to the September '69 collapse that opened the door for the Mets to become World Series champion. But the painful emotions are worst when the moment is still fresh. For evidence, let's check back in on Reggie, the otherwise nonreligious Pittsburgh Steelers fan who was described by his girlfriend, Penny, earlier in this chapter as "praying for the Steelers to get into the '96 Super Bowl." So when the Steelers lost that Super Bowl to Dallas, how did Reggie take it?

## The Ravings of a Losing Fan

During the two-week buildup to the Super Bowl, Reggie was in heaven. A waiter who refuses to work any shift when the Steelers are playing, Reggie's thoughts were Steelers this, Steelers that. He paid twenty dollars to get his fingernails painted in Steelers colors —not just the thumbs like some guys do, but all ten fingers. He bought another hundred dollars' worth of Steelers stuff. He grew a rough beard to look more like Pittsburgh quarterback Neil O'Donnell. He put two new Steelers Terrible Towels on his walls with his banners and pennants. On Super Bowl Sunday, he joined a big group of Steelers fans at a friend's house. That's when heaven dissolved.

"When the Steelers lost, I was disgusted," Reggie remembers. "I came home and ripped all the Steelers stuff off the walls. I took my fingernail polish off. I jumped in the shower and shaved off my beard. For a couple of weeks, I couldn't even look at a newspaper."

Clearly, Reggie wasn't much fun to be around. Fortunately for Penny, her job as a flight attendant occasionally gives her the chance to fly away from the rubble churned up by a sports catastrophe. But she knows that running away is not the best solution to their differences, and she tells Reggie her feelings about his sports behavior directly. When they argue about it, Penny admits that she sometimes resorts to one known way to strike fear into Reggie's soul. She threatens to rip up his coveted photos of him holding the authentic Stanley Cup won by his Pittsburgh Penguins a few years earlier.

"I first got to touch the Stanley Cup hours after they won it, when it was taken out at the airport where fans were celebrating the team's return home," explains Reggie. "Hockey players go their whole careers dying to get near the Stanley Cup, and there I was touching it! But that was nothing. Later, I was dating someone whose friend worked in the Penguins' office, and he let me borrow the Stanley Cup for a few minutes. I had eight photos taken with me and the Cup. I drank out of it, lay in bed with it. I was like a kid on Christmas getting his favorite toy."

Reggie's prized photos weathered the domestic storm. To keep peace, Penny frequently gathers up dozens of newspapers left behind in empty airplane seats and brings them home to Reggie, so he can enjoy the special treat of reading sports sections from far-off cities. And yes, she was the one who escorted him to the manicurist for that custom-designed, Steelers fingernail polishing.

When I talked with women in my survey about how their guy acted around sports, I often found them willing to accept his Game Face behavior as part of his personality. But they still got angry, frustrated, or just plain sad for two reasons. First, when he's busy acting out his Deion Dancer or Cool Cal, she's often doing all the household chores that must get done that weekend, or she's keeping up with their kids, whom he hardly notices until the commercials. Second, unless she chooses to sit down with him and put on her own Game Face (which more and more women are starting to do), she's simply not sharing his company for those coveted hours when they could be together.

And she misses him.

But here's the kicker. What she misses even more are signs of his Game Face behavior when she *does* get to spend time with him away from sports. OK, maybe not the extremes. As one woman told me, she loves gardening but doesn't feel she has to scream "SCORE!!" when a new bulb shoots up. And she doesn't need to see him pound his fist into a wall when they realize they picked the wrong wallpaper for the kitchen.

But his ability to get excited, to feel and express real joy and sorrow over the events of their day-to-day life together—that's what she wants. And she can't understand where it goes after the game. She yearns to feel a part of his vital life energy, to experience his desire to participate with heart and soul on the playing field of their relationship. If he can strive to become the Number-One fan of the Buffalo Bills, she reasons, why can't he focus the same commitment on being the Number-One fan of *me?* Instead of gearing up for the next game or rehashing the one just finished, why doesn't he want to learn more about what's happening in my work, with my life goals, my hopes for the future? Instead of asking me why I don't want to get into sports as much as he wants me to, why can't he spend time getting into what really interests me so we could share that together?

## A Timeout for the Male Readers

Let's table our discussion for just a moment. If you're a typical male sports fan, proud and pleased of your fandom, you may find yourself getting a bit impatient, annoyed, defensive, or just wondering where all this is going. You may be thinking or saying: What's the big deal? So what if I go a little crazy over a big game? I work hard all day. I need a release, someplace where I can let go. I'm not harming anyone. Sports are exciting. They get me pumped, give me something to look forward to, make me happy. How could anyone not feel totally excited when his team wins a big championship? How could you not feel angry and upset after they lose a big one? And even if I do act differently watching a game, I'm not like that every minute. I pay attention to her, too. We do things together. I don't watch sports every hour of every day.

If you hear your voice in any of these comments, be assured that I recognize truth in every point you make. I ought to. I used to say many of them myself in my days with sports, and what I haven't said myself I've heard dozens of other guys say.

I was a sportsaholic from the time I was nine years old, back when you had to work a lot harder to be a sportsaholic. I would begin each Sunday about eleven o'clock in the morning by shutting all the living room drapes tightly to make sure no glare of sunlight infiltrated my TV-watching sanctuary. Living near Boston, I'd start the day watching *Candlepin Bowling,* a uniquely New England phenomenon involving narrow pins and competition between ordinary-looking people. If it was September, I'd then watch the highlights show of Notre Dame's Saturday football game. Then I'd move on to perhaps a late-season Red Sox game, mixed with parts of the NFL doubleheader.

As I hit my teens, the exciting new technology of UHF television brought Bobby Orr and the Boston Bruins onto my TV screen every Sunday night, extending my sports day to a solid twelve hours. That would give me just about enough sports excitement and drama to get me through Monday morning's return to school.

I remained a passionate follower of Boston teams through high school and college at Boston University, in my Cool Cal style. I rejoiced in many of the great Celtics championship teams, and I suffered through all those Red Sox near-miss championship moments, including Bucky Dent's home run that sank the Red Sox in the '78 playoff loss to the Yankees.

I loved sports so much growing up that I decided I would make them my work, and I did. I was a sportswriter for twelve years, mostly with the *Charlotte Observer,* where I welcomed the opportunity to feed some of the nation's most passionate basketball fans plenty of what they hungered for. I still remember that freshman basketball player at North Carolina listed in the team's initial press guide for the season as *Mike* Jordan. Around the locker room and in the media, most people called him Mike; a few referred to him as Michael. My proper newspaper protocol told me that we should use one name or the other, so I asked him: What should we call you, Mike or Michael? "I don't care," he said. "Whatever you want." Well, I decided that he looked like a Michael, so I wrote that from now on we should all refer to this new basketball player as *Michael* Jordan. I guess the name stuck.

I don't spend much time in the sports world anymore, but I know the turf. And I know the people. I know fans because I've been one, and when I invite exploration about how sportsaholics act, I do so with understanding and respect. Rather than looking for ultimate right or wrong, I'm suggesting that you sift through pieces of your sports fandom and what it means in your individual life.

Your willingness to hang in with this game plan of discovery about sportsaholism ranks you in the upper echelon of devout sports fans in terms of curiosity, openness, and flexibility. We'll continue to take many of the points you may be wondering about (or want to debate) and zero in on them the rest of the way. In the next chapter, we're going to look at just how sports can become an addiction.

# FOUR

# Drama, the Drug of Sports

*I spend the majority of my time playing, watching, read-
ing, or thinking about sports. It's too much, but I can't
help it. I really believe it's an addiction. It's like a vicious
cycle, where one season ends and another begins.*
—Greg, a sportsaholic in Winston-Salem, North Carolina

OK, so you act a little crazy when you put on your Game Face and
watch your favorite team play. You devote a whole lot of time and
attention to sports, maybe more than you realized. And your wife
or girlfriend may get annoyed at you sometimes when you get
carried away with a big game or skip a family gathering. But can
*sports* really be an *addiction*?

If you're a man who really loves sports, you may find yourself
shaking your head at the idea. And even if someone can get
hooked on sports, you might argue, there's nothing wrong with
that.

The term "addiction" usually conjures up serious, dark, even
scary images: alcoholics ravaging their bodies while ruining their
work and family lives; drug addicts piling up huge debts and
turning to crime to support their habits, then suffering through
detox and withdrawal; long-term smokers coming to grips with
cancer or heart disease after years stuck on the nicotine habit.

Being a big sports fan is nothing like that, you may say. Sports
are about fun, enjoyment, excitement, and drama—not passing
out and forgetting what you did when you got drunk. They're

about camaraderie with friends and fellow fans—not crouching alone in the kitchen or bathroom to snort or shoot up. They're about kicking loose and letting off steam over a game— not endangering the lives of others by driving stoned on the highway.

Women who know sportsaholics have heard such arguments many times, and they may find it hard to launch a winning rebuttal. To guys who've surrounded themselves with sports most of their lives, this line of reasoning makes perfect sense. And there's even more to their case.

Sports are an outlet, a hobby, a treasured leisure activity, something to learn and become an expert on, something to look forward to, something to talk about, something to feel good about in a world that can often appear blasé or bleak. Sports provide a sense of history and continuity to life. In hearing of the death of Mickey Mantle, we can recall the first time we saw him hit a home run and reflect on our own path of life in the years since. Sports bring people together, not just two or three friends but large communities bound by a common sports following.

As a former twenty-five-year sportsaholic, I would suggest that being a sports fan today can be all of these things. *And* it can be addictive.

The drama of sports can hook you like a drug, one you may never want to give up. And while sportsaholism certainly doesn't ravage the body the way alcoholism or chemical dependency do, it can have negative life consequences that may include:

- messing up relationships
- consuming so much time and energy that you invest far less in work, family, and other life experiences
- experiencing emotions vicariously through your team's winning and losing, instead of with the people and events in your own life
- stifling career development and general life purpose, as you align yourself more with your team's goals and fate
- limiting you socially, cutting you off from anyone except other fans
- serving as a substitute for religion or spirituality

You may recognize one or more of these effects in your life, but still question sportsaholism. In our culture, we're often trained to see things in "black/white" or "either/or" terms. Men, especially, tend to place things in concrete categories. Being a sports fan feeds right into this thinking. When two teams play, one wins and the other loses. There's no gray area in between. So when the issue of sports addiction is raised, some men may naturally feel inclined to pin down the concrete definition that fits them:

- I'm addicted to sports and, though I should probably do something about it, I may not want to.
- I'm not addicted to sports so I've got nothing to worry about.

If you're inclined to follow such "either/or" thinking, consider putting it aside for a moment and trying on the concept of "both/and." In other words, give yourself the space to see how some behaviors can be both good *and* bad, right *and* wrong—depending on how and when you exercise the behavior, to what degree, and the importance it assumes in the total picture of your life. With this approach, you've got more maneuvering room to consider how sports can be fun, exciting, dramatic *and* hook you in ways that cause problems too serious to deny or laugh off.

This outlook may require you to think bigger, to allow more truths into your heart and mind. It may also lead you to a grander conclusion. Rather than seeing some sports fans as sportsaholics and some as nonsportsaholics, you might consider the possibility that I reached after surveying hundreds of Sportsaholism Questionnaires: Most men drawn to take this questionnaire are sportsaholics *to some degree!* To some degree, most passionate sports lovers probably engage in sports fandom in one or more ways that cause tension, conflict, or limitation in their lives.

So rather than trying to decide if you've gone completely over the edge as a sportsaholic, explore the addictive tendencies you've already identified and try to gauge the *degree* of your sportsaholism. Here's an exercise to help you do it. Turn to your Sportsaholism Recovery Playbook, and let's begin.

## PLAY #3:
## SPORTSAHOLISM CHECKLIST   THE SHORT FORM

Here's a quiz with yes or no answers! It can be taken by either the sportsaholic or the woman who knows one and makes her best judgment of the answers that fit him. This checklist is based on my own personal experiences and exploration, interviews with psychologists and addiction counselors, as well as books and guides about addiction and recovery by leaders in the field. If you think of another question you want to add on, go for it.

Remember, as well as answering yes or no, think about the *degree* to which the question may be true for you or the sportsaholic in your life. It's your (or his) degree of sportsaholism that will be your best guide in the weeks, months, and sports seasons ahead.

1. Do you get annoyed or angry when someone interrupts you while watching a game?
2. Do you get defensive when they question how much time you spend with sports?
3. Do you argue with them about how much time they spend doing something they like?
4. Do you prefer the drama and excitement of sports to intimacy with your partner?
5. Do you often say, "Just one more game," or, "As soon as I see the scores update"?
6. Do you feel cravings for the next big game when it's hours or even days away?
7. Do you get more worked up over the game than the daily ups and downs of your life?
8. Does your team's fate affect your mood for days, weeks, or months afterward?
9. Do you experience withdrawal when your favorite season ends?
10. Do you avoid people who don't like sports, or get bored by conversations that don't include sports?
11. Do you sacrifice sleep to see the late game or get the West Coast scores?
12. Do you wake up needing to check the latest sports scores before doing anything else?
13. Do you know sports statistics better than your budget, family birthdays and anniversaries?
14. Do you neglect household chores or your children to watch more sports?

15. Do you block out disturbing questions about your life with soothing thoughts of sports?
16. Do you daydream about sports when you're unhappy at work, rather than map out a new career?
17. Do you find trying to cut down on sports for someone you love doesn't work?
18. Do you sneak in sports time your spouse doesn't know about, or lie about how many hours you *really* devote to sports, even in the exercises in this book?
19. Do you say you could spend less time with sports but deep down not believe it?
20. Do you fear that life with less sports time would be boring, empty, and joyless?

If you answered a resounding "Yes!" to ten or more of these questions, then you know you're a sportsaholic. If you answered yes "to some degree" to at least five-to-ten of these questions, you're probably a sportsaholic *to some degree*. And even if you answered no to almost all the questions, there's something about your relationship with sports that doesn't sit right for you, or else you probably wouldn't have gotten this far. Rather than worrying about the definition of sportsaholism or whether the label fits you, just ask yourself if you see negative consequences from your sports habits. If you do, they're worth examining.

You probably noticed that many of the questions in this checklist are similar to the others you already answered in the Sportsaholism Questionnaire in Chapter 2. You may have found yourself answering them more easily or honestly this time. Sometimes the direct approach is what we, as men especially, really need to separate fact from fiction, or see what's in front of our nose. You may also not be very surprised by your answers. One way in which sportsaholism differs from other addictions is that you get started much younger, so you've been practicing much longer. You know the story of "sports and you" inside and out.

One research study conducted for the NFL revealed that 43 percent of serious pro football fans report that they were hooked on the game by age eight, according to Sara Levinson, president of NFL Properties. Many sportsaholics reveal that attending their first game at the age of six or seven ushered them into a sports world they've never left. And as they get older and take on the more mature ways of the world—especially marriage—they recognize that sportsaholism may affect them much more seriously than it did when they were twelve.

## Marriage Can't Match His Sports Passion

Greg, an auditor in Winston-Salem, North Carolina, is the sportsaholic whose words about his sports addiction opened this chapter. He follows the Atlanta Braves and New York Yankees in baseball, and Louisville and South Carolina in college sports. He's also taken an interest in the new pro teams a couple of hours down the highway in Charlotte, the NBA's Charlotte Hornets and the NFL's Carolina Panthers.

He estimates his sports time at twenty-five hours per week. He not only participates in Fantasy Leagues but runs them—two in the office and two more in his neighborhood. He watches *SportsCenter* or a comparable sports-news program every night. Regular news, he watches hardly ever. He has some sports clothes, but it's a modest collection by most sportsaholic standards. He gets emotional over his teams, especially South Carolina's frequent losses, which leave him feeling cheated, angry, frustrated, and depressed for days.

When dating a new woman in his life a few years ago, Greg found that he felt the same kind of interest and passion toward her that he did toward sports. He was interested in everything she liked. And although she was raised in a foreign country, she showed some interest in sports. But today, when asked what else in his life grips him with the same passion as sports, Greg answers, "Nothing," despite the fact that he's now married to that same woman he once felt as intensely about as he did about sports. What happened?

Greg explains: "We both travel for work, and when we're home, it's usually Saturday and Sunday. When are the biggest games? Saturday and Sunday. With sports, I just have to have them. I've been that way all my life. I do my best to cut down so we can have quality time, but our versions of cutting down are very different. Sometimes when I watch, she has work to do. Ideally, that would always be true. But sometimes she just gets real quiet, or she'll stomp upstairs thinking, What's the point in bringing it up again? When she does bring it up, I usually get defensive and tell her it's a big game. If I'm in a good mood, I'll tell her she's right, or sometimes I'll even go to the park with her.

"We tried to find something new to do together and decided on chess. But it turned into a competitive thing, like sports. I won a few times and she said, 'No way.' Last weekend we went out shopping together and there was a game on. I knew I'd get back for the end of it, but while we were out, she said she needed to go to another store for pants. I told her the store wasn't open on Saturday (I don't know, *maybe* it wasn't). I did get back for the end of the game, of course. Sometimes when I stay home and watch a game when we could have done something together, I feel really guilty. I tell myself I could have just caught the highlights, but I can't. It's that drama . . ."

## The Drug of Sports

Ah, the drama of sports. What else in life is so clear-cut? What else in life is so neatly arranged in segments that we can plan around? What else always ends with a definite conclusion, with a clear winner and loser every game and every season just one champion? Despite this tidiness, the buzz comes from never knowing exactly what's going to happen. Even with overwhelming favorites, upsets are always possible—or at least a hope to cling to. Sports happen live and they're packed with action, excitement, intensity. The games are brought to us on bigger-than-life screens, with sportscasters elevating every matchup and every play to monumental importance.

Where sports become an addiction, drama is the drug. It is the alcohol, the cocaine, the nicotine. It gives us the high and keeps us craving more. How do my Philadelphia Eagles stack up against the Cowboys? How will my San Francisco 49ers fare on the road at New England? Will my Denver Broncos ever get back to the Super Bowl before John Elway retires? When will my New York Mets get back to the World Series like the Yankees did in '96? How did my Boston Celtics lose another close one in the final seconds?

Drama lures us into following our teams and watching their games, and our investment in the outcome fuels our emotions. Like Reggie, the devoted Pittsburgh Steelers fan, we act a bit crazy during the game because of how badly we want our team to win. We put ourselves on the line, and as the big showdown approaches, we're more nervous than the players. If they win, we'll be ecstatic for weeks. If they lose, we'll be thrown into a fit of depression. *The drama on the field becomes the drama of our life.*

As a drug, the drama of sports is readily available in regular, hearty doses. That one big game between our Chicago Bears and those dreaded Vikings can provide us with dozens of intense highs and lows in a short three-hour sitting. Big plays, changing leads, dropped passes, key sacks, last-second field goals. Drama is sprinkled within every game, every season, every championship run. Just the start of spring training in March is enough to trigger a Cleveland Indians fan's desire to see how his team is shaping up, to wonder how they'll look in April and how they'll fare come October. The NBA draft revs up the drama for a New York Knicks follower long before the new season, because the right draft pick could bring his team that one missing championship ingredient.

A fan hooked on sports finds just as much drama within the individual matchups, rivalries, and competition. How will my man Shaquille O'Neal do against David Robinson? Who'll gain more passing yards, Dan Marino or Steve Young? Who's going to win the home-run race? It's all full of drama that makes us excited, anxious, proud, angry, jubilant, frustrated.

We cling to drama, the drug of sports, because it makes us feel alive. It gets us pumped up, juiced. It gets us high. And with overlapping seasons, we can get high any time we want. Baseball begins before basketball ends. Football begins before baseball reaches playoff time. Basketball and hockey start up while football is still in full swing. With the saturation of TV sports, we count on witnessing our own team's drama almost every game. Nationally, we expect to be fed the most dramatic events of every sport, every season. With so many games, we can adopt faraway teams like the Super Bowl champion Green Bay Packers or the Los Angeles Lakers, and we know we'll see them often enough in our home in Peoria to get just as hooked on their championship hopes.

Even when we tune in to a game where none of our favorite teams is playing, we can still tap into that never-ending supply of drama. All we have to do is pick someone to root for, and to a serious sports fan that's as natural as driving a car. While we may not get *quite* as emotionally invested as we do watching our New York Yankees, we'll still get a kick from the drama of that Baltimore-Detroit baseball game—especially if we're rooting for the Yankees-rival Orioles to lose. When a fan joins a group already watching a game in progress, he usually asks: Is it a good game? In other words, is the score close enough to promise an exciting finish that will give me a hearty dose of sports drama?

Sportsaholics say they enjoy sports for many reasons. They appreciate the skills, strength, grace, and agility of the athletes. They get into the strategy of baseball. They like basketball's fast pace. They get pumped up by the action and contact of football. But take any game in any sport and suddenly switch off the scoreboard at halftime, then announce that no score will be kept, no winner or loser determined. Watch how many people stick around to appreciate the athleticism and style! Without the competition between teams and players that creates real drama, no one would watch. We wouldn't be talking about sportsaholism.

The drama gets inside a sportsaholic's physical, mental, and psychological being. He sits riveted by the action, unable to get up for anything but the barest essentials. When the outcome's determined, he lingers in his euphoria or depression for hours, his emotions not simply worn on his sleeve but on his face and in his general attitude.

Clearly, drama is what hooks a sportsaholic, popular myths to the contrary:

*Sports Myth #1: Sports fans get so worked up over the games because they bet money on them.*

Gambling is a major societal addiction, and gambling addicts certainly gravitate to sports to place bets. But *gambling* is their addiction, not sports. A sportsaholic's addiction is the drama of sports and the emotions they naturally bring out, not wagering on the outcome.

In the Sportsaholism Questionnaire, Question #30 asked how often and how much respondents bet on sports. A full 40 percent of all survey respondents reported that they *never* bet on sports, and 23 percent more said their betting was limited to office pools, Fantasy-League entry fees, or a special one-dollar bet with a friend. Other respondents did sometimes bet on a game, but only a handful mentioned big bets of hundreds or thousands of dollars. As one sportsaholic put it, "I would never bet on games I watch. That would cheapen it for me."

*Sports Myth #2: All sports fans are alcoholics, or at least drink regularly when they watch a game.*

You know the image—wild and crazy fans huddled in sports bars, guzzling two beers for every touchdown. The myth is that men only watch sports as an excuse to get together with the guys and drink. Or, to watch sports and fully experience the flavor of it all, they need a few drinks under their belt and one always in hand—just to be in the right spirit, you know.

But in the national survey, the answers to Questions #16 and 17 about drinking habits while watching sports painted a different picture. It revealed that 38 percent of all respondents never drink alcohol. Not with the game, not away from the game, not *ever.* Some indicated that they had benefited from AA or other recovery programs. Another 33 percent of survey respondents called themselves occasional drinkers who never had more than one or two drinks during a game.

So alcohol and sports do not go together as commonly as peanut butter and jelly. Yes, many guys do drink with their buddies at

the game or in sports bars. Others do indeed pop open a six-pack
to keep them company for an afternoon of TV football at home
alone. But they're in the minority. Millions of other fans sit at
home watching sports holding nothing stronger than a diet soda.
They're addicted to what they're looking at.

*Sports Myth #3: Men's addiction to sports is just like women's addiction to soap operas.*

There is some similarity, especially as it relates to living life
vicariously through the characters involved. Many women (and
men) who love soaps develop intimate relationships with the people they watch on TV. And soap opera followers certainly experience emotional cravings, along with withdrawal if they miss an
episode of their favorite show.

But soaps offer melodrama, not drama. The interaction of the
characters is scripted, while sports are live. Soap plots are fiction,
sports are real. Soaps go weeks or even months without resolution
to even the simplest of questions, while sports reach a clear resolution with every game. Sports are more active and elicit a full range
of emotion, including joy and elation, feelings seldom experienced through soap operas that play on loneliness, rejection, anxiety, and depression. Sports hold a far more prominent place in
our culture, with all-sports TV networks and the dominance of
sports in our day-to-day conversations and in the language we all
hear.

Men try to use soap operas as a counterattack to women who
criticize them for their sports addictions. They figure that if they
can pin an equal addiction on women, they'll take less heat for
their sports indulgence. But their case simply doesn't hold up.
After all, in these days of all-sports-talk radio stations, how many
all-soap stations do you know?

*Sports Myth #4: Men get hooked on football because of the violence.*

Sure, some guys really light up when a defensive back smacks
into a receiver as he's about to catch a pass, or at the sight of a
quarterback getting buried by a fast-charging linebacker. But most
of the hitting at the line of scrimmage doesn't even get on camera.

Football's celebrated players are offensive stars who dazzle us with their passing, running, catching, leaping, and diving. We go for the guys who score points and give our team a chance to win, players like Jerry Rice, whose grace and skill make them very good at *avoiding* physical contact. Defensive players, even those who personify violence, are seldom mentioned in the same breath as Rice, Brett Favre, Steve Young, or Emmitt Smith.

Also, with football's regular season packed into just sixteen games, the natural drama of sports becomes intensified. Cut the baseball season to one game a week and sixteen games for the season and watch how exciting that game would suddenly become!

*Sports Myth #5: Watching sports is a great way for a man to relieve stress and tension.*

Excuse me, but how calm, relaxed, and worry-free does the sportsaholic you know look when the game's on? For most fans, watching sports *creates* stress. It's an adrenaline rush. It gets the juices flowing, churns up the emotions. For many men, it's almost like having an orgasm! The drama of sports jump-starts someone who's usually laid-back and apathetic, rather than slows down someone who's hyper and stressed. That's where the term "couch potato" becomes a distortion of reality. Some men get as much exercise watching a game as they get at the fitness club.

When men say that watching sports relieves stress for them, they probably mean that the game gives them an opportunity to forget about their own problems for a while. In that way, sports are an escape, or a panacea for real pain or depression in their own lives. When the game ends, however, those problems are still there.

## Aren't We All Addicted to Something?

Many sportsaholics know about other addictions from firsthand experience. Through the national survey, I heard from many recovering alcoholics and gambling addicts. A few admitted to similarities between their former addiction and their sports obsession. But others balked at the idea of one more "ism" and bemoaned a culture they call "addiction-happy." We're all addicted to something, they would argue: work, shopping, sex, TV, computers. We need fun and a diversion, and even if we are hooked on sports, at least it's the lesser of many evils.

Holly, an assistant farm manager in a small town in Nebraska, asked for a Sportsaholism Questionnaire with the full intention of giving it to her husband. She believed he fit the definition of a sportsaholic perfectly, but somehow she couldn't bring herself to hand him the survey to find out for himself. "He is a recovering alcoholic who has chosen not to drink. We have gone to more counseling than you'd care to hear about. So I know that if I asked him to fill this out, he'd not be pleased," Holly explains. "I think he gets too emotional over the wins and losses of the game. But if I mention it at all, he says, 'I don't need your lecture!' Because of his anger, I rarely bring it up. It's very frustrating."

But others familiar with addictions have willingly addressed the issue of sportsaholism. Arnie assists drunk drivers as a counselor in a California jail. He knows addictions from professional training, and he woke up to his own sportsaholism years ago after a sports-related neck injury prompted him to reassess his life priorities. Now he says he comes across many men whose lives have suffered from their sports obsession. He cautions male sports lovers whenever he can, inviting them to ask themselves: Do I actually prefer the excitement of a Michael Jordan dunk to the feelings I get from being with someone close to me?

"One guy told me that he was a big Oakland A's fan, and they were ruining his life because their constant losing kept him in a bad mood all the time," Arnie relates. "His wife said, 'Choose me or the A's.' He chose the A's."

Students in an introductory course on addictions at Old Dominion University filled out the Sportsaholism Questionnaires as part of a class lesson by instructor Pat Fitzgerald, who found the women students especially receptive. They can see how a male friend is addicted, but they've found that complaining doesn't help. And the problem grows.

"We see often that women who marry alcoholics say, 'He wasn't like that when I married him.' Well, he was, he just didn't show it," says Fitzgerald. "In the same way, the sports guy hides it until he's married because so many women hate sports. It's hard for a woman to call up a therapist and say, 'I need an appointment because my husband spends too much time watching sports on TV.' But it's happening."

## Addiction Study Focused on Husband

When a wife knows the ropes of addictions and counseling herself, her husband can find himself scrambling to stay out of the corner. That's how it is for Cheryl and Wayne, married four years and living in Mesa, Arizona.

Wayne, a thirty-eight-year-old service adviser at an auto dealership, admits he's a sportsaholic but doesn't see anything wrong with that. Spectator sports have been a major part of his life since his early childhood in an orphanage outside Cleveland. At age seven, he couldn't sleep the night before a group outing to his first Cleveland Indians game. Slugger Rocky Colavito, Wayne's hero, hit a home run in the game. When he was a bit older, Wayne remembers lingering behind the fences of the Cleveland Browns summer training camp, waiting for errant footballs that cleared the fence after a field-goal kick. He'd chase them down, and even got to take a few home.

By working hard for years on a paper route, Wayne saved enough money to buy his very own Browns season ticket when he was only fourteen. He recalls the thrill of watching Hall of Famer Jim Brown, and he delighted at the sight of a Browns defender trying to "corkscrew Terry Bradshaw's head into the ground. I was right there," he reports proudly. "It was awesome!"

Wayne was a high school quarterback, modeling himself after Oakland Raiders quarterback Kenny Stabler. He even grew a scraggly beard like Stabler's and added the Raiders to his intimate list of favorite teams. All his friends loved sports, and he thrived in a city that takes its sports seriously. But an earlier marriage prompted him to leave Cleveland and move west, first to San

Diego and then to the Phoenix area. He quickly learned that in hot, retirement-friendly Arizona, sports just don't turn people on the way they do in frigid Cleveland.

"In Cleveland, when you went to see the Browns play a *Monday Night Football* game, you'd scream so much that you had no voice until Thursday morning," Wayne relates. "You knew you were in a game there! Down here in Arizona, they don't get that rowdy. I have no friends here who are as passionate about sports as my friends back in Cleveland."

Wayne admits that sports caused friction in his first marriage, that his wife threw out all his sports souvenirs when they broke up, and that he's lost all contact with his two sons from that marriage. But that experience didn't discourage his love for sports, and he's been yearning for the chance to rekindle his romance with his Cleveland teams and see more of the Raiders. That's why he ordered Primestar and its dozen or more sports channels. Now if he can just convince Cheryl to let him watch . . . "She's shocked," he says, "at how strong an addiction this is."

Cheryl knows about the bite of addictions. She's into her sixth year of recovery from cocaine dependency, a habit that she says destroyed her first marriage. Now she's studying to gain an associate's degree in drug and alcohol counseling, so she can help others stay clean and sober. She has lots of homework, including her observations of Wayne's sports obsession. It's a busy household, what with two children under age six, several dogs and rabbits, and Cheryl's mom. But Cheryl homes right in on her husband's sports habits.

"I can see sports are an addiction, in many ways identical to other addictions," Cheryl admits. "If he doesn't get all the scores, he'll flip to four channels to find them. When he's watching a game, everyone around him has to be totally quiet. Sports come before the family. He knows scores from years ago, injuries to key players and when they occurred, all the statistics. But he doesn't know my social security number, or checkbook number, or important dates in the family. When we go away on vacation, the first day back he has to read all the sports sections, catch up with all the scores. When it comes to sports, he's just got to have 'em."

For many men, they've got to have that drama and rush from sports more than anything else in their lives. In the Sportsaholism Questionnaire, the answers to two related questions revealed the full intensity of sportsaholism's grip. To follow along, look back to how you, or the sportsaholic in your life, answered Questions #15 and 29, **"What else other than sports grips you with the same interest and passion? What else other than sports can you talk about with as much enthusiasm?"**

In the national survey, the second most common response to the question about a comparable passion to sports was "nothing." In terms of finding any conversation topic to talk about with as much enthusiasm as sports, "nothing" ranked as the number-four response, well ahead of books, religion, and even sex!

**SURVEY RESULT: What else other than sports grips you with the same passion and intensity?**

1. family/spouse
2. *nothing*
3. work
4. music
5. sex
6. politics
7. movies
8. outdoor activities
9. reading
10. food

**SURVEY RESULT: What else other than sports can you talk about with as much enthusiasm?**

1. family/spouse
2. work
3. politics

4. *nothing*
5. music
6. national events
7. movies
8. religion/spirituality
9. books
10. sex

As a woman who knows a sportsaholic, you can take some encouragement that "family/spouse" ranked first in both categories. Yes, he knows you're out there. Maybe he can even talk about you or your children with as much gusto as he describes Shaquille O'Neal's thunderous dunks. Now, he might not talk up life at home to his pals *as often* as he debates whether Steve Young or Brett Favre is the best quarterback in football, but at least you're making the highlight films.

For *some* men anyway. Many others simply don't get excited about any conversation unless sports occupy center stage. This is true whether they're talking to you, their buddies, their coworkers, their parents, their brothers, their sons, or the guy they just met watching CNN sports at La Guardia Airport while waiting for the flight to Chicago. ("You really saw Michael Jordan at his restaurant once? What was he like?")

If you're a big-time sportsaholic, sports provide your passion, your excitement, your lifeline. Nothing else compares. When something turns you on as strongly as sports, why *would* you want to talk about anything else? Or think about anything else? Or do much of anything else? Men's passion for sports poured out in the national survey, as they explained why they defined themselves as sportsaholics.

*Sports are the most thrilling, exciting, and emotional thing I do during the week.*

*My entire life—what I do, where I go—is centered around what games are coming on.*

*I feel excited whenever a season begins and sad when it ends.*

*I go to bed thinking about sports and calculating sports scores and updated standings.*

*During football season, I talk, eat, and dream it until I'm consumed by it on Sunday.*

*If there's hitting, throwing, catching, shooting, running, sweating, punching, or bleeding, I love it!*

*Sports are in my blood, in my heart, and in my brain.*

You may recognize yourself or the sportsaholic in your life from many of these comments. You know just how deep this wellspring of love for sports runs. That love is why so many men live their lives *for* sports, or live their lives *through* sports. This is the definition of sportsaholism suggested in Question #1 of the Sportsaholism Questionnaire.

A person who lives his life *through* sports is someone who gets more emotionally involved with his teams and what happens to them than he does with the people, events, and circumstances in his everyday life. He gets his major joys and suffers his most painful sorrow through sports, and just doesn't feel as deeply about anything else.

A person who lives his life *for* sports is the type who regards sports as one of his primary life focuses. He plans his schedule around sports, wriggling out of many a potential time conflict with social or family commitments to keep the deck clear for big games. He counts down the days and hours to important sports events, and he invests in the latest technology to watch them. He tolerates work, does what's absolutely necessary around the house, but on most days looks forward primarily to sports. Following sports makes him happy, fully engaged in life.

In the national survey, 42 percent of all respondents called themselves sportsaholics by this definition. But 58 percent said no, they're not sportsaholics. From reading their answers to the rest of the questions, I would say that some were sportsaholics to only a *small* degree. But many, many others who placed themselves in the "no" column reported the same problems we've been discussing: arguing with their spouse or partner over their sports habits; wide mood swings from following their teams; little or nothing else in life that got them excited.

So why did they contend that sportsaholism was not real for them? We may find part of the answer by keeping in mind something else about addictions. To listen to the problems that sportsaholism may be causing in your life, you must also pay attention to those other voices, the ones that keep telling you there's nothing wrong, nothing you need to do. Here's how addiction experts categorize those voices, with examples of how they might sound coming from a sportsaholic:

### Denial

"If I want to watch sports all day, that's my business. I don't care what you say, I know it's not a problem."

### Rationalization

"Watching sports is the only relief I get from the stress of my job. Sports get me through the week."

### Minimizing

"You're overreacting again. If I skip out on doing something with you so I can see the game, I always try to make it up to you."

### Externalizing

"Look, if you knew what life was like with my wife and kids, you'd want to spend most of your time with sports, too."

### Other common deflections

"You knew I was like this when you met me."
"At least I'm not out all night drinking and messing around with other women."

"It's only for six months out of the year."

For many sportsaholic candidates, another favorite deflection is to point to that "other guy," the one who's clearly worse off than him. This "other guy" is the inspiration for many of the definitions of sportsaholism arrived at by those respondents who denied that they were sportsaholics themselves. I share some of those definitions here, with total respect and appreciation for those who came up with them. They're simply reflecting what most men have felt at one time.

### How would you define sportsaholism?

"Someone who doesn't go to work or school, just sits around every day watching sports."

"Someone who has a bookie and watches indoor lacrosse on ESPN2 at midnight."

"Somebody more involved than me in Fantasy Leagues, gambling, and season tickets."

"Someone who has to tape football scrimmages and break down the tape."

If you're a woman trying to get through to the sportsaholic you know, such deflective talk may leave you struggling to summon any hope. You may feel even more strongly that you can never compete with sports, that his attitude toward sports will never change, that their place in his life will remain rock-solid forever. The drug of sports, as you know, is indeed strong and powerful, and sportsaholism has no formal intervention or treatment program.

Still, some men have broken through the wall of sports. In their consideration of sports in their lives, they have found that extra room to maneuver, that openness of "both/and" thinking. They understand that they can still love sports *and* recognize the real problems caused by their overindulgence and obsession. They've seen how they had placed sports on a pedestal, above their relationships, their own winning and losing, their own goals, and their need to rebuild from their own life's setbacks.

These men have made changes: big changes and small changes; subtle changes and powerful changes; easy changes and hard changes. You'll hear some of their stories in Part IV. And through-out the following chapters, you'll be working with more exercises in the Sportsaholism Recovery Playbook to see how you can make new choices and improvements in your sportsaholic environment.

But it's important to recognize and talk about the way things are today. The more you hear the sportsaholic in your life say that the one with the real problem is that "other guy," the more convinced you may be that the "other guy" is him. Convincing *him* to look at it that way is a tough task. That's what Andrea finds when she approaches her husband with her feelings of rejection and resentment regarding his sports devotion. Andrea's com-ments about her husband's enthusiasm while he watches sports, and his apathy otherwise, opened Chapter 3.

"I rarely share my feelings with him verbally, though I'm sure he has some idea from my actions," she says. "When I do say anything, he curtails his obsession for a short time out of guilt. But before you know it he's back to it, sometimes sneakily. When I went to give him the Sportsaholism Questionnaire, I was nervous and shaky. He knows sports aren't helping things, but it is an addiction. I can't change him. He can only change himself when he's ready."

It's true, sportsaholics can only change themselves, and only if they choose to. But change seldom occurs in a vacuum. Usually, something or *someone* pushes or nudges us into it, at least initially. Then we take the next steps. For a sportsaholic, that nudging usually comes from the voice of a woman he knows. He may hate hearing that voice. He may wish it would go away, that he could turn the volume down on it like he does with baseball commenta-tors and their overkill commentary.

But this is one voice he can't control with a push of the remote. As long as men keep bringing sports into their living rooms, fam-ily rooms, and bedrooms, women will give voice to their feelings about it. Sportsaholism, to any degree, plays a role in how men get along with women. Men may bargain with women, belittle them, plead with them, try to convert them—but somehow, some way, they have to deal with women around sports.

And women have to deal with men and sports. They may wish they didn't have to, either, but we're all in this one together. It doesn't help to retreat to our separate and private corners over the struggle of sports and relationships. So let's keep exploring the turf together, moving now to another question of frequent contention: Just how much time is he devoting to sports, and how it is impacting your relationship?

# FIVE

# Keeping the Game Clock Running

*To spend time sitting at home watching sports as the world goes by is not fair. I wish we could be more spontaneous, go out and try new things. I wish they'd limit the sports time on TV or ban it completely!*

—Judy, girlfriend of a sportsaholic
in Dayton, New Jersey

Tick, tick, tick, tick, tick, tick. The game clock is on, and it's not counting down the final seconds of another Super Bowl. The clock is on *you,* sports fans. It's keeping track of all the time you're really spending on sports. It's gathering up evidence to bring into the court of inquiry in your relationship. What will the total count be? How much is too much, and who gets to decide?

When couples argue about sports, time is usually at the heart of the disagreement. You spend way too much time watching sports, she tells him. No way—if anything, I wish I could spend *more* time, he shoots back. We never go out on weekends because you're spending so much time with football, she complains. Well, we went out a lot last summer during baseball season, he counters. She says: Can we please have dinner now as we planned? It's after seven. He replies: The game's going into overtime—can't it wait another twenty minutes?

In this chapter, we'll address the thorny issue of time, beginning with the answers to Question #2 on both questionnaires. If you're participating as a couple, look back at how each of you answered the question **"How many total hours per week do you (or does he) spend playing sports, watching sports at games or on TV, listening to sports, reading about sports, talking about sports?"**

Are we talking about a fifty-hour sports habit, or a five-hour diversion? If you're a couple, how closely do your estimates match? Hopefully, you arrived at your answers independently, so they reflect your individual perceptions unfiltered by the other person's attitude. Most survey respondents, men and women, came up with a number. However, many couples estimating his sports time discovered a wide gap. For example, she says he spends at least thirty hours with sports, he says it's only ten. She says forty, he says twenty. And going higher . . . she says a hundred, he says twenty-five!

Some of the discrepancies could be explained; maybe he had a job in the sports media and didn't count his "work" time as part of his sports total, whereas she did. However much their estimates differed, the couples and individuals who responded to the survey often appeared to have fun with this question. Of course, not everyone offered an estimate in actual hours. When asked the total time the man in their lives devoted to sports, women often responded with a comment rather than a number:

> *How many hours are in a week?*
>
> *As many hours as the sport and the season will allow.*
>
> *Whatever it is, it's too much!*
>
> *It would be more time if I didn't express my concerns and he didn't work a second job.*
>
> *It's all day Saturday, all day Sunday, and Monday night.*

So those differences in actual time estimates clearly reflected differences in *feelings*. His fifteen hours of total sports time may *seem* like fifty to her, because they fall into their limited window of available time together. His forty hours may feel like only twenty to him because, as the saying goes, times flies when you're having fun. Perhaps he's in denial about how big his habit has become.

Or maybe he's simply not taking into account his many forms of sports fandom, and he's underestimating his sports time innocently and honestly.

Some men clearly took pride in how much time they spent with sports, demonstrating that uniquely male phenomenon of wanting to be a bigger and better fan than the guy down the block. One respondent calculated that since a week has 168 hours, his sports devotion must take up *169* hours. I took that in jest, mostly. But I decided to check out another male respondent who claimed that he spent a hundred hours per week on sports, after *cutting back* due to family needs and responsibilities! When I talked with Scott, a transplanted Philadelphia fan living in the suburbs of Washington and working as a systems engineer, he insisted his estimate was accurate.

## The Makings of a Hundred-Hour Sports Fan

"When I first get to work at six-thirty A.M. with my bagel, I go on the internet for ESPN and *USA Today* sports news," begins Scott. "I listen to sports-talk radio whenever I can during the day. When I take the kids somewhere, I've got the car radio on some kind of sport. At home, it seems like there's never enough hockey, football, or baseball on TV. But I really have cut back. I used to watch or listen to sports every waking hour, and when all the games on TV were over at night, I'd dial-hop the radio for other games out west and fall asleep with it on. I don't do that as much now."

Scott certainly ranked on the high end of male respondents, although I'm sure there are many other hundred-plus-hour sportsaholics out there. Maybe you're one of them, or you know one. On the low end, the national survey drew respondents who reported spending as few as five hours per week on sports. The national average of all survey respondents was *twenty-two hours per week*. For women living with a sportsaholic, their average estimate of his weekly sports time was *twenty-four hours per week*. For many fans, it appears, sports have become the equivalent in time and energy of holding a second job!

Now you're going to find out how reliable *your* estimates really are. Before you begin, let me urge you not to be too concerned about where you stand relative to the national survey average. Remember, *how much time we spend on sports matters less than what impact sports may have on us over time.* And everyone's life situation is different. For many individuals and couples, a ten-hour weekly sports habit may not cause any problem. For others, those same ten hours may be triggering real tension and conflict. Likewise, an estimate of thirty sports hours per week may not afford any reason for panic. It all depends on the individual involved. It's time to open up your Sportsaholism Recovery Playbook.

## PLAY #4:
## THE SPORTS TIME LOG

Set up a chart with the days of the week noted across the top and large blocks to fill in data under each day. Your computer system may have a program that will help you create an excellent chart, though colored pencils and a ruler work just as well. Dressing up the chart in your favorite team's colors may be a good incentive to stick with it! At the top of the chart, write down the dates of your log week. Hang the chart in an easy-to-reach spot. The refrigerator door works well in most households.

Starting with today, begin a thorough and accurate record of how many hours you really put into sports. Try to count everything, including:

**Games you attend in person**—Jot down all time you spend at the game site, including tailgating, pregame warmups, batting practice, etc., as well as time traveling back and forth to the game.

**TV**—Calculate all time spent watching games on TV, including pregame shows, halftime shows, and highlight shows—at home, in sports bars, restaurants, or wherever sports on TV catch your eye. Don't forget all time with ESPN's *SportsCenter* and any other sports news program or all-sports network. And yes, the six-to-eight minutes of sports news on your local news program, CNN sports updates, and sports features and interviews on commercial networks do count.

**Radio**—Include time listening to games, pregame shows, highlight shows, features, interviews, commentary, and especially sports-talk radio.

**Newspapers and magazines**—Record time spent reading sports sections, stats, sports magazines, fan-club magazines or newsletters, as well as sports stories in general interest magazines and catalogs of sports merchandise.

**Fantasy Leagues**—Be sure to add the total hours consumed by draft preparation, draft time, updating stats, thinking about whom to play and whom to bench, talking trades, making trades, contemplating and implementing all personnel decisions.

**Sports betting**—How much time do you spend studying odds, betting-tip magazines, and injury reports, as well as placing bets, talking to betting contacts, and tracking office pools?

**Talking sports**—Remember to count up hours spent talking about sports to spouse, family, friends, coworkers, strangers in an airport, etc.

**Thinking sports**—No, you can't monitor your *every* thought. But you do know when you've killed a half hour or more contemplating the big Ohio State–Michigan game without any newspaper or radio reference to prompt you. Aim for honesty.

**Playing sports (optional)**—Our focus is on spectator sports, so this may not belong in the count. Certainly, fitness routines such as walking, running, swimming, biking, or Nautilus workouts are not part of a sportsaholic lifestyle. That's healthy exercise. But consider including in this log time spent playing competitive sports as part of an overall picture of sportsaholism. If those two rounds of golf with friends or five hours per week playing basketball at the Y create the same strain at home as a football doubleheader, it will help to include them in the time log. But if you regard these activities as part of your fitness program and it's not an issue at home, leave them out.

**When to undertake the log**—If you're the sportsaholic, you might say it's not fair to keep the log during football season if you're into football more than any other sport. Your average time for a week in November certainly is not your typical average for the whole year, right? But if your football time is the hot topic of contention in your relationship, then this is the best time for you to keep a log.

Try to let go of that natural sports-fan instinct to get an accurate yearlong statistic. This isn't about right or wrong, anyway, it's about what's happening in your relationship as a result of your sports devotion and what you want to do about it. If you want to keep another log some time in June or July for a more balanced look, fine. But do the first log now, while the issue's hot. To get the best possible cross section of your habits during this time of year, it will help to keep the time log for two weeks in a row and get an average. This will compensate for once-a-year events like the World Series that inarguably inflate most fans' time.

### FOR THE WOMEN:

As a woman who knows a sportsaholic, you can be an active participant in this exercise. You can kindly remind your sportsaholic to record sports time when he forgets, or point out sports time he'd be inclined to leave out. Father-son dinner conversations over the fate of the local college team can be easily overlooked, for instance. As with all the exercises in the playbook, this can be fun if you approach it with a positive attitude. If a game he's watching lasts longer than expected, you might note, goodnaturedly: "Overtime! That's thirty more minutes on the time log!" As a woman, you can also participate in one of two other ways:

1. If you spend a fair amount of time with sports yourself, keep your own Sports Time Log. This can help clear up arguments about how much sports time is willingly shared together versus how much time he's watching alone.
2. If your sports time is almost nil (or you're participating in this exercise alone), check your answer to Question #16 in the Women Who Know a Sportsaholic Survey, the one that identifies a personal interest you practice as passionately as he follows sports. If you answered "gardening," then keep a Gardening Time Log for the week. Or a Reading Time Log, or Shopping Time Log. This will give both of you reference points as you further explore the role of sports time versus quality time together in your relationship.

**Note**—If you're a sports fan who does not have a woman waiting to see how your time log comes out, use this exercise to track your sports devotion for yourself. You may decide to make changes in your sports time now, or you may learn something you didn't know when you filled out the questionnaire.

### FOLLOW-UP:

At the end of two weeks, take the chart down and look it over either by yourself, or as a couple. See any surprising numbers or overall trends? How does the total estimated hours you recorded in this exercise compare to the estimate on your questionnaire? More important, what does this sports total represent in the full picture of how time is spent in your household?

Figure out how many waking hours per week are available outside of work and other recognized commitments. Couples should arrive at a total number of hours available to be spent together or as a family, time when both of you are free of mandatory responsibilities. Now look at what portion of that time goes to spectator sports.

Suppose you determine that you have forty free hours to spend together, and his sports time comes out to thirty-two hours. That means you only have eight hours left for time together. Or let's say his sports time comes out to fifteen hours, but you both have so many outside commitments that your window of possible shared time is only eighteen hours to begin with. That's just three free hours together! You're already pressured, with very little time to spend together, and sports make it impossible.

On the flip side, the time log and follow-up breakdown of hours in the week may show you that sports account for only twelve hours and you have fifty hours of available time—which means you've got thirty-eight hours left for yourselves, if you decide to use them together. This may add a new perspective to your previous arguments. It may be that sports-watching isn't the only obstacle, and you may want to consider what else is causing tension between you. And bear in mind that everyone's different. A couple who cherishes their individual passions may feel that the ten hours they have left for each other feels right to each of them.

To conclude this exercise, take a few minutes to review what you've learned from the time log and discuss how you feel about the time consumed by sports in your lives. If you come up with new ideas about how to spend your free time together, or how to rearrange your weekly patterns, jot them down in your Sportsaholism Recovery Playbook.

If you're a couple spending much of this follow-up period arguing about your differences on this issue of time, don't be alarmed. You're right in sync with the majority of survey respondents. Listen to some of their responses to Question #3 from both questionnaires, **"How do you feel about the time and attention you (he) devote(s) to sports?"**

Remember how, in Chapter 3, we found that most men agreed with women that they acted differently watching sports from the way they did in their everyday lives? Not so in this case. Of the men who took the Sportsaholism Questionnaire, 85 percent reported they felt *great* about the time and attention they devoted to sports. But among the Women Who Know a Sportsaholic, only 10 percent said they felt happy and satisfied with the attention he gives to sports, probably because they love sports themselves. Not all the remaining 90 percent are rebelling against sports. As Celeste explains of her sportsaholic husband in Rochester, New York: "I married him for better or worse, for richer or poorer, in sickness and in health—*and* in baseball and football." But the vast majority of women respondents were dissatisfied, to put it mildly. Here's a sampling of comments from the hard edge:

*I find it very annoying. He consistently talks sports to me like I care.*
—VERONICA, A SALESPERSON
FROM MARLBOROUGH, MASSACHUSETTS

*It has made me lose respect for him. He is no longer a balanced, well-rounded partner in life.*
—BRENDA, AN ACCOUNTANT FROM LINCOLN, NEBRASKA

*I feel our relationship is not high on his priority list—it ranks somewhere behind sports, news, job, beer, and food.*
—MARILYN, AN ADMINISTRATOR
IN CHARLOTTESVILLE, VIRGINIA

If you're a woman who's tired of all his excessive sports-watching, you can see that you've got lots of company. More and more women are feeling that enough is enough! One group of women in New York meet in an Upper East Side restaurant every January on Super Bowl Sunday in a "Football Widows Party" to share common complaints of the last five months and to celebrate the end of at least one sports season. You can bet that party-goers don't offer many complimentary toasts to their men.

Now let's see what the men in the survey had to say. Yes, they love sports and feel great about those twenty or thirty hours they spend watching their Baltimore Orioles and Ravens. If sports-watching stands as their primary interest in life, it's an interest they take great delight in:

*As long as it doesn't interfere with my job or my health, keep it coming!*
—EDWARD, A MEDICAL PRACTITIONER FROM AURORA, OHIO

*I wish I didn't have to work as much so I could spend more time on sports.*
—DAVE, A STUDENT FROM LINCOLN, NEBRASKA

*I don't know what I'd do without sports.*
—MORT, AN ACCOUNTANT IN ARLINGTON, VIRGINIA

But while men indicated that they felt fine about their sports habits, they had a pretty good idea that the women in their lives didn't share their enthusiasm. In response to Question #6 in the Sportsaholism Questionnaire, **"How does your spouse, girlfriend, or family feel about all your attention to sports?"** almost half the men acknowledged that their loved ones don't much like or appreciate all the time they spend on sports. Among the other half, some fell into the category of sports-friendly relationships, where she whoops it up over the 49ers as much as he does, while others admitted that they simply didn't have a current relationship.

And, of course, it's possible that some of the men are in denial about the stress and strain their sports habits cause in their relationships. Sometimes, a man simply doesn't know his sports devotion bothers his wife or partner because she hasn't found a way to tell him. But when a woman does confront her sportsaholic with her feelings, he notices. In answering Question #7, **"How do [women] express their feelings about your sports attention to you?"** men described their reactions as taking the form of verbal complaints, teasing, and pouting; some women give men the cold shoulder, leave the room abruptly when he turns on the game, or change the channel right in the middle of the action!

These methods of "communication" only serve to annoy sportsaholics, especially with their poor timing. The sight of his woman plopping down beside him and snarling, "You never pay me any attention anymore," just as the Green Bay Packers and Oakland Raiders begin the fourth quarter of a crucial game can make any man gnash his teeth in frustration no matter how much he loves her.

Similarly, if you approach your man right after the game, you're also met with fierce resistance. That's because no matter how the game turned out for his team, he needs an emotional debriefing period. If his Packers won the big game against the Raiders, he wants to celebrate and see his joy mirrored in everyone and everything around him. Should a woman come around to complain, his feeling of well-being is threatened and he gets hostile or defensive. His message: Don't bring me down.

And suppose his beloved Packers lost the game to the big, bad Raiders. If she voices her discontent minutes after the final gun, he's still reeling from anger and despair. He may not have decided whom to blame for this unjust and unnecessary setback, and that's a critical step in managing his negative feelings. He genuinely feels that life stinks about now, and all he really wants to do is complain about just how bad it is. Her feelings, no matter how valid, may force him even further into the abyss and may even prompt him to turn on her with his need to vent, blame, and act out his pain.

How a woman expresses her feelings can annoy him more than the feelings themselves. Sarcastic comments don't work. Example: "Gee, look, you're watching another *football* game. Isn't *that* a surprise!" Neither do put-downs. Example: "I cannot believe how long you've been sitting there watching that game. You're *so* immature!" Here's another tactic that gets men looking for a red penalty flag to throw on the floor: She notices that his Bears are losing and immediately declares herself a die-hard fan of the opposing Vikings, so when he suffers through his team's defeat, she's there waiting to rub it in. Ultimatums during *Monday Night Football* don't score many points, either. Example: "Next weekend you get one game all Saturday, Sunday, and Monday or I won't cook any meals for a month!"

But for women, the feelings that lead to such outbursts burn intensely, especially when he's on his twenty-eighth hour of spectator sports for the week. To bottle them up right when they're bubbling to the surface sounds unhealthy or unfair. After all, this isn't the first time this scene has been played out in their home.

The resentment of his sports time and devotion is something she may carry with her not only during those thirty-eight hours of weekly sports time, but during the other 130 hours of the week.

If you're a woman living with a sportsaholic, look back to how you answered Question #6 of the Women Who Know a Sportsaholic Survey, **"How do sports affect your relationship with him?"** If you're like most women in the survey, you probably referred to the tension in trying to squeeze intimate time into your busy schedules and his sports obsession. Or you spoke of a wall between you. As you read your answer to this question, ask yourself how clear you've been with him about what you see and feel regarding the impact of sports on your relationship. Whether you've been together six months or six years, it's critical that you share your perspective about sportsaholism. If you don't, he'll either never know or he'll conclude that you don't care enough to do anything about it. Just be careful to select a time when the game's not on, and allow a brief cool-down period after an emotional sports event.

And you know what? Many men *want* to know how you really look at their sports habits. They may already feel guilty about it and realize that they're probably going to have to make some changes eventually. They may just be waiting for you to prompt them. But the longer the stalemate festers, the harder it may be to reverse the pattern.

## Sally Remembers: A Time Without Sports

A homemaker in Pittsburgh, Sally tells her retired husband, Dean, "Let's get a life," about every week. But Dean simply responds, "This is my pleasure," and doesn't change anything. She doesn't expect him to. She's endured his sports time since football began on TV more than thirty years ago. So when he watches one or more games, she reads, shops, walks, watches other TV programs, or goes to a movie. When she stays home, she tries to squeeze in dinner during halftime.

But at moments of peak frustration, Sally can still recall a happier time, a period when they lived together briefly in Madrid.

They didn't have a TV there, so his sports time was limited to one or two major events that he caught on TV in a public place. Otherwise, their time was their own to share, to explore, to talk . . . *but that was 1972!*

Many women in my survey have chosen not to endure life behind the wall of sports. When it becomes clear that sports hold the Number-One ranking in his life priorities, she may decide not to settle for second or third place. So she leaves him.

Couples counselors may suggest that relationships don't usually break up over a single factor like sports, but rather over a combination of many. Some also say that one problem may serve as a smoke screen for others that can't be brought to light. Yet both women and men in the survey confirmed that sports sure felt like the major reason for a divorce or separation. At the very least, it was the one they could see.

Dave, the University of Nebraska graduate student we mentioned streaking through his neighborhood dressed only in a Nebraska flag in Chapter 3, once broke a Valentine's Day dinner date with his girlfriend so he could watch the Cornhuskers play a big basketball game. She broke up with him soon afterward, and he admits that this incident just *might* have had something to do with it.

Women in the national survey were more direct. "Sports played the biggest role in ruining our communication and thus our marriage," wrote Margaret in Alabaster, Alabama. Rose, who dated a sportsaholic for three months in Austin, Texas, reported upon breaking up, *"I* was the game, and he was too busy with sports to play it."

If you're a couple reading this book together, you've made other choices. You've decided to look more closely at your conflicting perspectives on sports and the problems that emerge because of them. You're in this together in order to find ways of getting through to each other. And if you've tried to talk about sports (not teams and strategy, but problems and discontent), you know it's seldom easy.

You may be finding that these comments from survey respondents are stirring up some of the same old feelings and arguments. If so, now's a good time to pick up the Sportsaholism

Recovery Playbook. This next exercise will provide a framework for what you're already doing. It's designed primarily for couples, but if you're a man or woman reading this book alone, you can still benefit from writing down your feelings in response to the issues addressed in this chapter.

## PLAY #5:
## VIN SCULLY PLAYBACK

Vin Scully, for those who don't see much TV sports, is one of the leading pro baseball play-by-play announcers. It's his job to tell you exactly what's happening in the game, leaving it up to the commentators to analyze it. In this exercise, you'll each get to play Vin Scully, and you don't have to know much about baseball or sports to do an expert job. All you have to do is listen attentively and repeat back everything you hear clearly, thoroughly, and accurately. Many relationship teachers and therapists suggest related exercises to help couples communicate better. Harville Hendrix's books *Keeping the Love You Find* and *Getting the Love You Want* offer excellent examples that you may want to check out after finishing this book.

To begin this exercise, the man takes on the Vin Scully role first. The woman gets one minute to talk about how she feels about one of the issues related to sports. Stick to the material recently covered, such as your feelings about the time and attention he devotes to sports or how sports affect your relationship. It's important to share these feelings in a calm, respectful manner. No verbal attacks are allowed. During the one minute while you speak, he sits quietly and listens intently, as if he's watching a play in a game and getting ready to report on it.

At the end of the minute, the man becomes an active Vin Scully and reports back to the woman everything she said. As the man, be sure to leave nothing out. Imagining you're broadcasting on radio rather than TV will help—on radio, it's necessary to describe it all. Also, resist censoring, changing, or analyzing anything you play back. You are reporting on her ideas, opinions, and feelings. You're not the color commentator assigned to tell her what you think about what she's saying.

When you've replayed all the points she raised, you should check with her to make sure you got it all straight. Example: If she said she wished you would cut your sports time down ten hours per week, it's not quite right if you report back, "You want me to watch less sports." You should say it as she did: "You wish I would cut my sports time down ten hours per week." If you can't remember an important detail, you may ask her. If she notices anything that you left out, she can bring that to your attention, and you return to your playback role to repeat this idea to her.

You know you've been a good Vin Scully if you've been able patiently to stick to your job, though you may have been tempted to blurt out, "That's not true!" or, "You do things I don't like, too, you know!" Simply to listen to your partner without return volley can help you understand her much better. And being able to report back to her what she said enables her to feel heard and valued. It's a gift, possibly as big to her as anything you give her for her birthday.

After a minute breather, it's time to change roles. You as the woman then become Vin Scully, and the man has the opportunity to speak to his feelings related to the issues in this chapter. This isn't time for him to defend himself or launch into a tirade about your shopping habits. He might try talking about how he feels when you interrupt him during a game, or how he feels when you criticize him for doing what he loves. He should speak in the same respectful tone you used when he was Vin Scully, and he should tell the whole truth. He wants you to understand him.

After his one minute of speaking, you become Vin Scully and report back to him every relevant point he covered. Again, you should refrain from commenting on or analyzing what he said, nor should you countercharge or revise his words to suit your beliefs. Example: If he tells you that he feels that you don't want him to enjoy life when he hears you call him immature for loving sports, that's what you should report. Saying instead, "You get mad when I call you immature," doesn't describe the full picture. It should be, "When I call you immature for loving sports, you feel that I don't want you to enjoy life."

When you've finished your Vin Scully Playback, you should check with him to make sure you didn't leave anything out, and that you got it right. If not, you should follow up with him until you get it all. Again, this is a gift. How often does he have his thoughts or feelings reflected back to him unedited and unrevised? How good must it feel to know you're working to listen to him so you can understand? You're not saying you *agree* with him any more than he necessarily agreed with what you shared. But at least you're both really hearing one another, and you may find that this exercise dramatically improves your future communication.

What will become apparent to both of you is that if you pick quieter, nonsports-related times to talk about your feelings or concerns, you will enjoy clearer, more satisfying communication. Find a time that fits both your schedules —early Saturday morning, for example, often presents a good opportunity, before you begin a weekend of chores, family activities, and sports.

### FOLLOW-UP OPTION:

If you're both willing, you may decide to do another minute of alternate speaking, with the other person in the same Vin Scully role. Focus on listening so that you really understand your partner and can begin to empathize. You don't have to agree, but this sharing can open the door to new understanding and possibilities between you. You may want to finish each round of sharing by simply saying to your partner, "I understand you." Use your playbook to jot down ideas that the exercise generated which might be useful later. You can turn to this exercise anytime you find an argument brewing.

If you're a woman doing this exercise alone, simply write down in your playbook your feelings in greater detail about his sports time and attention, or its role in your relationship. Imagine that you are getting the full listening attention of the sportsaholic in your life. If this is an experience you never actually get with him, just imagining it can be a powerful lift. Men doing this exercise alone may also want to imagine a woman they know (or have known) listening to their feelings in ways she may not have been able to do before.

## Still Stuck?

So now you've had a reality check. You've pinned down how much time sports really consume in your life and relationship, and how both of you feel about that sports devotion. And as a couple, you've practiced listening to each other's feelings about sports without rebuttals or countercharges. You may feel encouraged, inspired, and more clear about how each of you sees things. You may be ready to work out a different role for sports in the household. That's progress, and we're just getting started!

However, you may also feel just as stuck as you were when you picked up this book. She's thinking that it doesn't matter what she says or what you both learn, he's never going to change his sports habits. He's thinking that even if he did sacrifice some sports time for her, she still wouldn't be happy or stop nagging.

It's natural to feel doubtful and discouraged. We're just

scratching the surface of the impact of sports in your lives, and often the scratching can, at first, make you itch more. Stay with it. Even if your particular sticking point has yet to emerge, there's much more ground to cover. Remember, you're not trying to find a better way to manage your monthly budget. We're talking about sportsaholism, and its hold on men is strong and not easily shaken.

It is an addiction.

PART TWO

# The Arena:
# Men, Women, and Sports

# SIX

# A Sports-Shrouded Marriage

*If he died tomorrow, I guess I'd throw the sports section in
the casket before they buried him.*

—Marcy, a sportsaholic's wife in
Winston-Salem, North Carolina

Sometimes you have to wonder how couples tangling over sports
can get along at all. If you took an inventory of all the ways in
which women and men may differ, you'd find every one applies
to their disagreements over sports.

Do you believe men and women communicate differently? Do
they have different ways of expressing emotions? Do they regard
the art of compromise differently? Do they have different needs
for intimacy, and different definitions of spending time together?
Do they see the role of family differently? Do they react differently
to exercises in self-reflection and understanding, such as the ones
in this book?

As you probably know from your own experiences, every one
of these differences manifests itself in the arena where women
and men grapple with sports. See if you spot yourselves in any of
these typical domestic sports scenarios.

## Communication

She says: "Gee, it's a nice Saturday afternoon. I think it would
be great to spend the afternoon at the park together, don't you?"

He says: "There's a big game on." (Translation: "It may be nice out, but I've got something more important to do.")

### Emotional expression

He's been watching games all weekend and it's late Sunday afternoon. She's angry about it and has told him so many times, which makes *him* angry. She expresses her anger by complaining, making sarcastic comments, rolling her eyes, and storming out of the room. He expresses his anger by saying once: "Sports are what bring me pleasure and help me relax. Don't bug me!" From then on, he fixates his eyes on the TV screen and never looks up.

### Compromise style

He agrees to miss the live telecast of one of the four weekend football games he really wanted to see so that they can go to dinner with friends. He's taping it so he can watch it when they get home late that night. She's let go of three other ideas she had for them this weekend, and while they're at dinner she's feeling grateful that he's made this one concession. Meanwhile, he's imagining what's happening in the game and feels that he's getting the raw end of the deal.

### Intimacy differences

Her definition of spending time together: talking about their day or week, or sitting quietly for a few moments without outside distractions. His definition of spending time together: her watching the game with him and asking him to teach her the rules.

### Family role

She wants their kids to be physically active and intellectually challenged. She wants them to enjoy family vacations together, discovering national parks and historic monuments. He wants their kids to be physically active, as long as that means organized, competitive sports where he can root for them to win. When he settles down to watch a game at home, he expects them to leave him alone. He also assumes they'll be as excited as he is about his vacation plan—checking out three new baseball parks!

### Self-reflection

She enjoys new opportunities to learn more about what makes people tick, and she plunges headlong into new exercises on how better to understand and improve her own life. He regards such exercises as overanalyzing, sort of like Tim McCarver's baseball commentary, and believes time would be much better spent trying to remember the entire lineup of the '69 Mets—including platoon positions.

Now these may strike you as big-time overgeneralizations, and I'll admit that I may be stereotyping a sportsaholic's behavior slightly. But these are real—I've met or heard from quite a few couples who have demonstrated exactly these kinds of differences over sports. These differences are not inborn, however—they are based in large part on our socialized training and the roles we play.

Even with all the sports-related differences spilling out in relationships these days, sportsaholism is only now beginning to emerge as a legitimate issue in discussions of marital discord. As you probably know from firsthand experience, sportsaholism can create just as much marital tension as any of the hot relationship topics that regularly make the covers of women's magazines. But back in the mid-1980s, sportsaholism never even arose as an issue during my own marital counseling. Strange, because it was a classic sports spat that brought us in for help. I'll take you back to that day.

## My Super Bowl Flashback

It's the 1984 Super Bowl, Raiders versus Redskins. Like most American men, I've been planning my day around the event for weeks. I want the Redskins to win, but even before halftime it becomes clear that the superior Raiders will prevail. Like many

Super Bowl contests that don't live up to the hype, this one is boring and tedious, an occasional moment of action wrapped around long blocks of beer commercials and delays to treat injured players. But not for one second do I consider turning it off.

I am a sports fan, and this is the Super Bowl. For most men (and many women), that's enough said. I even have an added excuse: I make my living as a professional sportswriter for the *Charlotte Observer*. Even though I do not have to write about the game, I know that on Monday morning and most of next week, people everywhere will be talking about the Super Bowl and expecting me to be thoroughly knowledgeable about it. I need to keep watching out of professional duty. At least that's what I keep telling myself.

My wife walks in and asks the score. I mechanically report it to her, never looking up from the screen.

"Well," she says, "since it's such a lousy game, why don't we run off to a matinee movie? You've been watching this for five hours already, with all that pregame crap. For one Super Bowl Sunday, it would be nice to do something together."

"You know better than that," I snap.

And for the better part of ten years, she had known better. A sportsaholic could not have asked for much more from a woman. When we lived together in Boston in 1975, she walked with me to Fenway Park almost every night to see the Red Sox on their march to a pennant and World Series. In June '76, two days after our wedding, she amused herself alone as I pulled the drapes tight against the midday sun in our motel room to focus on the Boston Celtics wrapping up another basketball championship. If she noticed that I got more excited over the Celtics winning than anything else during the honeymoon, she was nice enough not to say.

She even let me teach her how to keep score and understand the rules of baseball—well, some of the rules. And as I launched my dream career in sports journalism, she found things to do on all those cold winter nights I was off covering basketball games. I lured her into my sports world so far, she even became a sportswriter *herself* for a couple of years.

Yes, when it came to my single-minded devotion to sports and all the time and energy it consumed, she had known better than to complain. But no longer. Especially not on this Super Bowl Sunday.

In response to my snippy remark, she flips off the TV switch just as the third quarter gets going. As she coaxes me toward the kitchen to continue the argument, I carefully wait until her back is to me and turn the TV on again, with the volume all the way down—a critical maneuver in preremote days.

My strategy is simple: Since I know that our kitchen has a serving window that opens onto the living-room area, I will position myself so I can see through that window, and I'll make sure she doesn't have the same view. That way, I can sneak a few peeks at the game while we're talking. You never know, the Redskins could come back. Besides, I have to know the full story.

For the rest of the third quarter and into the fourth, my strategy works perfectly. Our fight cools to the point where I can just nod my head or mutter a few apologies as she runs through her complaints. And she unknowingly cooperates by slumping to the floor, so there's no danger of her seeing the TV beyond. As she talks, my thoughts are focused on fleeting hopes that Joe Theismann, the Washington quarterback, can rally the Redskins back into the game. I'm straining to see a long Theismann pass completion when she catches me.

"I don't believe this!" she hisses.

She screams. She shoots up from the floor. She stomps her way through the kitchen and races to the living area. She approaches the TV at full speed, and with the quick, sure hands of a shortstop, she yanks out the plug without shutting off the switch, pivots, and storms out the door, slamming it hard behind her.

I wait for a few seconds, wondering what I should do next. Should I run after her? Should I write her a note of apology and put it on her pillow? Should I consider for a few moments why I'm so obsessed with sports? I reach my decision.

Quietly and mechanically, I get up, plug the TV back in, and proceed to watch the rest of the one-sided Super Bowl, and all the postgame interviews, awards ceremonies, highlight shows, and analysis. A few weeks later, we enter our first round of marital counseling. Two rounds later, we divorce.

• • •

I wouldn't say that sports alone broke up my marriage more than ten years ago. My ex-wife and I came together as teenagers, and many factors led us to go our separate ways in our thirties. But I can say that my addiction to sports clouded my vision of my role in our marriage and what I wanted in my life, and it certainly got in the way of intimate communication between us. I didn't understand then what I do today. I value everything I've learned since that time, and I have few regrets. But today I hope my experience and the examples of couples from the survey will help others recognize the impact of sportsaholism sooner and make more informed choices.

One point worth noting is that underneath those sports arguments, we often find underlying problems that need to be uncovered and addressed. Couples counseling can be useful in bringing these issues to the surface. But if sports represent the action in your relationship struggles, pursue that. Exploring your sports arguments can lift the lid on other concerns that may be simmering in the marital pot.

## Marcy and Nick: Back from the Brink

Marcy is the woman quoted at the start of this chapter. An interior designer, she's been married to Nick for twenty-seven years. A fiftyish couple, they knew that sports would play a major part in their marriage when he watched an entire college football bowl game on their honeymoon. She likes sports to a point. She's played competitive tennis for years, and she's even been known to sit down to watch a baseball or basketball game with him now and then.

An attorney, Nick grew up a New York Yankees fan but switched allegiances to the Atlanta Braves when he settled in North Carolina. He also follows the Charlotte Hornets and Carolina Panthers, but the local basketball and football teams from Wake Forest University really get his sports juices flowing. And his violent reactions to major losses convinced Marcy that the problem was very serious.

Marcy: "When Wake Forest was losing, Nick would throw things. I'd cower in the corner and whisper, 'Please win. Please win.' There was a total lack of communication between us. It was hard to compete with that adrenaline he'd get from watching sports, an adrenaline he didn't get from anything else."

Nick: "I needed sports to relax. I was unaware or unwilling to admit that it was really interfering with our relationship."

Marcy: "When it all got to be too much a few years ago, I told him I was leaving. He was watching some basketball game or something, and he barely heard what I said. He asked me if I was going to the store. I said, 'No, I'm out of here. I'm *leaving!*' "

They landed in couples counseling. In time, they discovered that their problems extended beyond sports. Marcy learned that she had trouble expressing her needs and that she'd walk away from trouble between them, denying that anything was wrong. She says she's much better about speaking to what she wants today.

Because sports was the arena in which their problems manifested, Marcy and Nick worked together on compromises they could each accept. Today, Nick says he might watch one game instead of two, or part of one game instead of a whole game. He admits that if he had understood earlier how obsessed he had become with sports that "things could have been so much better during those years when I was ridiculously involved."

They still have disagreements about his sports time. He still follows his teams closely, and she still complains. As you may recall, this chapter opened with Marcy's comment about throwing the sports section in the casket when Nick dies.

Nick: "When she complains, sometimes I feel it's justified and sometimes I don't. I listen to sports-talk radio sometimes and hear these guys carry on all day about sports, and I wonder how she thinks *I'm* addicted."

Marcy: "He's about thirty percent better than he used to be, but I accept that. We all have good qualities and bad qualities. We both made changes."

When men and women argue over the time and attention *he* devotes to sports, she's often contributing to the problem with issues of her own. Maybe she's not as clear as she thinks she is in communicating what it is she wants in her life or in their relationship. Maybe she's unsure of how to ask for it. If her self-esteem is low, she may not value herself enough to believe she deserves to take priority over sports. To please him or coexist peacefully with him she may also be burying her own needs so deeply that she really doesn't even know what she really wants.

## Finding a Passion of Her Own

Keith is a mediator, Mary Anne is studying to be a social worker. A fortyish couple married three years, they live in Northport, New York, where his attention often gets pulled toward the Knicks, Yankees, and Jets. He also plays basketball competitively. Both agree that he's not a serious sportsaholic now, but earlier in their relationship, sports did come up often and intensely.

"She tested me constantly," Keith explains. "Could I get away from football on Sunday? It seemed like she needed to believe she wasn't getting in with a football addict. I felt defensive, like she was somebody's mother saying to her son, 'You're watching too much TV—it's Sunday, go out and play!' Gradually, she found that I mostly just watch the Jets. Not watching that second football game on Sunday afternoons—that was passing the test."

Mary Anne believed she had good cause to be wary of Keith's football-watching habits. The reasons go all the way back to her childhood. "My dad would sit watching football and throw peanut shells on the rug. My mom would come in and clean them up," she remembers. "I learned about subservience from them, and I associated it with sports-watching."

Not surprisingly, Mary Anne grew to "detest football—a bunch of bullies lashing out at each other." But before Keith, many of her boyfriends loved football. Problems ensued, including the day Mary Anne was ridiculed by one boyfriend's male pals for daring to step into the football-watching room with them, sit down, and start reading a book. Frustrated and lonely, Mary Anne tried pretending to like sports with some of the guys she dated because they certainly didn't seem interested in anything *she* liked. Later, she learned that was the wrong approach, and she needed to look at herself for the answer.

"I understood how women can lose themselves in relationships to the point where they don't even know anymore what their real interests are," she says. "I see this with a lot of the teenage girls I work with, where she can tell you what her boyfriend likes but not what *she* wants."

As Mary Anne learned more about what she wanted, she cultivated a passion for antiquing. It's her "high." She appreciates how Keith supports her in following her passion, and how he listens to what she wants in other ways. Yes, she still objects sometimes when he watches football, but she recognizes that he's practicing moderation and has found that taking care of her own life has helped her work out issues with men.

But even for women who know what they want, finding any activity that satisfies them as deeply as sports satisfy him can be difficult. For evidence, let's look at the national survey response to Question #16 from the Women Who Know a Sportsaholic Survey, **"What personal interest of yours do you regard with the same passion he has for sports?"**

Women in the survey mentioned pursuits such as reading, gardening, work, shopping, and spending time with friends. But the most frequently mentioned response to this question was "nothing." There was nothing she could point to with the same pride and enthusiasm he had for sports!

**SURVEY RESULT (Women): What personal interest of yours do you regard with the same passion he has for sports?**

1. *nothing*
2. reading
3. work
4. time with friends
5. exercising

6. children
7. gardening
8. shopping
9. household projects
10. music

Some of the women who answered "nothing" to this question did so with a certain pride and indignation. It's not that they didn't have interests in their lives, they explained. Rather, they didn't have anything that they took to the *extreme* that he takes sports. They weren't *addicted* to their special interest, didn't practice it to the exclusion of almost everything else in life. They didn't block out their spouse and family for full weekend days and nights.

Other women, though, indicated that they were so busy doing what they loved that they didn't concern themselves with their man's sports obsession. Theresa is married to Ned, the advertising manager who opened Chapter 2 with his assessment that he wasn't a sportsaholic, even though his wife said he was. Theresa works full-time staffing a home health-care agency for people with AIDS, and she spends twenty additional hours helping out at a women's center for victims of domestic violence. She considers sports a waste of time and does not join Ned in any of his forty-plus hour weekly sports habit, but she says that with their separate endeavors, they have found a balance in the relationship.

"We have a life together and a life separate," relates Theresa. "We have friends as a couple and friends individually. When we socialize together, he talks sports and I talk social issues. But we do things together and have a great time. After twenty years, we've adjusted."

## PLAY #6:
## LOBBYING FOR YOUR SPECIAL INTEREST

This is a subject worth talking about on your own, so take out your Sportsaholism Recovery Playbook. You'll be working as a couple, but this one can be handled by either a man or woman participating alone by writing your answers in the playbook.

The woman begins. Taking your answer to Question #16 as a starting point, take two or three minutes to tell your man about your most passionate, special interest in life. If you answered "nothing" in the questionnaire, talk about what your special interest *might* be if you had one, something you always wanted to pursue but haven't for whatever reason. Why does this interest excite you? How do you feel when you're doing it? What does it do for you? Remember, you're lobbying on behalf of this interest, not to convert him to it, but to help him understand you more fully. So make your case strongly and clearly. The man's role is simply to listen and allow you to lobby. (If you're a woman participating alone, simply write this response for two or three minutes in your playbook.)

After two or three minutes, switch roles. Now, you as the man get to talk with the same conviction about why sports are your number-one special interest. Make your case as strongly and as objectively as possible. Remember, you're not a congressional lobbyist pressuring her to vote for five more sports cable channels for your home. Rather, you're lobbying for her understanding. You want her to know better how you really feel about your love for sports. The woman's role here is to listen intently, something she may not be able to do in the midst of your arguments about sports.

**A different approach**—For many couples, this lobbying may be old news. He's lobbied and lobbied, but nothing changes. If that's true in your relationship, you may want to table this portion of the exercise and try a different twist. For his two or three minutes of speaking in this exercise, rather than talk sports he can choose to talk about whatever he would regard as his number-two interest in life (reading, music, movies, work, cars, etc.). Those willing to try this option may find that it will level the playing field in those arguments over sports versus whatever she likes. And as a man, you may come to regard your number-two interest with a new level of respect and seek a higher profile for it in your life.

If you're a woman living with a sportsaholic, you may find yourself getting more annoyed than anything else, especially if you're married with two or three kids in your sportsaholic household. You're probably thinking, Special interest? When would I have time to find a special interest? While he's spending most of the weekend watching sports, I have to clean the house, do all the chores, cook meals, and watch the kids by myself. I work during the week, and weekends are for catching up at home. I'm lucky if I have enough time to read a couple of magazines or watch a TV movie, never mind going out antiquing or bird-watching.

If this describes your world, you're not alone. That's just the picture that often emerged from the women's survey in response to Question #14, **"When he watches a game alone, how do you spend your time?"**

You can see how the survey results below shatter the myth about football widows. You know, the one that says that during those long hours men watch sports, women are out shopping, which men would suggest is just as addictive as sportsaholism. Women tell a different story. They're not grabbing their purse and heading out to the mall, not to return until *most* of the football is over. Far from it.

> **SURVEY RESULT (Women): When he watches a game alone, how do you spend your time?**
>
> 1. household chores
> 2. reading
> 3. watching other programs on another TV
> 4. socializing with friends
> 5. shopping
> 6. taking care of the kids
> 7. cooking
> 8. crafts projects
> 9. outside job
> 10. exercising

Instead, while he's sitting in the sports-watching zone of the house for hours at a time, she's circling nearby. She's doing laundry, vacuuming, cooking, washing dishes, making grocery lists, planning meals, taking care of the kids. Even when she takes a break, she often stays right there in the house: reading, watching other TV programs, doing crafts or needlework projects. And she may even watch some sports with him.

No wonder a woman feels such resentment toward the time

her man spends with sports! Not only is he more excited about sports and more devoted to his team than to her and their family, but seeing him sitting there glued to the game while she cleans the house aggravates her more. "He skips out on his share of chores," she fumes, "and while he's having a grand time lying on the sofa yelling about the game, I'm slaving away!"

On the flip side, the man may be thinking, Not only does she give me grief about sports, she has to keep coming into the room to tell me how upset she is at crucial moments of the game! With strong feelings like these bouncing off the same walls for hours, week after week, it's no surprise that sports-related arguments can boil over into yelling and screaming.

## Vicky and Jim: Continuing Fireworks

Vicky and Jim are a married couple in their mid-thirties who have been together for twelve years. They live in Salt Lake City, where Jim's brand of sportsaholism includes a job in the sports media. That means he's gone for eight or more hours a day at work, which happens to revolve around sports. When he comes home, it's more sports. Since Vicky also works as an accountant, this greatly disturbs her.

"I get angry," she says, "because when I come home after working at my job all day, I have to turn around and cook dinner, clean up, pay the bills, open the mail, do the laundry, et cetera, all by myself."

When they argue, Vicky points a finger at Jim's upbringing. His father was a football coach, and Jim's younger brother is now an assistant coach for a college football team. In Jim's childhood home, sports ruled. Vicky claims her husband never learned the basics of helping out around the house. Beyond the issue of chores, Vicky and Jim share the common sportsaholic argument about how emotional he gets over sports. This is a hotter issue for them now, since before they moved into their new home, they never had cable TV. Now Jim can watch his brother's team play more often on ESPN, not to mention the NFL team for which one of his best friends is an assistant coach. It's those games involving guys he cares about that especially get Jim's emotions churning, and the more explosive he gets, the more upset Vicky becomes.

"I feel I'm being accused by her, like a defendant on trial," Jim argues. "My basic stance is there are other people who are much worse than me. I see them all around town after the Utah Jazz lose. They're taking it much harder than I take my teams' losing."

But Vicky doesn't buy this comparison, and Jim admits that his reactions are severe. Sure, it's easy to get worked up when you personally know people involved with your team. But Jim wonders if he gets more emotional over those games than his brother and best friend themselves.

"I get nervous, excited, and edgy watching their teams. When they win, I feel satisfied and exultant. When they lose, I feel sluggish and despondent," Jim confesses. "I judge myself by their play. I would love to know how I can enjoy sports without having them affect the way I view myself. Their success or failure governs me way too much."

In Part III, we'll explore why men get so emotionally invested in the fate of their teams. We'll talk about how men can balance their responses to sports events with their response to what's happening in their personal lives. We'll also hear from many men whose emotions are no longer dictated by their team's wins and losses, or at least not to the degree they once were.

For some couples today, it's not his screaming about the game that disrupts the household. It may not even be the juggling of household chores or taking care of the kids. Sometimes it just comes back to that issue of time. In a couple's busy life, they only have so much time to spend together, and every hour he watches sports is one less hour they spend together.

## Ruth and Jerry:
## The Window for Intimacy Slams Shut

A fiftyish couple, Ruth and Jerry live just a couple miles down the road from Notre Dame in South Bend, Indiana. Ruth is a teacher, so she has Saturdays and Sundays free. Jerry's a ticket agent for Amtrak, where Saturday is a busy day—what with fans coming from all over the country to see Notre Dame games. He's off on Sundays and Mondays. That leaves Sunday as their only day together. But in the fall, Jerry loves to watch pro football on Sunday. In the winter, he revels in the constant TV exposure of his favorite Chicago Bulls.

It's been this way Jerry's whole life. Growing up in a rural community in Pennsylvania, he played football, basketball, and baseball all the time. He regularly attended Pittsburgh Steelers and Penn State games with family and friends. Now that he lives in South Bend, he's gotten to know the Notre Dame fans who come in on the train, so he roots for them, too. His sports family keeps expanding, and when Sunday comes he can't imagine leaving *that* family behind.

"Sports are my enjoyment, my relaxation. I'm comfortable with them, except for my wife bugging me," Jerry relates. "But I think I'm better about it than I used to be."

Ruth's not handing out any ribbons for Jerry's sacrifices just yet. To her, fighting for equal time remains a continuous struggle. She watches a few games with him to placate him, but she's quick to point out that she'd much rather be doing something else. Sometimes she asks him if he could just tape the game so they could get out and take in the day together, enjoy more of life's firsthand experiences. But she doesn't see herself getting through to him.

"I've told him that if I could bounce a basketball, I'm sure he'd find me more exciting," sighs Ruth. "I can give in some and let him watch, but he has to give in, too. If he does, it's usually after I throw a fit. And the winters here last so long. That's what really makes it hard."

Ruth's willingness to appease Jerry and watch some sports with him during those long, cold Sundays is typical of many women, as evidenced by the majority of responses to Question #11 in the Women Who Know a Sportsaholic Survey, **"When you watch sports with him, what percentage of the time are you doing it for your own enjoyment, and what percentage of the time just to join him in his world?"**

Women in the survey indicated that they watch sports just to join him 58 percent of the time. While some women do watch sports because they enjoy them, many others say they will *only* sit down to watch a game for a while because it's a way to spend time with him.

That percentage raises questions about just how many women sitting in football stadiums or watching at home actually care about sports as much as the guys with them. NFL research indicates women make up 36 percent of pro football's TV viewing audience, according to Joe Ferreira, NFL director of broadcasting research. But could it be that most of those women are just casual fans, going along for part of the ride on Sunday to keep the peace or share some company with him? Sure, some women get as excited as men about Steve Young and the 49ers, but hard-core women fans are still a minority. Many men in my national survey indicated that they'd been searching for years for that *one* woman who likes sports even half as much as they do.

It's not just NFL Sundays that strain a sports-shrouded marriage. College-football Saturdays also add to the tension. TV doubleheaders take up entire afternoons, and with night telecasts, football blankets all waking hours on an autumn Saturday almost as snugly as basketball in winter. College fever is particularly severe in college towns, where on any given Saturday it seems as if everyone's going to the game or talking about it. If you're a woman who hasn't caught the fever, you can feel alone—especially if the man in your life is a college sportsaholic.

## Susan's Lament: No Weekend Travel

Susan is a mental health therapist who lives in Columbus, Ohio, home of football power Ohio State. Her husband Bernie, a lawyer, loves the Buckeyes; she doesn't. In their dating period more than twenty-five years ago, she went to a few games with him and even pretended to enjoy it. Now she doesn't pretend. The last time she went, her lack of sports knowledge was obvious not only to Bernie but to everyone within earshot. Embarrassed, Bernie said it ruined the day for him. He still attends all Ohio State home games, serving as a volunteer usher at the stadium, which means leaving home extra early. When he gets home, he's usually so wound up from the game that Susan no longer plans social events with other couples on Saturday night.

The college season only lasts four months, but fall is an important time of year to Susan. She likes to travel, you see, and she's concluded that they can't go away together during football season. So she's had to let go of her hopes to visit the Grand Canyon in autumn, and Greece will have to wait, too. Planning around Ohio State games just doesn't work. Bernie counters that they do take some trips together—when the Buckeyes go on the road. Every two years, for example, they visit Chicago when Ohio State plays at Northwestern.

"Sometimes," muses Susan, "I'd just like to go to Chicago without the football game as the reason."

Do you recognize these frustrations over time and scheduling? Not only do sports consume several hours per week, but each season lasts several months. And when a sportsaholic likes all the major sports, the seasons overlap. There is no break, no letup. The sports calendar seems even longer than twelve months and 365 days. For Marilyn in Charlottesville, Virginia, there was only one way to get through to her husband, who spent nearly all his free time in front of the TV. She took off her wedding ring and plunked it down on top of the set.

Even with a hobby of her own, a woman often finds she can't fill up all the lonely hours he devotes to sports. Let's say he spends thirty-six hours a week on sports. She likes gardening. Well, she's just not going to fill up all those hours in the garden, unless she's caretaker of some billionaire's estate. And more important to most women, even if she's filling up most of his sports hours with an activity of her own, she still yearns for that deeper intimacy with him. What happened, she may wonder, to his commitment to spend quality time with *her*?

There's no easy solution, but effective communication is a step in the right direction. If you're a couple tired of the same arguments about not spending time together, try these two exercises together in your Sportsaholism Recovery Playbook.

## PLAY #7:
## SPORTS RATING SYSTEM

If you're a woman, you know that you enter scheduling negotiations with your sportsaholic with three distinct disadvantages. First, he's usually got more on his sports schedule than you have on your calendar, and a typical game runs longer than most things on your list. (Example: A football game lasts about twice as long as a movie.) Second, he generally knows the sports lineup well ahead of time, while yours is likely to change weekly or daily. Third, your plans for a specific movie or play are usually a one-time thing, while his list includes sixteen weekly Steelers games. That's why women often get discouraged when trying to hash out time commitments with a sportsaholic. Here's one way to even things out:

He agrees to devise a sports event rating system that will categorize everything he wants to watch or attend. He sets ratings for all upcoming events at least a month in advance, with occasional weekly revisions for previously unscheduled major games. The rating system might look something like this:

**CLASS A:** Must-see games. If he's a New England Patriots fan, he would probably list all their games in this category, as well as an occasional major matchup like the Dolphins-Cowboys. The Super Bowl, World Series, and NBA Finals also may fit in this category, as well as games involving his college alma mater.

**Class B:** Games that would be nice to see (anytime the 49ers are on, or the Bulls in basketball) but he would honestly admit that he could live without them. Major national college games might fall into this rating.

**Class C:** Those games he watches just because it's football (or basketball, or whatever) and they were judged important enough to crack some network lineup of telecasts. Often, these games catch his eye because they come on just before or just after his main team's game, and it helps him keep that sports high going longer.

The woman in the household devises a similar rating system for events or activities she wants to do together each week. A friend's wedding is Class A, and so is their daughter's school play. The new Tom Hanks movie that just got rave reviews also might make the A list. In Class B, she might include a shopping excursion to look for new household furnishings, or a discussion about their next vacation. For Class C, she might mention cleaning out the attic or another activity that could be scheduled for any time.

Then, at a designated time each week, the couple sits down together for a weekly scheduling session. If he has a Class A game at the same time as a Class B event on her list, he gets to watch that Patriots game. But her Class B shopping excursion should take precedence over his Class C football game between the Falcons and the Bengals. If you both have Class B events at the same four-to-seven-P.M. Saturday slot, you negotiate and compromise as you would try to under any circumstances. With this system, you've at least got some structure and a few reference points to get you started.

**Point of caution**—Obviously, this rating system will not resolve or head off all arguments. The ratings are arbitrary, subject to each person tilting decisions toward her or his side with a higher rating. Sometimes common sense simply must prevail. But if the rating system reduces your arguments by 20 percent, isn't it worth it?

## PLAY #8:
## TRYING SOMETHING NEW TOGETHER

Many couples told me that they tried to find a new activity to share as a way of spending more time together, but most of the activities involved sports— competitive sports! Vicky and Jim, the couple mentioned earlier in this chapter adjusting to cable TV for the first time, joined a church softball team for couples. Vicky expected an emphasis on socializing and fun. The male coach stressed winning. Jim liked it. Vicky didn't.

Other couples reported similar results when they tried any sport or game that involved a winner and loser. Avoid the same mistake! I'm certainly not discouraging exercising together. Hiking, biking, canoeing, skiing, working out—these kinds of physical activities might be perfect for you. Just don't get into anything competitive. That feeds right into his addiction to the drama of sports, and he will, of course, want and need to win.

Also, be sure to find an activity that's really new to both of you, something neither of you has tried or mastered. The goal in discovering a new interest isn't to compromise. You're already compromising in other ways, which we'll explore fully in Part IV. Look for something new that you both can learn and participate in.

Maybe you'll decide you want to learn more about animals and wildlife. You might start by becoming more familiar with the zoos, wildlife centers, and nature trails in your area. Perhaps you'll choose to do volunteer work in the community together. In that case, you'll want to see where help is especially needed, perhaps with the homeless, disabled, or elderly. Or maybe you just want to have fun, and you'll decide to take up swing dancing together.

This new activity isn't something that has to take up a lot of time, either. This isn't a plot to cut off his sports supply. Your goal is to commit to spending perhaps a couple of hours a week together on common, uncharted ground.

Spend a few moments discussing and agreeing on your new shared activity. Write down your ideas in the Sportsaholism Recovery Playbook. Decide on the first step you will take together, and when you will pursue this new venture each week.

## Time to Lighten Up?

As you probably know from your own life, not all sports-related disagreements erupt with the magnitude and seriousness of Middle East conflicts. Divorce doesn't necessarily hang in the balance every time the Sunday-night football game kicks off. Sometimes a woman's refrain of "Oh no, not another football game!" is meant to be taken in jest. Sometimes when a man clasps his hands together and begs, "Just let me watch the rest of this half," he's trying to take the tension out of those same old arguments, not manipulate you to get his way.

Sometimes our extreme attitudes and prejudices toward sports just spill out in truly funny ways. When they do, it's OK to stop and laugh at them now and then. In fact, it's encouraged. Remember that laughter can be therapeutic. And if you're able to laugh *with* each other rather than laugh *at* each other, it will bring you closer together.

I'm not suggesting that you laugh away your legitimate problems with sports and relegate sportsaholism to the realm of one big cultural joke. By reading this book, you're demonstrating your willingness to explore the tough spots in your sportsaholic household. We'll be digging into more of them later. But an occasional breather, a bit of comic relief, can go a long way in helping keep your perspective.

So let's look next at some of those moments when sports enter the relationship arena and you just have to laugh.

# SEVEN

# The Things They Do for Sports

*They say it helps to simulate your home environment in
the delivery room, so the Cubs were on the radio when both
my boys were born.*
  —Carolyn, wife of a sportsaholic in South Bend, Indiana

You have to understand, Carolyn's husband, Peter, grew up idol-
izing Cubs Hall of Famer Ernie Banks. In fact, when Peter was a
boy growing up in a small Indiana town, everyone called him
Ernie. Yeah, he played lots of baseball, but the nickname actually
took hold the day he ran away from home at age five. He got as
far as the center of town, walked into the barber shop, hopped
up on the stool, and told the barber that Ernie Banks was his
cousin.

When Peter and Carolyn started dating, he hit a major stum-
bling block. She had grown up near Cincinnati, where she had
the nerve to attend games at Riverfront Stadium and root for the
hometown Reds, one of the main rivals of the Cubs. Peter put it
to her simply: For us to get married, you have to convert to the
Cubs.

"At first, I thought he was kidding," she recalls. "But then I saw
how serious he was. His goal was to bring me to Wrigley Field to
see a game in daylight, so I'd never go back to the Reds. This was
in '84, and the Cubs won their division. That impressed me. And
the environment at Wrigley *was* different. I started following
them, but I still don't like Harry Caray."

So they got married fourteen years ago and had two sons, neither of whom is named Ernie. For the first one they agreed on T.J., because the initials would look cool on the back of any sports uniform. For the second son, Peter pushed the Cubs connection and campaigned for Ryne—for Cubs second baseman Ryne Sandberg. No way, Carolyn said. They settled on Taylor.

Eddie faced a similar predicament while dating Paula, a Cincinnati native who dared call herself a fan of the football Bengals. Eddie grew up in Cleveland as a die-hard follower of the Cleveland Browns, before their '95 move to Baltimore. Eddie soon learned that conversion was impossible. Paula took her Bengals very seriously, not like those "me too" women who start watching football to score points with guys. After their courtship as fellow students on the neutral grounds of Ohio State, he decided he'd go ahead and marry her anyway, but he held off the proposal until the right moment.

One day they went to Cleveland together to see a Bengals-Browns football game, where they could root for their opposite teams. An hour before the game, Eddie asked to borrow Paula's camera to take a photo of the field—with no action going on. "Why do you want to do that now?" she asked.

But as she followed the direction he was pointing the camera, she caught on. The scoreboard message center flashed Eddie's question: PAULA, WILL YOU MARRY ME? "Well," she said, "you're stuck now because you got it in writing." The Browns clobbered the Bengals that day, and for this one time Paula didn't mind coming out the loser.

When Paula and Eddie completed the surveys, they were preparing for the birth of their first child, who would move into their second bedroom, which doubled as Eddie's sports-memorabilia room. The walls and ceilings were covered with banners, photos, license plates, and pompons. Eddie worried that Paula would demand that he take them all down when the child was born. Not so. A few months after the birth of their son D.J., Paula reported that the room was "half baby, half sports. I've got a couple of Bengals things in there, too, so we'll keep the sports motif for now. They say babies should be exposed to bright colors, and with our team colors we've got orange, red, and blue."

## Please, All I Want Is That *One* Championship

Eddie deeply mourned the departure of the Browns from Cleveland, a move he protested by shaving off his mustache so that every time he looked in the mirror, his missing facial hair would serve as a symbolic reminder of the missing team in his life. He had hoped to see the Browns win a Super Bowl someday, just as he's been hoping to see an Indians World Series championship, or even the Cleveland Cavaliers taking the NBA title. It's been years of waiting and hoping, hoping and waiting. He often thinks back to how fate plopped him down in this sports city, instead of others where championships are more than a dream.

"I was born in Scranton, Pennsylvania, and my dad was an auto worker," he recalls. "When I was young, he faced a transfer to another plant. It could have been Pittsburgh, and if it had, I would have seen four Super Bowl championships for the Steelers and the '79 World Series title for the Pirates. It could have been Detroit, where the Pistons won back-to-back NBA championships. But no, he had to relocate in Cleveland! Just about every other city you could research has won some championship, even Seattle and Portland. But not Cleveland."

Obviously, Eddie suffers the defeats of his Cleveland teams deeply. Paula usually takes his emotional displays in the same playful spirit she accepted his marriage proposal, but sometimes she complains that he takes it all too seriously. Eddie agrees. He hopes he can do something about it—someday.

"I have to get that monkey off my back," he says. "If one of my teams wins a real championship, I really think I would finally feel fulfilled to the point where I could reduce the role of sports in my life substantially."

Addiction experts might call that "bargaining," a sportsaholism deflection technique similar to those we saw in Chapter 4, sort of like the alcoholic waiting for the perfect "drunk" before he'll quit drinking. But hey, you never know. Sports results can trigger bizarre behavior from otherwise sane, serious sports fans. And many fans totally believe that how they behave *during* a game will impact their team's chances of winning. Fans put together their own elaborate game plans that are as carefully devised as anything mapped out in a locker room.

Take Russ, for example. A thirty-six-year-old clerk, he roots for his Dallas Cowboys from his home in Troy, New York. While he's watching, Russ will not eat or drink anything until the game is over. Once he slipped up at halftime of an apparent Dallas romp and had a snack. When he returned well-fed for the second half, the Cowboys blew the game. From then on, he's always observed a strict fast until game's end.

Also, Russ now recognizes the importance of staying in his seat and not moving for the entire three-hour (or more) span of a game. When the Cowboys held an apparently safe lead in the final seconds of a game against Detroit, Russ again gave in to overconfidence. He got up, put on his coat, and told his dog (named Dallas, of course) to get ready to go out for a walk. At that very moment Cowboys quarterback Troy Aikman fumbled, the Lions scored, and the Cowboys lost. "I never move from my seat for the entire game now," brags Russ, who figures that if the Cowboys need him to sit still for three hours, it's the least he can do to help the team.

Other fans find that getting up and leaving the TV room in the middle of the action can boost their team's chances of winning. Or maybe it's just the only way to calm their nerves in sweating out the outcome. Ted, a sixty-two-year-old Kentucky Wildcats basketball fan whose sports memorabilia room has relics dating back to 1948, admits that whether listening on radio or watching on TV, sometimes he turns away from the Wildcats because the tension is too much for him. So he takes a break to walk his dog in his neighborhood in Hopkinsville, Kentucky. But even in walking away from the game, he figures he's helping his team. His dog's name is Lucky, and when Lucky and Ted return from their walk with the game still in progress, they usually find that Kentucky's lead has increased—thanks to the good luck they brought them.

Gordon, a twenty-five-year-old Houston Oilers fan in Houston, suffered intense guilt after his team's most famous collapse: blowing a 35–3 lead and losing a playoff game to the Buffalo Bills. As

Gordon stormed the house punching walls, he knew he had only himself to blame. "I talked to my dad on the phone at halftime," he confesses. "We had never done that before during a game. We were all pumped up talking about the Oilers making the Super Bowl. That was a big mistake. The only other time I was depressed like that was when my grandmother died. It was a couple of weeks before I could read the sports page or watch ESPN, because I knew I'd be reminded of the game."

## Raising the Children of a Sportsaholic

Gordon probably owns one of Houston's most complete collections of sports merchandise from all the local teams. He once managed a sports-merchandise store near the Astrodome, so the prices were right. His souvenir corner in their home is decorated and maintained like a shrine. It doesn't include any sports clothes for kids, mostly because he and his wife, Jenny, do not have any children. But they've talked about starting a family, and debated what the first child should wear as an infant.

"We were walking through a store in the mall recently, and I saw all this Winnie the Pooh stuff. I loved it," Jenny explains. "So I said that we've got to get this stuff for our child someday whether it's a girl or a boy." Gordon's response? "No, it will be sports clothing for our child."

In a Jackson, Michigan, household several years ago, Carl wasn't worried so much about what his first child would wear as he was concerned about the timing of the birth. Carl's a serious Michigan football fan, you see, and his wife Diana was due just about the same date as the annual showdown with Michigan State. In fact, she went into labor the morning of the game, and an hour or two before kickoff her contractions were just ten minutes apart.

"We had to make a crucial decision," remembers Carl, an auto dealer. "Could she wait until after the game to deliver? Should we go to the hospital and skip the game? I asked her what she wanted to do, and she screamed: 'GO TO THE GAME!' We were planning to attend the game with a physician friend, so we thought, What the hell. We joked that she could give birth at halftime, and the baby could see the second half."

Their baby girl held off her initiation into sports, not arriving until after the game. Michigan won, so everyone was happy. At least Carl didn't insist on naming his daughter after one of the Michigan players, as Peter had tried to do with his favorite Cubs players in the example at the start of the chapter.

Giving his child a sports name is a common request for a sportsaholic who becomes a father. Sam and Chelsea, a couple in their twenties living in Florissant, Missouri, went through the debate as they prepared for the arrival of their son. An operations manager for an electronics firm, Sam's a serious Cowboys fan, so he naturally wanted to name their son Troy or Emmitt after Dallas stars Troy Aikman and Emmitt Smith. Chelsea, who works for a travel agency, hates football. "One guy gets the ball, a bunch of guys jump on him, and they get up and do it again," she says. She nixed the Cowboys name idea, and Keith was born.

But some husbands win this tussle over names. Fred, a hotel manager in Port Orange, Florida, roots for the Chicago Bulls. When his wife, Melinda, was expecting, Fred clearly expressed his intention that, boy or girl, the child would get part of Michael Jordan's name. In this case, Melinda loves sports too, so she went along with the program. They named their daughter Chanler Shea-*Jordan*. Had it been a boy, it would have been *Jordan* Michael.

When a child is born into a sportsaholic household, the influence doesn't end with a sports name, or even with lots of toddler clothes from the sports-merchandise catalog of Dad's favorite team. The youngster's father also wants to ensure that his child sees his or her first TV games early and often.

Curt, a buyer for a marketing firm in Madison, Tennessee, identifies with the Dallas Cowboys so much that he drives a car decked out in Cowboys blue and silver with team flags and license-plate frames. Since Curt wears Cowboys jackets, hats, shoes, gloves, and scarves, it wasn't surprising that he had his daughter wearing three or four different Cowboys outfits before her first birthday, with a cheerleading outfit on hold for the following year. (Curt also bought Cowboys shirts and a collar for his dog, but that's another story.) When his daughter was about eight months old, Dad also taught her how to raise both arms high in the air in a touchdown signal when asked, "What do the Cowboys do?"

One Nebraska fan who called me inquiring about the survey explained his different twist to the same story. He taught his three-year-old daughter the arms-raised salute to mark a Nebraska touchdown. She was trained to give that sign whenever the family yelled and screamed for one of the Cornhuskers' frequent touchdowns. Here's how she understood her first lesson about sports and life: parent screaming = touchdown salute. During the off-season, Dad was watching a speech by President Clinton on TV, and something Clinton said made him yell and scream in response. Sure enough, he found his daughter raising her arms in the touchdown signal.

## Saying "I Do" or "I Will" at the Game

Many men, single or married, fantasize about proposing or getting married at a sports site, as Eddie did when he proposed to Paula at that Cleveland Browns game. It's a growing trend, one that even emerged in a beer commercial a few years ago, where football announcer Keith Jackson took over the play-by-play of a wedding that needed a little excitement. The Pittsburgh Steelers allow one couple to broadcast their marriage proposal on the Three Rivers Stadium scoreboard at every home game. The announcement always comes right after the halftime show, so people know to look for it.

In the survey, several respondents reported that they had really wanted a sports-stadium proposal or wedding, but backed down because they didn't believe their intended would go for it. Of course, if *she's* the big fan, the idea has a better chance of working out. Lucy, a twenty-four-year-old purchasing agent and self-confessed sportsaholic in Mesa, Arizona, was attending a Harlem Globetrotters game one night when one of the players started flirting with her. It was all part of the act, of course, which ended with her boyfriend taking the mike and asking Lucy to marry him. "The rest of the game, players and referees ran by congratulating us," she recalls. "And when we left, everyone we walked by either just stared at us or stopped and asked us if it was a joke."

If you're single and looking, you can still hope for the sports proposal or wedding fantasy to come to life. One Nebraska fan proudly admits that he dreams of finding a woman willing to get married at Memorial Stadium at halftime of a Cornhuskers game. And he'd want them both to be all decked out in the school color of red.

Mike, age twenty-two, single, and a Dallas Cowboys fan in Leetsdale, Pennsylvania, has the entire wedding scene all mapped out and ready to roll. All he needs is the bride. "We would get married at halftime of a Cowboys game at Texas Stadium," Mike imagines. "My fiancée, of course, would be a Cowboys fan. There would be blue and silver balloons everywhere. After I kissed the bride, I would send her deep and toss her a long pass for a touchdown, and we would run off the field together."

If you're married and realize it's too late for that perfect sports proposal or wedding, you can still fantasize about sharing a peak moment at a sports site. A few respondents in my survey admitted they imagined having sex in one of the glass-enclosed skyboxes in Toronto during a Blue Jays game, something that many Toronto fans and media with binoculars have spotted and eagerly described a few times.

## The Things *Women* Do for Sports

Men don't have the market cornered on outlandish behavior or ideas about sports. In the national survey, 12 percent of respondents to the Sportsaholism Questionnaire were women. They described themselves as bigger fans than most men they knew. In fact, a few women revealed that their husbands left *them* because he couldn't handle *her* sports expertise and devotion. In one woman's divorce settlement, the hot issue involved who got custody of their two season tickets to Purdue basketball games.

For sixty-something Peggy, a Texas native living in Farmington Hills, Michigan, Super Bowl parties can be too much to bear. Those *men* just don't know football like she does, and all they do is talk, talk, talk. When her beloved Dallas Cowboys make the big event, Peggy hightails it right out of Michigan. She flies to Dallas just to watch the game on TV on more friendly, knowledgeable turf—with her eighty-something, Cowboys–loving mother!

Another woman boasted of forming an all-female Fantasy Football League in her office. In the survey, such passionate women fans often scolded other women for refusing to hop on the sports-lovers bandwagon. When they encounter other women who don't get sports and don't want to, they're just as judgmental as any man. One woman in the survey wrote, "When I hear the giddy, silly questions women ask about sports, I feel embarrassed for my gender."

But even a woman who dislikes sports can do some funny things when she rebels against her male sportsaholic. Rochelle, a teacher in Suffolk, Virginia, got tired of standing in front of the TV trying to block her husband's view of the game. Flipping the dial to the Weather Channel just as a touchdown was about to be scored didn't work so well, either. So she grabbed the remote and hid it in her robe pocket. That made him work a little harder to get a game on.

Rochelle, though, couldn't resist wading into the sports scene when she heard that the new minor league baseball park needed a name. She called and suggested Harbor Park. A short time later, she learned she had won a contest she didn't even know she had entered, and first prize was two season tickets to all games at Harbor Park. Yes, she took her husband.

"He was so thrilled sitting there at the games that his face puffed up with pride like a bluefish," she relates. "I became the supreme queen in his eyes. He feels we're bonded when we go together, and because it's sports-related, I'm sure in his mind this is more meaningful than any other kind of bonding between humans."

## Life As a Baseball Game

We've all grown accustomed to the regular mixing of sports symbols, language, and images into "real-life" events and situations. Sports talk has been commonplace at work and in politics for decades, even before former pro football quarterback Jack Kemp's '96 vice-presidential campaign triggered a nonstop barrage of football metaphors. In politics, any highly touted speech gets called a "home run." In business, CEOs assessing a bad deal routinely discuss when it might be time to "punt," or huddle for a new "game plan" to "level the playing field" against the competition.

One of the most creative life-as-sports metaphors I've seen arrived through the national survey from Hank, a labor-relations consultant and sportsaholic in Mentor, Ohio. Hank broke down the stages of a baseball game and compared them to the basic phases of life. His outline:

### Innings 1–3

This is like childhood. You're feeling things out, preparing for the next stage. You usually can overcome those early mistakes. You're getting set to do what you can do.

### Innings 4–6

This is adolescence and early adulthood. You begin to make your mark and set the table for the balance of your life. You want to get the lead here, and the closer is near.

### Innings 7–9

This is later adulthood. You're either ahead and enjoying the finer things in life, or you're behind and you have limited time to change things and win the game, or in life, to end on a high note.

And where is Hank, at age forty-seven, on the baseball/life map? He explains, "I'm late in the sixth inning. It's been a rough six innings in many ways. I was a firefighter for sixteen years, which I enjoyed, but I got fired. I had a midlife crisis at forty, had a son born about then, entered a second marriage. Things are going great now. Maybe I'm ahead 5–2."

## Why They Take It So Far

As a woman living with a sportsaholic, you may be scratching your head again wondering just why men go to such lengths to weave sports so intricately into the fabric of their everyday lives. But is it really any wonder why they do the things they do for sports? When you reach for the sports section first thing in the morning, sports are going to impact your thoughts, words, and deeds. In answering Questions #51 and 52 in the Sportsaholism Questionnaire, regarding their time spent with the sports section compared with the rest of the newspaper, men reported that they spend an average of nineteen minutes reading the sports section and only fourteen minutes looking at the rest of the newspaper.

That's five minutes *less* for everything else in the daily newspaper: national news, world news, local news, features, commentary, lifestyle, obituaries, comics, advice columns, wedding notices, crime reports, advertising flyers, etc. A full 10 percent of all respondents reported that they never look at the rest of the paper at all. The news is just too negative and depressing, they say. They'll just stick to sports. Or *SportsCenter.* In the survey, a majority of men indicated they watch ESPN's *SportsCenter* at least once every day. Discounting those survey respondents who don't have cable TV and thus lack access to ESPN, 86 percent watch *SportsCenter* several times a week. And 22 percent said they seldom or *never* watch regular TV news.

Clearly, he prefers sports as his main world. And even when you're able to laugh occasionally about his excesses, that day-in, day-out onslaught of sports and his dependency on them reminds you of its seriousness. So you try to jolt him, get him to break away. "It's only a game," you say. "Get a life!" you urge.

But he only digs in more deeply. In fact, he wants *you* to join him in that world. "Just try it," he says. "You'll like it." If you took the time to learn about sports and understood the rules, personalities, strategies, and history, you'd want to follow it your-self. He tells you that your put-downs about sports and how much he loves them come from lack of intelligence. You haven't given sports a real chance, he argues. Everything you say about sports is way off base, because you just don't know what you're missing.

# EIGHT

# You Don't Know What You're Missing!

*Women ask really dumb questions about sports like, "Who's Michael Jordan?" I actually had one ask me that. I'd like to educate them about sports.*

—Raymond, of Omaha, Nebraska

It's true, men can say nasty things about women who don't know sports. They may sound sexist or judgmental, but it's what they believe: Women don't know the difference between a home run and a touchdown. They think the New York Knicks play baseball. They always ask what inning the football game is in, or how many quarters are left in the baseball game. They can't understand simple football strategy. They don't know the names of the big stars.

There's more: If women don't know sports, they're not following current events so they're just not educated. They have no sense of history, either. They pick teams to root for because they like the pretty uniforms or the cute quarterback. Whenever they open their mouths and make a comment or ask a question about sports, they say something stupid or silly.

Many men fantasize about meeting a sports-savvy woman, then bemoan what they find instead. But despite men's harsh put-downs, watch what happens when a woman comes up to her sportsaholic and tells him she wants to learn more about sports, or get to know the players, rules, or strategy. His eyes light up. He smiles. He beckons her closer. He puts down the newspaper or the remote. He speaks eloquently and with great conviction. He acts, as one woman said, like a kitten lapping up milk.

In fact, he plunges so deeply into the role of happy sports teacher, she can't figure out how to get him out of it. It starts with one simple question: What are those number signals that the catcher flashes to the pitcher before every pitch? In response, she hears a two-hour report on the history of pitching, from Sandy Koufax's fastball years ago to Tom Glavine's slider today. And, of course, he'll explain the distinction between a change-up and a split-fingered fastball, what's wrong with the designated-hitter rule, and whether you can ever get the accurate speed of a good fastball on the radar gun.

Occasionally, she may even find something in his lesson that she can understand.

Before you know it, he's buying two tickets for a Yankees-Orioles game and taking her to the ballpark in plenty of time to watch batting practice, so she can study the proper techniques of hitting. He's educating her on the difference between the hit-and-run and the squeeze play, and showing her how to keep score with all the proper coding. Every so often, he pops a surprise quiz to check her progress. And if she gets good grades, he's as pleased and proud as any parent of a child bringing home straight A's. He also expects her to want to know more.

"You don't know what you're missing," he's been telling her. Now he's going to show her exactly what he means.

## Sports Apprentice on Trial

A trial lawyer who lives in Kearny, New Jersey, Barbara's in her first year of marriage with Lennie, a sports reporter and sports-aholic whose game-watching tendencies to get profane and throw things were mentioned in Chapter 3. Barbara entered the relationship with a respectable degree of sports awareness from years of following college basketball and even pro football. As soon as they moved in together, Lennie began offering her advanced lessons on all sports, and the curriculum was as challenging as law school.

"There was an initial novelty for him in my knowing a good bit about sports," Barbara explains. "It was as if Lennie was saying, 'Look at the girl. She knows about sports. Isn't that cute.' He is still genuinely surprised that I know some of the rules. But now I think he expects me to keep up-to-date on trades and daily developments of my favorite teams. If I don't, he seems a little disappointed in me."

If you're a woman who begins dating a sportsaholic while you're still a sports novice, don't be caught off guard by his eagerness to show you the ropes. And expect that he'll want to push you quickly through the elementary material so you can soon become his sports buddy.

## Training a Foreign Student

Sue is a native of Vietnam who fled to the U.S. as a fourteen-year-old with her family as the war in Vietnam was ending. She caught on to many American ways quickly, but sports were a tougher subject, and also a painful one. She would often find herself alone, her boyfriends spending hours engrossed in such "foreign" pursuits as football, baseball, and basketball. When the guys noticed that she didn't get sports at all, they'd go off to watch the game with their men friends. Sue ended those relationships.

But then she met Steve, a serious sportsaholic with a forty-plus-hour weekly habit and a background in sports broadcasting. As we learned in Chapter 3, Steve's friends call him Stork because he gets so nervous watching games that he hops on one leg. Early in their relationship, Sue gave him an opening by showing just a little interest in sports. His first response was to throw her kisses from across the room. Then Stork hopped right on over to begin teaching.

"Before I met Steve," she begins, "when I looked at football I just thought to myself, What a bunch of bozos. What are they doing out there? But he taught me all about the game. I think it's exciting now. I recently went to an Oilers game, and I found that

I much prefer being there in person to watching it on TV because you can see it all. He wanted to take me to a baseball game, but I put my foot down. Baseball is just too slow."

So why do men leap so quickly to the call of a woman who wants to know what this sports stuff is all about? The motivational factors are strong, the benefits numerous.

- **Assuming teacher-pupil roles**—By playing teacher, he creates a forum in which to share his expertise and natural enthusiasm for sports. Also, in this role he can relive some of his treasured memories of learning sports from his father. Those are probably some of the strongest and fondest memories of his life, the reasons for which we'll explore in the next chapter. Teaching sports to a woman also allows him to operate in the male-superior position, which could lead to a healthy balancing act, especially if he often plays pupil to *her* as teacher in child-raising, cooking, sewing, and emotional awareness.
- **Turning down the heat**—The logic works like this: If she starts learning about sports, then she'll want to watch them more. If she watches them, she may start liking them. If she likes sports, she won't bug him about the time and energy he devotes to sports. He's off the hook!
- **Treating her like one of the guys**—A girlfriend or wife who gets into sports becomes a true companion for a sports lover. He can take her to games. He can watch at home with her. He can even talk sports with her sometimes. Maybe he can even let her watch with some of his male sports buddies, and trust that she won't say anything to embarrass him. He has always found that when it comes to sharing sports, a man can never have too many friends— especially when he can include the woman in his life.
- **Connecting intimately**—Beyond becoming one of the guys, the woman who starts getting into sports gives her man a sense of genuine intimacy in their relationship. As we'll explore in Part III, many men hide behind the wall of sports to avoid intimacy. But deep down, most men really do yearn for a strong connection with their partners.

Sports may be the only place they believe they can find it, and to those who believe that, sports are the most satisfying grounds for an intimate connection.

- **Revealing what she's missing**—If a man believes that sports are the greatest thing on earth, it naturally follows that everyone should love them. Who more important to get in on all the fun, drama, and intensity than the person closest to him? He regards sports as a joy in life, perhaps one of the few pleasures in a depressing world. As he sees it, the woman in his life should not be denied this pleasure any more than she should be denied the mutual pleasures of sex.

If you're a woman who knows a sportsaholic, you've probably heard all about what you're missing if you don't get turned on by sports. In our culture, you can't escape hearing the praises of sports. But usually you just hear the surface stuff. Men tell you how great it is to watch Michael Jordan take over a basketball game. Or Jerry Rice make an art form of catching footballs. Or Ken Griffey Jr. crank home runs and run the bases like Willie Mays. You may hear about that unbelievable comeback the Bills made to beat the Oilers in the NFL playoffs a few years ago, or how the '69 Mets came from way behind to beat the Cubs in the pennant race and stun Baltimore in the World Series.

After almost every game, the sportsaholic is bubbling over with some story of heroic deeds, astounding plays, dominant victories by powerhouse teams, or shocking upsets by up-and-coming spoilers. It can seem as if he's constantly auditioning for a role in a TV infomercial about the virtues of spectator sports. It wouldn't be thirty minutes long, either—perhaps more like ninety minutes. Couldn't you just picture him doing it? Wouldn't it be easy to come up with the video highlights of his actual sports-watching moments?

But to tell the whole story, the script for that advertisement also needs to explain more completely just what sports do for him in life. To gather the best material, let's look at the national survey results of Question #4 on the Sportsaholism Questionnaire from Chapter 2, **"How do sports enhance the quality of your life?"**

This question, like the others, does not offer multiple choice answers. But in reading through the responses, I was struck by the consistent themes that emerged. With minor differences in wording that still conveyed the same message, respondents described the benefits of sports in their lives in five basic ways:

1. fun/enjoyment/entertainment
2. intense emotions from the drama of the games
3. clear focus for life/something to look forward to
4. relaxation/relief from daily problems, concerns, boredom
5. conversation/camaraderie with friends and fellow sports fans

Sounds like a pretty full package, doesn't it? No wonder he keeps telling her, "You don't know what you're missing!" As a woman dealing with a sportsaholic, you hear that message over and over, in its many forms and variations:

"Just let me tell you what the Packers did in the *Monday Night Football* game after you went to sleep," he might tell you.

"Come over for just one second and see the replay of this unbelievable touchdown pass Dan Marino just threw," he'll coax.

"You're not gonna believe how my Fantasy-League team just jumped from third place to first," he'll report.

"Look, honey, the camera's zooming in on the Pittsburgh coach's wife cheering from the fancy VIP box again," he'll chuckle.

"Check out this new mouse pad I got for my computer," he'll urge. "It's done up like a football field with the Dallas Cowboys star at the fifty-yard line!"

In his campaign to win you over to sports, he will call upon many allies. Pro-football marketeers, for one, are on the lookout for ways to gain new women fans and to deepen their bond with casual women fans. The NFL recently introduced a new line of sports apparel aimed directly at women. Sure, women do buy and wear some of the same Troy Aikman uniform jerseys and Miami Dolphins T-shirts that guys wear, but new official NFL sleeveless tank tops and shorts are designed for women to feel comfortable wearing outside the stadium gates—to health clubs, beaches, wherever.

I remember a few years back when CBS still owned part of the TV rights to NFL football. In promoting the upcoming Sunday games, CBS ads throughout the week portrayed a couple at home. The football-loving guy talked up the big upcoming matchups with great enthusiasm and inside knowledge. As his disgruntled wife roamed the house behind him, casting disapproving glances and trying to distract him from the TV, the guy would end the promo by saying, "I'm a big fan!" After keeping the same theme with these characters for a few weeks, CBS introduced a new twist. Suddenly, that once-disgruntled wife was sitting right beside her sports-lovin' guy in front of the TV, and *she* was hyping the upcoming games with her own passion and know-how. The new ending, spoken in unison: *"We're big fans!"*

Closer to home, you will also feel the pressure of your sports-aholic trying to convince you to switch from local news to *SportsCenter,* just in time for one of Keith Olbermann's funny lines. Or you'll see one of those commercials with Michael Jordan or Charles Barkley that's designed to convince you that the sports world is not just a bunch of dumb jocks. And then, when your sportsaholic engages in one of those intense and animated sports conversations with one of his male sports friends, you can't help wondering, I still don't get why, but they *do* always seem to enjoy themselves, or, I wish he would get this excited about our anniversary, but if sports are what gets his juices flowing, maybe I should just get into them a little more . . .

## Hitting the Choice Point

Sooner or later, you know he's going to try to convert you from sports outsider to insider. Ideally, he does want you to share this special world with him. He wants to hear you ask him questions about the games, the players, his team. He's eager to play your teacher. He hopes you can learn enough to know the basics, so you won't have to ask those silly and embarrassing questions (but not so much that you think you're an expert and threaten his sports-wizard status). He envisions you going to games with him, watching games with him, talking sports with him during intimate moments over a meal or in bed. He imagines a domestic life where he's never again stung by complaints about his beloved sports. Because you will be right there with him.

The sportsaholic has a vested interest in converting you. And at some point, you're going to have to make a choice: Do you give in and play the role of pupil, learning such useful bits of information as why football teams punt on fourth down? Or do you stand fast and declare sports out of bounds in your own life, then see if you can nudge him toward changing *his* ways?

The questions don't end there. If you choose the first option and say yes to sports, how much do you take in? Will it be OK for you (and him) if you watch basketball and baseball, but draw the line at football? That's still five months of long weekends apart. Also, will your compromise on sports leave you feeling that you've given too much of yourself away? And if he's really addicted to sports and you endorse his behavior by joining him in it, aren't you playing a codependent role?

If you say no to sports, will the permanent sports split ultimately lead to a total break in the relationship, and is that really what you want? Or will you two be doomed to a sports standoff, where you aim sarcastic comments at each other from opposite corners?

## Jenny's Choice: Sports or Divorce

We met Jenny in the previous chapter, where she was eyeing Winnie the Pooh clothes for their first child, while her husband Gordon insisted any child of his would wear official sports apparel. They're a young couple who met as college students in Texas and married soon thereafter. Early in their three-year marriage, Jenny hit her choice point. She had grown up in a sports-dominated household, which she didn't much enjoy. And now her husband was urging her to watch football with him.

"I hated it," Jenny admits. "I was very unhappy."

But she didn't want to see her marriage turn sour over something like sports. She looked for guidance from others who had been through a similar experience. She didn't have to go far. Because Gordon's father also was a passionate sports fan, Jenny decided to ask Gordon's mother how she dealt with the issue.

"She told me it was the same for her at the start of her marriage," explains Jenny. "She decided that if the marriage was going to last, she would have to learn sports, and she did. So after talking to her, I started asking questions about sports."

Jenny has found that she actually enjoys watching the Houston Rockets in basketball. Baseball she can appreciate in person but not on TV. But football is still a big problem. Even if she gets past her basic dislike for the sport, she finds that a close Oilers game makes her so nervous that she gets nauseous and has to leave the room. So Jenny's trying to make do as best she can, though she warns that when she and Gordon do start having children, she expects *him* to make a choice to spend less time with sports.

For most couples, the choice point is most likely to come about six months to a year into the relationship. That's about the time when most major issues rise to be reckoned with, and when couples decide how to take them on, or if they're willing to try. The emerging gap over sports often fits that predictable timetable.

In the first few months, the couple is focusing on their physical, emotional, or psychological attraction to each other. When it comes to sports, she may decide to go to a game with him early on and pretend to enjoy it more than she really does, or shrug off his sports obsession as no big deal. And maybe he'll skip a game or two in the beginning, so she won't get turned off like other women he's dated.

Then, before the first anniversary of that initial romantic encounter, reality settles in. Now they've moved in together, or at least they're sharing larger blocks of weeknight and weekend time. That's sports time, and he's not holding back his interest anymore. He's cuddling up with his favorite teams and riding those intense emotional ups and downs. She's not faking interest anymore, either. She's letting him know that she finds this sports habit of his quite annoying and often disruptive.

And she chooses which way to go over sports. Or whether she wants to go forward with the relationship at all. In the national survey, I found that many couples had been toting their major disagreements over sports around for several years. Their early choice point had left them in polarized positions that became more entrenched and more hostile over time.

For many couples, the choice point may hit earlier than six months, perhaps even on the first date. Attitudes toward spectator sports often turn up high on compatibility lists for both men and women, right up there with sex, money, children, and politics. It's something each person may need to know right away. If she's suffered through sportsaholic relationships in the past, she's on the lookout for any sign of sports memorabilia in his car or home. When he first flicks on the radio or TV in her presence, she's waiting to see what he'll do when he comes across a game: Will he stop right there, or keep on going for news, music, or some other palatable, nonsports-related entertainment?

For a man still hearing the echoes of complaints and put-downs from other girlfriends over his sports habit, his eyes and ears are tuned in to her initial response to sports: Will she smile and make a comment that shows at least *some* sports knowledge, or squirm in her seat as if she's enduring a root canal?

## Saying Yes to Sports—And Meaning It

When Leroy and Jan of Somonauk, Illinois, met a few years ago, Jan had been married and divorced once, and Leroy had been divorced twice already. He is a big sports fan. In addition to his passion for football and baseball, he has also worked in sports broadcasting. It's just *possible* that the time Leroy spent with sports negatively affected those previous two marriages. This time, he vowed, he was going to be clear from the outset. In seeking a new relationship, he wrote a personal ad that included a reference to baseball, and when he met Jan he gave it to her straight.

"You know," he said, "I really love sports."

"That's fine," Jan replied. "I don't have a problem with that."

"No, you don't understand," Leroy continued. "I *really* love sports."

Well, Jan's ex-husband of twenty years had no interest in sports at all, and she hadn't had any desire to watch them either. But she decided to give sports a try. Friends who knew them didn't hold out much hope for the new relationship. But the teacher-pupil role clicked for both of them. By the time they planned to spend their honeymoon in the Washington, D.C., area, Jan eagerly consented to take in a Washington Capitals pro hockey game.

"He has been very helpful and encourages me to learn more, and that's sparking my interest," Jan enthuses. "I like watching most sports, especially baseball, basketball, and volleyball. I still have a little difficulty with football. But Leroy is absolutely wonderful about explaining plays and rules to me. And more important, he never makes me feel less than intelligent. He simply answers my questions in ways that he knows I can understand."

Wanda, a twenty-one-year-old customer service representative from Fredericksburg, Virginia, is another woman who's thankful that she went with the sports flow right from the start. Wanda's husband took her to her first baseball game soon after the wedding, and she quickly got into baseball's players, strategy, and history. As a new fan of the Baltimore Orioles, she didn't miss out on any of the thrills of Cal Ripken's historic breaking of Lou Gehrig's record for consecutive games played.

"Being a bit of a baseball fan," she says, "it brought tears to my eyes."

The choice point over sports is not necessarily a one-time thing. As couples stay together longer, their habits change. When a sportsaholic suddenly finds himself with access to Primestar, he doubles or triples his sports-watching time, and she faces a new choice point—increasing her own sports time, or telling him it's back to basic cable. If a couple begins a family, those casual Sunday football doubleheaders, when she'd watch with him a little between catching up on her reading, suddenly don't appear so benign when she's running around taking care of the kids.

Even if the woman makes an initial investment in learning sports, over time the couple may find that they still have a major gap in *passion* toward sports. Let's say he lives and dies with the fate of the New York Yankees, Knicks, and Giants. She watches maybe a third or half the time with him, understands some of what's going on, and can talk to him about what they're seeing, like when the Yankees play in the World Series. But maybe she doesn't think the Knicks losing in the playoffs is worth tearing up the house over. Sooner or later, it becomes clear that they're having two very different experiences with sports, not fully sharing as they first believed. He's a sportsaholic, she's a casual fan. So another choice point comes along.

Sometimes sports get dragged along a marital road that gets bumpier from other new ruts. Suppose a woman goes back to grad school and comes home full of excitement and energy about her path to an MBA. If he greets her with a total lack of interest in her course work and instead keeps babbling about the Chicago Bears' hot new running back, she may quickly sour on his sports devotion. Or if she's been criticizing him for not standing up to his boss and demanding a higher salary, he may suddenly decide that this is a good time to pay more attention to the rebuilding efforts of the Philadelphia Phillies.

And as women say, the choice involved is often *his*. She's made it clear that she needs him to curb some of his sports habits and make room for greater intimacy or she may leave him. Cheryl may be reaching that point. She's the addictions counselor in training whose sportsaholic husband, Wayne, has become her major case study, as revealed in Chapter 4. Cheryl reminds Wayne that his first marriage failed and that this is his second chance—so don't blow it.

"I'm going to move forward in my life with him or without him," declares Cheryl. "He has a choice."

For other couples who have hung in together over many years, nothing ever seems to change regarding sports. It's a problem and it doesn't go away. He loves sports, she doesn't. He says, "You knew I was like this when you married me." She thinks, Maybe, but I didn't know how much more alienated and frustrated I'd get as time went on. She may have tried to let him teach her sports once, but that only reminded her just why she wanted nothing to do with them. She *does* know what she's missing with sports, and she's quite content to go right on missing it.

## Women Who Hate Sports

Just as men can sound judgmental talking about women who don't follow sports, so can women sound judgmental talking about men who *do*. In the national survey, the longest answers from the Women Who Know a Sportsaholic Survey came in response to Questions #21 and 22, asking for women's basic attitudes toward sports and why they think men love sports so much. Many women wrote for pages and pages on this subject. If you're a woman living with a sportsaholic, check back to how you answered these questions. Here are a few responses:

> *I've always thought that men watching sports was pathetic.*
>
> *I'm bewildered by sports' ability to influence otherwise rational and mature men.*
>
> *I resent sports as a metaphor for the exclusion of women in society!*
>
> *Sports are a total waste of time and emotions. They have nothing to do with the real world, with being a good father, a caring and compassionate person, and a productive member of society.*

When you turn the volume down, you can hear through these comments many of the same themes we've been exploring so far and will continue to look at in Part III. Women may not know which Oakland A's pitcher gave up the dramatic World Series home run to the Dodgers' Kirk Gibson, but they have a pretty clear hit on what men are up to in their relentless pursuit of spectator sports. Here's a quick overview of some of the common themes women pointed to in describing why men love sports:

- They can feel real emotions without the intimacy with other people that usually comes with them.
- They can join a private male social club, where they can talk and act in ways they can't around women.
- They can escape from everything in life they don't want to deal with.

- They can relive their experiences of playing sports as boys and pretend they're in the big games today.
- They can vent their aggressions and release some of the stress from work with their hootin' and hollerin', their screaming and cursing.
- They can sharpen their competitive instincts that they need in other domains of life.
- They can tune in to a fantasy world that's much more interesting than life.
- They can feel a sense of achievement through the success of their team, helping them feel better about themselves and life around them.

Not all women who complain about men this way really hate sports themselves. In fact, many women have played sports and follow them at least a little for their own enjoyment, or, in the case of rising women business executives, a little sports knowledge helps them gain more acceptance in the male-dominated boardrooms. But women's approach to sports differs from men's in two important ways. First, women often prefer to *play* sports rather than watch them. Second, rooting for a special team is not the source of their primary emotions. While the man feels his major highs and lows from the game, she may show joy and sorrow in response to five or more nonsports moments that same day.

Maybe women can't be completely objective about men and sports, but they sure have a front-row seat. For many women, watching men go wild over sports and figuring out why they do it is a study that began when they were growing up with sports-obsessed fathers and brothers. Watching the sportsaholic in their adult life offers new research material almost daily.

Some men might hear harsh comments from women and smell a conspiracy. They're imagining groups of angry women gathered together spouting judgmental remarks toward all men's behavior, and they may see this negative talk about sports as just another form of "male-bashing."

But the image I get from the questionnaires is very different. I see women from diverse occupations and backgrounds, from big-city attorneys and business owners to small-town office clerks and homemakers. I also see a rich diversity in overall attitudes and influences concerning men in general, and what can be expected in male-female relationships today.

More important, the dominant emotion that emerged in answer to the final women's-survey questions and comments did not appear to be anger, bitterness, or jealousy. Rather, what prevailed was *compassion*. Women may feel annoyed, hurt, and alienated, but in the end they say that they really hope men can come to understand the role of sports in their lives more clearly, and find room to grow and change.

When a man says to a woman, "You don't know what you're missing" with respect to sports, a woman may be tempted to answer him, "And you don't know what *you're* missing in real life!"

## A Sports Talk, Man to Women

I'd like to take this opportunity to have a man-to-women talk. Your observations about men and sports are right on target. Your feelings about how sportsaholism functions as a real addiction, and how it influences men's lives and yours, are entirely justified. Keep speaking those feelings. Even when men react with defensiveness, denial, and counterattacks, it's critical to stay true to what you believe. Even as our culture inundates you with fresh bursts of sports saturation in all its glory, hold firm to your understanding of what men's addiction to spectator sports can really do. You have broken through mounds of resistance and powerful prevailing wisdom to reach important conclusions that can help us all.

And you've got a heck of a lot more to learn!

You may think you have men and sports figured to a T, but if you sincerely wish to facilitate change for yourself and the sportsaholic in your life, you're going to need to keep listening and learning. You need to understand more fully *why* men turn to sports with such a fervent passion. You need to know how it all got started for them, and try to identify with their very real fears about letting go of their deep connection to sports. You need to listen to more of their own personal stories, told without the involvement and interpretations of women that we've seen so far.

That's what we're going to do in Part III. Think of the next three chapters as your opportunity to sit in the audience before a panel of men talking openly about sports in their lives. I invite you to listen to their stories fully, with an open mind and a caring heart. You just may find the key to reaching him and relating in a new way toward sports—and beyond.

## PART THREE

# Men in Hiding:
# The Safe Haven of Sports

# NINE

# Searching for Dad
# in Fields of Dreams

*Going to see the Mets at Shea Stadium with my dad was
the most wonderful dream I could ever imagine, and the
happiest moment of my childhood.*
                              —Daniel, of Charlottesville, Virginia

Do you still believe that the man in your life can't express his
feelings? Are you still yearning for just a glimpse of his true emotional core? Have you seen his Game Face rantings and ravings
hundreds of times while wishing that just once you could understand where that emotional vitality *really* comes from?

You have that opportunity now. We're going back to the roots
of that deep love and devotion for sports. We'll be visiting with
several men who share their rich childhood memories of the very
first game they ever attended. We'll hear the true meaning of
what it means for a boy to be initiated into this magical, mystical
world of spectator sports. We'll uncover the depths of bonding
they develop through sports with their fathers, brothers, sons,
friends, and most men they see and talk to every day. Through
this sharing, you'll learn much more about why your man, and
most American men, really love sports. And you may understand
a bit better why it's so hard for them to imagine how they could
ever let go of sports—even a little.

If you're reading this along with the sportsaholic in your life, you'll also be able to invite him to share his first-game experiences and other childhood sports memories. Even if you already know the story, or you heard it in his response to the Sportsaholism Questionnaire, I strongly urge you to walk with him through that time and place again. For almost any man, that's a story worth telling over and over. They may not remember much about their first day of school, or their first Sundays in church, but that first pro or major-college sporting event always brings back clear and joyful memories.

Before you ask your sports fan to relive that special day, look at how other men in the national survey described their first games:

*"It was the Baltimore Colts against the New York Jets in 1976. I loved the color, the noise, the excitement, the food, the huge crowd!"*
—DENNIS, OF VIRGINIA BEACH, VIRGINIA

*"It was Yankee Stadium in 1961, with Mickey Mantle and Roger Maris. It was like heaven!"*
—BARRY, OF CHANDLER, ARIZONA

*"It was the Boston Celtics and the New York Knicks at Boston Garden in '82, when I was eight years old. I will never forget how fast my heart raced as I stepped out of that dark, smelly hallway and glimpsed the Boston Garden interior for the first time. What a rush!"*
—TOMMY, OF CHICAGO

Other respondents described their first game as: *Exciting. Colorful. Amazing. Overwhelming. Loud. Awesome. Dreamy. Inspiring. Magical. Spiritual. Heavenly.*

On that day, a door opened for them. Inside they found a world full of color, noise, energy, excitement, drama, heroism, magic, and people—lots of people. How big was the crowd at that first game? Was it ten thousand or twenty thousand? Or maybe a capacity football crowd of eighty thousand? To a typical boy going to his first game, a big crowd is a gathering of a hundred people at school or church. That first step inside a ballpark, stadium, or arena can leave him mesmerized by the sheer mass of humanity. It's all bigger than life, or life as he had known it. And when he is ushered into the experience by his dad, this magnitude rises to even greater heights.

## A Train Ride to a New World

Ned is the advertising manager whose denial of sportsaholism and his wife's contrary opinion opened Chapter 2. He was only five years old when he got his first taste of sports. Growing up in Youngstown, Ohio, in the 1950s, he had already begun to listen to the Cleveland Indians on radio when his dad told him it was time to see a game in person. His dad worked for the railroad, so they would make the sixty-five-mile trip to Cleveland on an excursion ticket designed just for baseball fans.

"Those sixty-five miles felt like an eternity," Ned recalls. "When we got out at the terminal, we walked the last seven or eight blocks to the stadium. The blocks got longer and longer. Then we stepped into Cleveland Stadium with its eighty thousand seats, just a huge building. As a little kid, everything seemed triple in size. I was awestruck!"

Like most boys sampling sports for the first time, Ned immediately wanted to feast on it every day. And like most boys, he wanted his dad with him at this banquet of sports delights. Baseball provided the bridge. As a youth, Ned's father had been a batboy for the minor-league Youngstown Browns and later played fast-pitch softball for years. To this day, Ned has kept the old finger-mitt glove his dad used. After that first trip to Cleveland, Ned and his father shared the annual spring hope that the Indians would somehow rise and knock off the powerful Yankees in the coming season. Though it never happened, each spring father and son would tell each other that this would be the year.

"My dad and I talked baseball constantly," Ned beams. "He's seventy-five now, and we've had a forty-plus-year bond over sports that can't be beat."

## A Tradition Comes Alive

For a boy's first-game experience, any place is a special place. But when the site itself carries its own storied reputation, an extra bit of magic dances through the day. Doug's first game took him to one of the most famous football stadiums of the past seventy years: Notre Dame. During his boyhood in Belding, Michigan, Doug didn't simply learn about the legend of Knute Rockne and the Fighting Irish in books and movies—he heard it directly from his dad, Notre Dame class of '38.

Doug recalls that he was eight years old, maybe nine, when his father told him to get ready for his first trip to Notre Dame. After much waiting, that day in the early 1950s arrived rainy, snowy, and muddy. But the game would go on, and so would Doug and his father. Without modern expressways, the trip took five hours in the miserable weather.

"I can still remember how cold and muddy everything was, and then what a thrill it was to enter that stadium!" Doug enthuses. "When you sit down, there's nothing like it on earth. I got my hot dog and pennant, and then watching that Notre Dame band come out of the tunnel before the players run out, you have to be taken by it. I really believe that ghosts live in that place—Knute Rockne and the people that made college football. You can feel them. You see the films from the past, and everything still looks the same today as then. I've been to football games at Michigan and Michigan State, and there's simply no comparison. Since that day, I've been a Notre Dame fan all my life."

## Those Were the Days

For some survey respondents, first-game memories took them back to the time when radio was king. Going to the ballpark was their first chance to *see* what they had only heard and imagined. Gerald, a consultant in Southern California, grew up in Lebanon, Missouri. He clearly remembers that October at age six when he gathered around the family's big Atwater Kent radio with his father, older brother, uncle, and several neighbors to listen to Dizzy

Dean and the St. Louis Cardinals beat the Detroit Tigers in the 1934 World Series. Three years later, Gerald was sitting in Sportsman's Park in St. Louis for his first big-league game.

"What I remember were the lights," he recalls. "It was one of the early games of night baseball. The Cards won, Joe Medwick went five-for-five with four doubles. It was overwhelming. From then on, it was baseball in summer and basketball in winter for me."

Back in the East, Saul knows he'll never forget his first game at Yankee Stadium in 1935, when he saw Lou Gehrig smash a home run for the Yankees. A few years later, Gehrig died. "Why such a sad death for Gehrig?" laments Saul, now seventy-eight. "I still can't understand."

## New York, New York

In New York City, everything seems bigger than life, so sports are bigger, too. It's the sports town where legends like Gehrig, Babe Ruth, Mickey Mantle, and Jackie Robinson roamed. As a man, to look back and say you attended your first game in New York can make you feel like you're part of a museum exhibit.

In the movie *City Slickers,* three New York kind of guys approaching their forties go off in search of an adventure that might reconnect them with their essence as men. They wind up on a western cattle drive, and while riding their horses in wide open spaces, they ponder the burning question, "What is the best day of your life?"

The character played by Billy Crystal responds, "I'm seven years old and my dad takes me to Yankee Stadium. My first game! I'm going under this long, dark tunnel underneath the stands, and I'm holding his hand, and we come out of the tunnel into the light. It was huge . . . how green the grass was. Brown dirt and that great green copper roof, remember? We had a black-and-white TV, so it was the first game I ever saw in color. I sat there the whole game next to my dad. He taught me how to keep score, and Mickey hit one out."

For most men, there's no need for further clarification. They recognize this description as a universal experience. Even for those who can't remember details of their very first game, some early sporting event stands out as one of life's high watermarks. If your own sports coming-out story has a New York backdrop (as it does for millions of men all over the country), the image becomes especially poignant. For Lennie, whose attorney wife, Barbara, was the sports apprentice on trial in Chapter 8, *City Slickers* rekindled all the memories from his first game at Shea Stadium.

"It was Mets-Dodgers on August 18th, 1966," recites Lennie, who brags of an encyclopedic knowledge of sports. "Going to the park, all my dad could talk about was Sandy Koufax pitching for the Dodgers and how great he was, so I rooted against Koufax for the Mets. The Mets won, 3–2! When we got there, I was incredibly terrified by how big it was, and all those people. I was holding onto my dad's hand for dear life. When we went through the turnstile, I was OK. Then walking down the ramp, the first thing I saw was the lights and then that grass—I had seen grass before at home, but not like this. I went home and tried to find a crayon of that shade of green for my coloring book, but I couldn't find one."

Ben grew up in Brooklyn in the '50s. He lived so close to Ebbets Field that when the Dodgers were winning, he could hear the roar of the crowd from his house. His mother's boss once caught a home-run ball hit by Duke Snider, got it autographed by all the Dodgers stars, and gave it to Ben. He's held onto it ever since and says proudly, "I can still see the imprint of the bat on the ball."

When he was old enough, about seven or eight, Ben got to see his first game at Yankee Stadium. He remembers the Yankees losing, 4–1, and Mickey Mantle striking out three times. His father wasn't around much, so he was guided into this first experience by his mother. "I wasn't even into sports much then, and neither was she," Ben admits. "She just figured that's what you're supposed to do for little boys."

Keith is the mediator and New York sports fan whom we saw in Chapter 6 passing his wife Mary Anne's test by saying no to the second game of pro football on Sunday afternoon. For his first taste of sports back in '63, he rode the train into New York City from Long Island with his dad and two cousins for a Yankees doubleheader against Chicago. "I remember those white pin-stripe uniforms like it was yesterday," Keith recalls. "Tom Tresh hit three home runs for the Yankees, and Mantle hit one home run. With the Yankees scoring more and more runs, the games went on and on. Mom was worried waiting for us to get home."

## Daniel's Doubleheader

Daniel's enthusiastic comments about his trip to Shea Stadium with his father opened this chapter. That game was in 1970, but Daniel actually attended his first game the season before as part of his Cub Scout pack's outing to Yankee Stadium. He'll never forget the date: July 20, 1969. Not then a real baseball fan, Daniel remembers far less about the game than what happened in the seventh or eighth inning.

"The umpires put up their arms and stopped the game," remembers Daniel. "A voice comes over the loudspeaker: 'Ladies and gentlemen, we wish to inform you that Apollo 11 has landed on the moon.' There was a deafening roar. Everyone was standing, cheering, clapping. The game was halted for five or ten minutes while the cheering went on. This was Bat Day, so we all raised our bats in salute. The organist played 'America the Beautiful'—a miraculous moment."

His sports interest aroused, Daniel gravitated to the Mets rather than the Yankees, because the Mets were winning. In fact, they won the '69 World Series that October. Daniel fondly recalls his fourth-grade teacher bringing her black-and-white TV into the classroom for the final game. The next season, Daniel dreamed of seeing the Mets in person. His father made him a deal: If Daniel got all A's on his report card, his dad would take him to Shea Stadium. Daniel got the A's. His father got the tickets.

"The anticipation was building for weeks," he relates, "and the best part was that it was a Sunday doubleheader against the Cubs. I would get two games! We had box seats, twenty or thirty rows above the Mets dugout. As we walked down closer and closer to the field, I noticed how white the bases, the batter's box, and the baselines were—the whitest white."

He can still taste the hot dogs and the mustard, still smell the pretzels, still hear the *pop!* of a pitch as it landed in the catcher's mitt. Mostly, he remembers watching the time on the big Longines clock by the scoreboard. Like many boys then and now, Daniel grew up amid turmoil—his day-to-day home life had more painful moments than happy days. This was one day he wanted to last forever.

"It didn't matter who won," he admits. "Just being with my dad for that long was special—we had so little quality time growing up. So much mystery was being revealed to me that day. I felt like I was being shown the grandeur of life."

## A Male's Rite of Passage

Robert Bly was wrong in saying that our culture lacks any rites of initiation for boys growing into manhood. A boy today does not need to go off into the woods for three days, or track animals, or bang a drum to know he can survive as a man in American culture. All he has to do is grab his glove and go off to the ballpark with his dad. Many boys internalize this message early in life: If you learn about sports and follow them passionately and faithfully, you can take your rightful place as a man. You will belong.

So there's a lot more going on at that first game than the heroes and the home team, the hot dogs and the scorecard, the colors and the crowds. As a boy enters that first arena or stadium, he's really stepping through the gateway into a huge, thriving subculture of American society. As a boy and later as a man, to have sports in your life means never having to be alone.

In dark, lonely Brooklyn bedrooms of the '50s, a young boy could flip on his radio and listen to the Dodgers play, knowing that thousands of other boys and men were tuned in right along with him, with the same love and common goal—for the Dodgers to win the World Series. He could give a friend the nickname of Duke or Pee Wee, and everyone would get the reference to his Dodgers heroes. Or another boy could make similar references to his favorite Yankees, or Giants, or Cardinals, or Cubs, or pro football's Detroit Lions or basketball's Boston Celtics.

For any man who knows sports today, the sports subculture welcomes him at every turn. He turns on the TV at just about any time, and he finds a game. He flips on the radio, there's a sports-talk show. He picks up a newspaper, and all the latest box scores, statistics, and feature articles await him. He is plugged in, tuned to the same wavelength as millions of other men. He is part of something larger than himself. He is connected. His life has meaning beyond his small circle of family and friends.

When he travels, the sports subculture travels with him. He can walk up to almost any male stranger watching CNN sports updates on an airport terminal monitor and strike up a conversation by asking him for a score, or which team he follows. Inside the air-plane, he can ask the guy across the aisle to borrow the sports section of his *USA Today,* and he is greeted with a knowing smile. The connection over sports cuts across age, economic, and ethnic lines, and those men who aren't part of the male sports subculture often feel peer pressure to join in.

For a man who follows sports, the world is a little safer, a little more secure. The economy may falter. His job may disappear. His marriage may not last. His kids could get sick. He could get sick. The stock market may dip. A hurricane or snowstorm or flood may strike. But there will always be football, or baseball, or basket-ball, or hockey. He will always have his favorite teams and special players, and if they skip town, he can adopt another one. Every time he reaches out for sports, he feels that connection with other men. Men he can watch sports with, talk sports, argue sports. Men just like him.

And it all begins with that first game.

## PLAY #9:
## HIS FIRST GAME

If you're a woman who knows a sportsaholic, this is a good time to ask him about his initiation into the sports subculture. You can listen to that story of his first game. This is our next exercise for the Sportsaholism Recovery Playbook.

Find a quiet time to sit down together comfortably. For the woman, your mission here is to listen and learn about his early experiences with sports. In filling out the Sportsaholism Questionnaire in Chapter 2, he already reported on his first game memories in response to Question #38, so he has some recent material to call upon. But it helps if you ask the key questions now, face-to-face. This will jog more memories and make the whole experience more personal. So take him back to that very first game (or first few games) as you ask him to answer the following questions. Allow ample time for each response, and if you think of additional questions that would satisfy your curiosity, ask away.

**Note**—If you're a man reading alone, just record your memories in your playbook. Later, see if you can find a friend to tell the story. If you're a woman reading alone, seek out a male relative, friend, or coworker willing to share his first sports memories with you.

*How old were you when you went to your first game?*

*What year was it?*

*Where was the game?*

*Who took you?*

*How long had the anticipation been building for you?*

*How did you travel to the game?*

*What was the first thing you noticed when you got there?*

*What did it look like inside, and what was the crowd like?*

*Who played, who won, and what highlights of the game do you remember?*

*What did you have to eat there?*

*What else did you do during the game?*

*What sights and sounds stand out?*

*What kind of scorecards or souvenirs did you keep from that day?*

*How involved did you get in sports in the following weeks, months, or years?*

*In what ways did you bond with your father over sports back then?*

*How do you regard that first game today, and what role did it play in your life?*

## WRAP-UP:

Take a few moments to see if he would like to add any other stories, images, or information about this first-game experience and the role of sports in his childhood. Make notes in your playbook about the highlights you remember from his story. And thank him for taking you back to this special time in his life!

## Fathers, Sons, & Sports

If the sportsaholic in your life was like most boys, he looked to his father to guide him through this rite of passage. Boys yearn for any kind of connection or bond with their fathers, and by the time they reach age six or seven, they get the message that sports offer one way to gain that bond. For many men, it's the only way to achieve closeness. Ask men who follow sports today what they shared with their fathers while growing up, and many will answer, "Sports."

For a man looking back today, this realization can be both happy and sad. It's often joyful to recall those early memories shared with Dad over sports—learning sports, playing sports, going to games, watching games on TV, talking sports. At the same time, it can be painful to remember that the bond didn't reach beyond the white lines of the playing field. Sports may be the only thing a boy can talk about comfortably with his dad, or the only area of life where they can share their emotional sides. It can even represent the only realm where he can trust his dad to hold any meaningful knowledge or wisdom to pass down to him.

Want to know about sex? Or the history of the local community? Science? How to talk to girls? How to deal with fear or loneliness? For these needs, many boys know they must seek answers and guidance from someone else, if they can find anyone or dare to ask at all. And when the questions get too tough, boys learn from their dads how to retreat into that safe and secure world of sports. A world Dad can show them. At a young age, then, boys receive two basic messages about sports:

1. *Sports may be the one way to reach their dad and build any father-son connection.*
2. *Sports can serve as a source of excitement in life, and a refuge when life gets too tough.*

Often it's the desire to build some kind of bond with his dad that triggers a boy's first real interest in sports. From an early age, many boys observe a father who works long hours and may act sullen or angry when at home until he switches on THE GAME.

Then the boy sees a different man—one who is excited, engaged, expressive, alive. A boy's curiosity may lead him to check out sports for himself. More important, he wants to know about sports so he can communicate with his dad and be close to him.

So he hangs out with Dad when the game is on. He asks questions. He learns the rules. He memorizes names of players and their statistics. He gets his first baseball card, or sports board game, video game, or book. All along the way, his father urges him on, encouraging him to welcome sports into his life with open arms.

The boy is also encouraged (or sometimes pushed) to play sports. His dad puts up a basketball hoop in the driveway, shows him how to grip a football, plays that first game of catch in the backyard. He is placed in a youth soccer program or midget football league, and he gets firsthand lessons about the nature of competition, teamwork, and the sacrifice needed to achieve a goal. Maybe Dad is out there with him, maybe he's just a cheerleader or critic from afar. Either way, the boy also understands that excelling in sports is something he *should* want to do, something that will make Dad proud.

**SURVEY RESULT: Which sports do you actively play?**

1. basketball
2. golf
3. softball
4. tennis
5. football
6. baseball
7. bowling
8. racquetball
9. soccer
10. volleyball

But for the vast majority of male sports fans today, the dream of becoming a sports superstar fades as he grows older. It's survival of the fittest, and only the very fit survive. So maybe he gets to play a sport or two in high school, maybe he's not good enough to get beyond Little League. He can still relive those playing days when he watches big-time sports on TV, or imagine himself as the star he never became. But in terms of his training in sports and his connection with Dad, how far he goes as a player doesn't matter.

No matter how long a boy plays organized competitive sports, he will continue to watch sports on TV and in person. It's part of his training, his education, a way to continue bonding with other men, and quite possibly that one route to a relationship with Dad. A boy understands that even if he can't live out his father's dream by becoming the sports hero he wanted in a son, he can still gain Dad's approval by becoming a dedicated sports *fan*. Whether or not father and son ever play a little touch football together, they can still connect by watching the New York Jets every Sunday. And Dad can rest assured that he has safely escorted his son into that great male subculture, where he'll be able to relate to his brothers, friends, and the other men he meets for the rest of his life. He is initiated.

**SURVEY RESULT: Which sports do you most like to watch?**

1. football
2. basketball
3. baseball
4. hockey
5. golf
6. tennis
7. auto racing
8. volleyball
9. track
10. boxing

For many a father with little time or energy for his family, simply bringing his son to one game may stand in his own eyes as one of his most significant achievements. And even when a boy's father is not around at all, a boy usually finds that some other adult male will step forward to take him through this rite of passage.

Fred is the Chicago Bulls fan from Chapter 7 who made sure that Jordan was part of his child's name. The youngest of four boys in his own family of eight kids growing up, Fred relied on his brothers to guide him into sports. Because they were much older and already well initiated into sports when he was born, Fred learned about sports early. He even credits sports with helping him in his general education. In fact, he contends that he was able to read when he was only two years old by looking at the sports section all the time. And studying baseball statistics helped him learn math quickly. But his major lessons revolved around male bonding over sports.

"My older brothers all played sports, and I'd go out with them and be the batboy on their team," Fred remembers. "By the time I was ten, I had about five thousand baseball cards because I inherited all of theirs, including a '55 Yogi Berra and a '72 Roberto Clemente. Sports made us all closer, gave us something to talk about, bridged the age gap."

But for most of us as boys, Dad guides us into the sports world. And that's how we want it.

## No Rain, No Rain!

When I was growing up in Shrewsbury, Massachusetts, my dad worked two jobs and wasn't home much. But when he was around, he often listened to the Boston Red Sox on the radio. So I quickly became the biggest Red Sox fan in the neighborhood, and could tell anyone all the Red Sox names, nicknames, and statistics. And since we lived only forty miles from Boston, I yearned to visit Fenway Park, my own field of dreams.

My dad promised he would take me someday, but it seemed he would never have time. Finally, he set a date for us to go, a Wednesday afternoon in July 1963. For weeks, I had that date circled on my Red Sox yearbook calendar, and I counted down the days. On the morning of the promised day, it rained heavily. I worried that the game would be postponed, and in my nine-year-old perspective on life, I assumed that my dad would never be able to take me again. I would never, ever get to see Fenway Park!

I can't remember for sure, but I might have cried that morning. If I did, that would be the only time I ever cried as a boy.

Even if the rain tapered off, my mother, acting in that protective-mother mode that boys know so well, decreed that she couldn't even consider letting me go. It would be damp and cold and I would get sick, and that would be *her* fault as a mother. She told us that baseball would just have to wait. She quickly entered into a power struggle with my father, and in these tussles with my mother, I knew my father was less than a .200 hitter. But somehow, this time he came through for me.

We drove off into the rain, toward hope. We approached Boston and pulled within sight of that huge, always-lit Citgo sign that most New Englanders know as the landmark that tells them Fenway Park is near. Just then, the rain stopped. The clouds dissolved. The sun came out. The game was on!

Like all first-game experiences, mine was magical—sitting inside ancient Fenway Park with grass so brightly green it appeared to have been painted on. I was also fixated on the legendary thirty-seven-foot-high wall in left field called the Green Monster. The hated and superior New York Yankees were in town as the opponent. All my Red Sox heroes were so close on the field I was tempted to call down and invite them home to dinner.

For one of the few times in my lonely childhood, I felt truly alive. And just for me, the Red Sox in this one game bashed doubles off the Green Monster, made great fielding plays, and knocked off the Yankees, 14–7. I didn't cheer so much as sit in awe. If Dad and I spoke at all, it was only a few comments about the game.

In the next several years, my training in sports fandom was the focal point of my life's education. My father still wasn't around much and we didn't get to go to many other games for a few years. But when we did have a moment together, we talked sports. As Boston sports fans, we asked each other the burning questions of the day: Should the Red Sox fire their manager? Could the Celtics win another championship? Was Bill Russell a better big man than Wilt Chamberlain?

In 1967, we shared the totally unexpected joy of the Red Sox winning the pennant. Longtime losers, the Red Sox' unexpected rise to the top in a wild and crazy pennant race captured our emotions—not only for my father and me, but for all of New England. Sports reporters called it the Impossible Dream, and it's a dream that gave me a hunger for life that nothing else could. As the Red Sox pointed toward the championship, my dad even managed to take me to Fenway Park a few times, including a doubleheader against the Angels in which our team miraculously rallied from an 8–0 deficit to win, 9–8. For years afterward, my father and I would mention that game and our shared experience as our symbol of the Impossible Dream. As a common reference point, it had far more longevity than anything that happened in our own family.

But like most fathers and sons in sports-dominated households, our bond never moved beyond sports. Once a father and son establish sports as their one safe ground to meet on, the idea of moving into another realm can be scary, leaving them unsure of their footing. I remember when another subject threatened to creep into my conversations with my father. I was thirteen, the winter after that famous Red Sox pennant. My father and I had just exchanged a little small talk about sports when he mumbled, "There's something your mother wanted me to talk to you about." I knew right away that my father was about to try to teach me the "facts of life."

Well, it seemed pretty late in the game for this talk. While I certainly didn't know *all* the facts, I did understand that this subject, like any nonsports topic, was completely out of bounds in our relationship. My father appeared determined to go through with it, though, and he'd obviously be grilled by my mother later about what ground we covered. So I tap-danced through a couple of introductory points before quickly moving us to safer ground.

"I know all about that, Dad," I said. "So do you think the Red Sox will win the pennant again next season?" I have never seen my father look more relieved.

While we may not have picked up many of the intricacies of sex from our fathers, we did at least learn by example how to tune out girls and women who dislike sports. To prepare for future arguments about the value of sports and their proper role in life, boys received expert demonstrations from their dads. They learned all the skills needed to prove men were right and women wrong—and how to get the last word. We would hear Dad say to Mom, "This is what I enjoy. I work hard, and sports help me relax and have fun. Why don't you leave me alone and go find something you want to do?" And we store away a mental note that will prove invaluable later in life.

We also learn from our dads that the game can serve as a handy getaway from women and the challenges of relating to them intimately. Sharing feelings? Learning compromise? Setting boundaries for their children? Listening to her talk about her dreams and what keeps her from fulfilling them? That's scary stuff that can be very intimidating to a man. In his own training to be a man, chances are Dad didn't learn much about recognizing and sharing his feelings, or how to listen. He recognizes that he doesn't know the way, and men don't like that.

So, he figures, the more time he spends watching sports, the less time he'll be expected to play the intimacy game. And if he can convince his wife that watching sports is what he's naturally oriented to do as a normal man, she may come to accept that it's just not in his nature to learn the rules and strategy of what *she* wants him to know. When she sees that being devoted to sports is just the way men are, according to his belief, she'll let him off the hook.

In many households, a man's son becomes an unknowing pawn in this game. If Dad gets questioned by Mom about his insistence on watching football all Sunday, and his twelve-year-old son is watching with him, Dad can fire back, "What am I doing spending all day watching football? I'm spending quality time with our son!"

There's another dimension to this sports education, something harder to see. If the man of the house is obsessed with sports, he may also be demonstrating how he hides from his true self: his own personal hopes and fears; his own joy and pain; his own achievements and failures—the full range of his own human drama. He may also be showing his son how to hide from his own authentic spirit—his individual way of loving, his ability to live fully in the world as an involved participant of life.

When the world gets too confusing, too scary, too threatening, when a man needs a safe haven, he can always rely on sports. He can just plug into the game-by-game, season-by-season plight of his Pittsburgh Steelers, and all those life needs will be met. All his more difficult questions will be kept safely at bay. And, as a boy learns, going along for this vicarious ride will be more fun than he could dare imagine.

But when a man uses sports to hide from the major parts of who he is, he does not have the tools really to connect with his son, human being to human being. That's often why boys with distant or unavailable fathers retreat deeper and deeper into sports fantasies, dribbling the basketball in the driveway and imagining themselves putting up the game-winning shot in the final seconds of the championship game. This, he assumes, is where he will get his life energy. And that's why he clings to those shared sports obsessions and rare sports moments with his father. He really does want a richer, fuller relationship with Dad. But if this is all he can get, he better squeeze out every last drop.

## Field of Dreams

Most boys can't easily recognize, identify, or explain this yearning for a deeper connection with their fathers. But in adult years, the emptiness and void often surfaces. For many men who follow sports (and even those who don't), the movie *Field of Dreams* stands as the ultimate symbol of the deep sports connection a boy feels with his father, as well as his adult yearning to reconnect with it and maybe find something more. As a bonus, the movie comes attractively packaged in sports metaphor and scenery.

"If you build it, he will come," the mysterious voice tells Ray (played by Kevin Costner) in the movie. "It" turns out to be a baseball field carved out of Ray's Iowa farm. As he builds the field and continues to follow the message of the strange voice, he acts on faith, rising above the ridicule of others and his own doubts. Finally, he understands the purpose. The "he" whose coming was foretold turns out to be Ray's father, who had died years earlier in the midst of their father-son feud. When "he" comes back to this magical Field of Dreams, it is to play a game of catch with his son, fulfilling an unspoken wish Ray has carried for years.

*Field of Dreams* was voted the most popular sports movie in my national survey. Men found it inspirational, touching, and riveting. The movie's universal messages—to trust in your vision in order to create miracles and to rekindle deadened human spirit through belief and dedication to a cause—brought it mainstream success.

**SURVEY RESULT: What are your favorite sports movies?**

1. *Field of Dreams*
2. *Hoosiers*
3. *Brian's Song*
4. *The Natural*
5. *Major League*
6. *Bull Durham*
7. *Rudy*
8. *The Longest Yard*
9. *Pride of the Yankees*
10. *North Dallas Forty*

Even for men who don't live for sports, the movie touches them as a father-son story. But for a man who loves sports, the movie conveys the essence of what it means to bond with Dad over sports. Any woman who has watched the movie with her husband or boyfriend probably sat in amazement as her usually stone-faced man openly sobbed at the end.

## Hitting Closer to Home

For a few men in my national survey, this movie struck an especially deep chord. Joel, forty-two, is a former high school soccer star and collegiate wrestler who lives in Herndon, Virginia. He credits his father with teaching him most of what he knows about sports, all before he died when Joel was ten.

"When Kevin Costner's dad comes out at the end of that movie, it's very emotional for me," Joel begins. "When I was young, my dad had a massive coronary while serving as an airplane mechanic in the Navy. After that, he had hardening of the arteries and his legs ached all the time. But even then, he played catch with me every day. He would play as long as he could, until he had to sit down. I'll never forget him for doing that. He was mowing the lawn when he died of a heart attack, the day before my first Little League game."

Lennie, who reported holding on to his father's hand for dear life at his first Mets game earlier in this chapter, has seen *Field of Dreams* about thirty times.

"First time I saw it," says Lennie, "I almost passed out at the end. I lost my dad when I was ten. He was diagnosed with cancer and gone within a month. If I had one wish, it was to play one last game of catch with him. He died in the winter, and every day the next spring I'd go out in my backyard, pound my baseball into my glove, and say to myself, 'He's gonna be here. He's gonna come back.' He was my Little League coach, and my friend. We were inseparable."

The movie also touches the fathers of today, men who have followed their own childhood learning by bonding with their sons over sports. Dale, an Oklahoma father of boys ages three and five, promises them that he'll take them to the real Iowa baseball field among the corn where the movie was filmed, and they'll have a game of catch right there. Other fathers in the survey expressed a deep wish that when they died, their sons would remember them and their games of catch.

It's important to remember, though, that the movie is also about a father-son split and the painful void that results. The final scene's message suggests that a man can reconnect with his father and share the truth of his life after years of anger, emptiness, alienation, and resentment. As such, it provides a ray of inspiration and hope.

But the movie also reinforces a boys' childhood message that the only path that can *ever* lead to Dad cuts across the white lines of sports. In the final scene, Ray plays catch with his dad, sharing a moment of true peace, joy, and love. His wife excuses herself, because she figures the two men have a lot to talk about. You have to wonder. Even after all these years, can there be any common ground beyond sports?

Perhaps not, but Ray's yearning for a deeper connection with his dad can motivate fathers today to build more far-reaching bonds with their own sons. Many are succeeding. Hank, who presented his "Life As a Baseball Game" outline in Chapter 7, admits that as much as he enjoyed sharing wonderful baseball moments with his father, he wished they could have shared more than that. So when Hank's son was born seven years ago, he vowed to do better.

"I was an active father for him since day one," asserts Hank. "We can speak about many, many subjects that I could never speak about with my dad. At this stage of my life, I want to enjoy my son's growth more than anything else, to be there for him as my dad could not be there for me."

# TEN

# Life Sucks...But the Cowboys Won Another Super Bowl!

*My highest highs in life came from Nebraska's two na-*
*tional championships. I used to go into depression every*
*winter. I'd think, Oh man, life's terrible. I've got to do*
*something different. But the last two years I breezed right*
*through winter on a cloud!*

—Brent, Nebraska football fan

When a team wins a major championship, we hardly see or hear anything of their loyal and devoted championship fans. Sure, we catch the mandatory TV shots of the cheering, hugging, banner-waving crowd in the stadium at the championship game's climactic moment. We might see a front-page newspaper photo of the city parade honoring the victorious team.

But within twenty-four to forty-eight hours, those cheering fans in the ticker-tape parade become a blip on the screen, a former backdrop quickly replaced by the next urgent dramas: What will happen to the players and coaches of this newly crowned championship team? Where's the next city or sport waiting for its turn in the roving sports spotlight?

This is a grave injustice to the passionate sports fans of America. If you're a true sports fan, you know that you're as much a part of that championship team as any player, coach, general manager, or owner. As a fan, you did your part in making it happen with your devotion, your caring, your rooting. And with your years of dedication, you've waited for this moment at least as long as any of the "real" team members—usually longer.

Championship *players* get huge bonuses, snazzy rings, fatter contracts, and rich commercial endorsements. Championship *fans* get. . . . enough joy and satisfaction to carry them through life until next season rolls around. As a fan, you won't get rich, unless you're in that small minority that makes significant bets on your team. In fact, the championship probably *costs* you money, either on your trip to the game site or the money you plunked down on the highlights video, T-shirts, license plates, and other championship memorabilia. No, you won't make the cover of *Sports Illustrated,* but anyone can see that you've taken this championship into your home and heart as lovingly as you would a newborn child.

## Keeping the Spirit Alive

Warren is a forty-four-year-old sports fanatic in Watertown, Connecticut. On his Sportsaholism Questionnaire, he listed his occupation as "Electrical Contractor/Rabid Cowboys Fan." He's never lived in or near Texas, but he proclaimed the Cowboys his team during the days of Roger Staubach in the 1970s, when the Cowboys' national popularity earned them the nickname of America's Team. During the spring of '96, Warren basked in the afterglow of the Cowboys' recent Super Bowl triumph, the team's third championship in four years.

"I'm still on a high!" beams Warren. "I'm wearing my Cowboys watch, my Cowboys sneakers, my Cowboys hat, and my commemorative helmet with the Cowboys star on one side and the Super Bowl emblem on the other. I'm watching the tape of the fourth game from last season. I've got fifty Cowboys tapes, including one with their all-time highlights. The tape player stays on all winter. I know a guy who owns an ice-cream store a few towns away who's as addicted to the Cowboys as I am, so I go down there sometimes to talk to him and look at all the Cowboys stuff on the walls."

Warren takes special pride in his three souvenir Super Bowl

footballs from the Cowboys' last three championships. The first one was marked number 885 out of a production batch of one thousand, so he asked for and received number 885 for the next two Super Bowl footballs. It was sort of like having his own number on the Cowboys roster. That's only fitting, because from August to January, he *is* a Cowboy. When he's riding in his work truck, the radio is always tuned to sports-talk radio's WFAN. It's a New York station, but Warren counts on hearing some references to the Cowboys, and he loves listening to New York Giants fans bemoaning their losing ways. At home during the week, you can find him watching one of those tapes of past Dallas games or monitoring ESPN to record anything about the Cowboys. Then comes Game Day, when his wife and two kids steer clear.

"Everyone knows I'm in my office watching the Cowboys," Warren explains. "I don't care who's got what, or who's doing what—I don't want to be disturbed."

If you're a devout fan, winning a championship makes everything look better, taste better, smell better, feel better. After that big game, you take your wife and family to dinner, not just to celebrate but maybe to relieve some of the guilt you felt about disappearing behind your sports wall for the past five months. Everywhere you go, everyone sees you with that unmistakable championship halo over your head. Almost all your conversations circle back to how your team did it and, of course, how they're going to do it again next year.

The ups and downs of your life do not faze you. The weather may be lousy. Your job may still be boring. Your budget may be out of whack, and the family may not always live in perfect harmony. But none of that matters. You're riding along with a champion. You *are* a champion.

For these precious months, you're free of all nagging questions and doubts about why your team couldn't win the big one. Any painful memories of past failure go on the shelf. You carry with you the sight of your team celebrating after those unforgettable final seconds. You are in a state of euphoria, or at least relief at not having to face those awful feelings from losing.

## Victory Calms the Jailhouse

Ernie is another Cowboys fan living far from Texas in Fredericksburg, Virginia. He works in a correctional center, where almost the entire staff roots for the Washington Redskins. Ernie remembers the derision he faced in the winter of '95, after the Cowboys had lost the big playoff game to San Francisco. Of course, he didn't have to go to work to be reminded of losing the big one. He bore that wound wherever he went. The Cowboys' loss was his loss, their failure his personal cross to bear.

"I was devastated," Ernie laments. "All I could think during the Super Bowl that year was how that should have been Dallas playing. I can be very critical of my team, put a lot of pressure on them. In that 49er game, I thought, How could we have spotted them twenty-one points? I kept asking myself that all winter. So when we won it this time ['96 Super Bowl], I enjoyed it but not as much as I should have. It was more like relief at not having to go through all that losing again."

For every champion, there are dozens of losers. Losing teams and losing fans. None feel the sting as painfully as fans of the team that falls short in the championship game. Here's how the '96 Dallas-Pittsburgh Super Bowl felt to Patrick, a Steelers fan in Gaithersburg, Maryland: "Before the game, I was a realist and knew the Steelers didn't have much of a chance. But once the game started, I wanted them to play the perfect game, which I knew they would need to do to win. They stayed close, and I thought, They can win this game! When they lost, I tried to suck it up, but it felt like someone had kicked me in the stomach."

## Where to Turn for Solace?

Pro teams expect a lot from fans, from ticket-buying and TV-viewing to patience and loyalty. A team that wins a championship expects its fans to express their appreciation by buying up heaps of championship memorabilia and team souvenirs and clothing, not to mention paying a higher price for next season's tickets. But when they lose the big one, the team offers nothing to help their suffering fans cope with that horrible feeling of getting kicked in the gut.

Is it time for support groups for championship-deprived fans? Sports-talk radio is the closest thing so far. In those agonizingly long delays between playoff games, fans use talk radio not only to share their excitement but also to work out their anxiety about the task ahead. And when their team loses the big one, fans turn to talk radio to dump their anger, sadness, frustration, betrayal, and disbelief on an often beleaguered talk-show host.

Losing a World Series, an NBA playoff series or a Final Four game can hit a fan just as hard as football fallout. But there's something about football championships that often pack a stronger wallop. The NFL playoffs are built along single-game dramas. Your team must win every time to advance, and with any loss they're gone—unlike baseball's rounds of playoff series, where you can recover from a loss and still prevail and become champion. Also, a football season has far fewer games, so every game along the route to the playoffs counts much more. Consider that the NFL regular season extends for only sixteen games. In contrast, the 1995–96 NBA champion Chicago Bulls played eighteen games in the *postseason* alone! Those seven days of buildup to the next Sunday football game heighten the weekly tension in any sportsaholic household.

College football's drama is packed into an even smaller powder keg. Your favorite college team plays only eleven or twelve games in its season, then just *one* postseason bowl game that will determine its final fate—and probably your own mood for the next nine months. It's an intense scenario, especially for fans of the major contenders for the number-one prize. For much of the '90s, that intensity has been best exemplified by the fans of the University of Nebraska.

## A State of Red

While the Dallas Cowboys may be America's Team, the Nebraska Cornhuskers are Nebraska's team. Not just the university, not just the college town of Lincoln, but the whole state—all the men, all the women, all the children, all the towns so small that some high schools play football six-on-six, instead of the usual eleven players per side. The Cornhuskers belong to the people of Nebraska, and the people consider themselves part of the team. And they show it.

Red is the official team color, so red is what you see. It floods the stadium on game day, with almost everyone in attendance wearing not only red clothes but *official* Nebraska red apparel. Red dominates most fans' everyday wardrobe in schools, offices, banks, grocery stores, restaurants. Red flowers sprout up in gardens more than any other color. When the Cornhuskers play away from home, Nebraska fans drive their red cars and red vans and mount an invasion of red clothing and pompons in the opposing team's stadium. When Nebraska fans talk of going to Manhattan, they're not thinking of taking in a Broadway show—they're referring to their team's road game against Kansas State in Manhattan, Kansas.

Nebraska fans know all about the peak emotional experiences of championship moments. After enduring several near misses, including a close loss to Florida State with the championship on the line at the '94 Orange Bowl, the Cornhuskers and their fans finally broke through. At the '95 Orange Bowl, they won their first national championship. Then they steamrolled through the next season undefeated, capped by a Fiesta Bowl triumph in January '96 that made them number one in the land two years in a row.

The entire state celebrated and bonded over this shared achievement. As one fan said, "It felt like everyone in the state was your brother or sister." Another compared the Cornhuskers' return to Nebraska after their championship triumphs to the sight of a nation's troops coming home after winning a war for their country. In the 1996 season, however, Nebraska lost a pivotal conference playoff game to Texas and was denied a chance to try for three consecutive national titles. But win or lose the big one, Cornhuskers fans remain emotionally invested.

Brent, the Cornhuskers fan whose comments about the impact of the two national championships opened this chapter, leaves his home in Spalding, Nebraska, to join the caravan of cars on Interstate 80 headed to Lincoln for every home game. A teacher and coach, he was excused from the first day of school after Christmas vacation for three years in a row so he could complete his return trip from Nebraska's dramatic New Year's bowl games.

"I'm a football-aholic," Brent admits. "It's my love and my passion. I've had girlfriends, including one up in Omaha that I used to visit on weekends. I'd drive up there on Saturday night after a home game in Lincoln, and at dinner I'd lose track of the conversation because I was still thinking about the game. Just as my highest highs have been winning the two championships, my lowest lows have been through the team's big losses. The only other low like that was having a friend die in a car accident."

Many sportsaholics in Nebraska may have an easier time with their relationships with women, because women can be just as passionate about the Cornhuskers. It's part of the state identity, something you take with you even if you leave.

Betty, a medical-office supervisor, grew up in a Cornhuskers household in Fremont, Nebraska. Her grandfather has had season tickets for about forty years. She used to drive into Lincoln on game day without tickets, just to be where people were congregating. About ten years ago, Betty and her husband made a work-related move to Van, Texas, just down the road from Dallas. Finding that absence does indeed make the heart grow fonder, Betty has become an even bigger fan of Nebraska. She and her husband joined the Dallas-based North Texas Nebraskans. They surf the internet almost daily for Cornhuskers info, subscribe to Nebraska state magazines, and attend any Nebraska games near them.

"When we meet other Nebraska fans, it's like old home week —where are you from, who do you know," explains Betty. "Some people here make fun of us, but I'm very proud of our team and our state. The Cowboys fans here all go to their games dressed up like it's a night at the opera."

Nebraska football fans talk about their team and their state as if it's all one entity. And to many Nebraskans, it is. The Cornhuskers are Nebraska, and Nebraska is the Cornhuskers. When coach Tom Osborne drew national media criticism for his handling of players caught in off-field crimes, Cornhuskers fans reacted with righteous anger and defensiveness. In one voice, they seemed to say, If you put down our team, you put down our state, and you put down us.

This feeling is not unique to Nebraskans. Passionate fans feel the same way about their Michigan Wolverines or Penn State Nittany Lions in football, or their North Carolina Tar Heels or Kentucky Wildcats in basketball. When Kentucky won the '96 NCAA basketball championship, the next day's celebration filled up Rupp Arena, where the team bus drove right inside the darkened arena to the screams of Wildcats fans. "It was like Batman coming out of the cave," remembers Rena Vicini, an administrator in the school's athletic department. That fan-celebration scene was captured on video and sold as one of the many pieces of Kentucky national-championship memorabilia.

Championships bring out fans' deepest feelings of joy and elation, just as we imagined it as kids in the driveway basketball court, fantasizing of hitting the winning shot as the crowd went wild. Fans who've been with a winner can't wait to tell everyone else what the real thing actually feels like. "If your team has never won a national championship, you pray for that one title," explains Skip, who rode Florida State to a national football championship a few years ago. "When it happens, it's unreal. You're so excited you don't know what to do. You grab someone to hug, jump up and down, call someone you know, scream it out loud: 'I did it!' Nothing else matters until next season. Then you want to do it again."

But your team need not have ever won a championship, or even come close to one, to feel that deep pride and strong identity. College fans from Florida to Colorado, and pro fans from Boston to Seattle all know what it means to make their team number one in their lives.

**SURVEY RESULT: Which team do you most closely follow?**

1. Dallas Cowboys
2. Nebraska Cornhuskers
3. Chicago Bulls
4. New York Knicks

5. New York Yankees
6. Cleveland Indians
7. Baltimore Orioles
8. New York Mets
9. Pittsburgh Steelers
10. Houston Rockets

## Our Teams/Ourselves

Sports teams become a part of us. When our Oakland Raiders win, we win. When our Denver Broncos lose, we lose. When our Philadelphia 76ers prepare to select their number-one draft pick, part of our future is at stake. When our Charlotte Hornets trade their best players, we worry about how we're going to fill the void. When our Chicago Cubs or Boston Red Sox compete for most of a century without winning a World Series, we feel personally deprived.

We learn everything about our team's players. We buy their official uniform jerseys with name and number. We study their statistics. We plot with our general managers about the right draft picks to make, the prudent trades to seek, the most desirable free agents to chase. We know our team's plays and strategy so well, we feel we're a step ahead of our coach. One fan told me he wants to fax in plays at halftime for his team to use in the second half.

**SURVEY RESULT: Who are your favorite players?**

1. Troy Aikman
2. Emmitt Smith
3. Michael Jordan
4. Cal Ripken
5. Magic Johnson (retired)
6. Hakeem Olajuwon
7. Tommie Frazier
8. Michael Irvin
9. Billy Bates
10. Don Mattingly (retired)

This intense devotion is familiar to anyone who is a sportsaholic to any degree, and it's a major reason we become big sports fans in the first place. It's a hunger for involvement in something bigger than ourselves, a desire for achievement, the need for a single-pointed focus on a clear goal.

We all need and seek a strong and positive self-identity, a sense of who we are that we like and can feel good about. We find it through many sources, including our personal values and charac-ter, our faith, our achievements at work, our child-raising skills, our contribution to our community, our service to others.

As sports fans, we discover that we can gain some of that posi-tive self-identity vicariously through our connection to our teams. If our Chicago Bulls beat everyone else in the league, we feel better about *ourselves*. If my team is part of me, and my team does well, then I'm doing well. I've got my act together. I'm a winner.

We get the same reward by aligning ourselves with players. If my guy Doc Gooden is striking out batter after batter, when I hold up cards with the big K on them, I'm a part of his strikeouts. I'm achieving something. I'm better than the other guy. This desire for a positive identity also explains the rush toward Fantasy Leagues. We can boost our identity by *creating* our own team that wins for us and makes us feel better about ourselves.

But what if you're a fan of the New York Jets and the Jets are losers for years? Does that mean you're nothing? Not exactly. Any longtime fan who's been through his team's ups and downs knows at least one way to avoid dragging his own sense of self down with his sinking team. You identify the specific reasons why your team is losing: wrong coach, bad quarterback, weak defensive line. Then you get just as involved with your team's efforts to do what it will take to start winning, using sports-talk shows or fan clubs to make the winning suggestions!

It's called rebuilding. Every owner, general manager, or coach understands the process on their end. For a sports fan, the process also entails the effort to rebuild the more positive sense of self we get from being with a winner. Winning is not only considered desirable, it's regarded as the natural state for a sports team. My Jets *should* be winning more and get back to the Super Bowl someday. That's just the way things should be. No fan deserves to carry around the tag of loser. It's not right unless, a Jets fan would say, that fan roots for the Giants. Fans love to compete against one another through the exploits of their teams.

When losing becomes too heavy a burden, and abandoning your team unthinkable, a fan may also employ a simple but often effective temporary strategy. When your team loses, you say, *"They* blew it," or, *"They* can't get their act together." Whereas, when your New York Yankees win the World Series, you always say, *"We* did it! *We* won! *We're* Number One!" It's amazing how far a little distancing can go.

If you're a sportsaholic to some degree, you probably think or act this way sometimes. But at what point does your team's fate become the focal point in your *life?* If you say you live and die with your team, you may be saying that your strongest life emotions follow your team's highs and lows. Your greatest joy comes from your Cleveland Indians winning their first pennant in decades. Your biggest kick is seeing your Green Bay Packers return to the Super Bowl glory of an earlier era. Your greatest frustration may come from hearing that Shaquille O'Neal left your Orlando Magic for a better deal. Your saddest moment in childhood might have been the day the Brooklyn Dodgers left town for Los Angeles.

## PLAY #10:
## YOUR MOST MEMORABLE SPORTS MOMENT

Let's get back to the Sportsaholism Recovery Playbook and see how the major happenings in your sports world impact you or the sportsaholic in your life. If you're working as a couple, find your comfortable spot and set aside five to ten minutes. It's time for the man to tell the story of his most memorable moment as a sports fan. (Note: If you're a man reading alone, just write down your answers in the playbook. If you're a woman reading alone, try to find a sports fan you know who is willing to share this experience with you.)

This moment could involve one of the teams you root for, or perhaps your favorite player. It can be a wonderful moment or a horrible moment, an inspirational moment or a sickening moment. It can be a moment from a long time ago, or the big game from last season. Some questions you might ask yourself (or your sportsaholic) to help bring the moment into focus:

*Why was this moment so memorable to you?*

*What factors or events led up to it, and what happened afterward?*

*How was this moment captured by TV, radio, newspapers, and magazines?*

*Who shared this moment with you?*

*How did you mark the occasion, and what mementos did you keep?*

*When was the last time you felt that way about anything else in your life?*

*What could ever happen in sports that would be even more memorable to you?*

### WRAP-UP:

Take a few moments to cover any additional questions or record other memories. Jot down a few notes in your playbook to record these highlights.

Pay particular attention to the question that asks what else in life gave you the same kind of feelings as your most memorable sports moment. Just as your team's championship may deliver your highest high in life, your most memorable sports setback may prompt your lowest low in life.

I spent years wrapped up in the fate of the Boston Red Sox and Celtics, years that gave me some wonderful highs. But in my early adulthood, I experienced my lowest lows in life from two Red Sox failures—losing the seventh and deciding game of the 1975 World Series to the Cincinnati Reds, the night after Boston's stirring twelve-inning, Game Six victory; and losing the '78 American League East championship playoff game to the Yankees in Fenway Park.

It's not enough to say those heartbreaking losses impacted my mood for a few weeks or months. It's more honest to admit that those setbacks colored my entire attitude toward everything around me for years. I was grouchier. I wasn't as hopeful about life. I didn't smile as much. I waited and hoped for the Red Sox to reverse their fortunes the next time around so I would feel better about life. And that never happened.

## Singing the Playoff Blues

Stewart, a property manager in Oceanside, California, grew up in Los Angeles following the Rams. In fact, he admits that his whole life centered around his team. The Rams won a lot of games, but every season from 1973 to 1980, they lost in the play-offs. Either Dallas knocked them off, or Minnesota squeaked past them. Once they even got to the Super Bowl, where they lost to the Steelers. Those playoff setbacks brought Stewart nothing but a heartache.

"They were so close every darn year, and some of those playoff losses to the Vikings were just unlucky," laments Stewart. "This is a painful memory I try to repress. But their losing truly bothered me to the point that my outlook on life suffered for many years. Even today, though I realize that it's all meaningless, the thought of the Rams' playoff losses is very upsetting."

Any painful memory in life can linger with us for years: a death in the family, the day we lost a job we loved, a valued relationship that ended abruptly. Likewise, any truly happy experience can leave a lasting imprint: the birth of our first child, a lucrative business deal, taking in the majesty of the Grand Canyon. How do those peaks and valleys compare in their day-to-day impact to those big wins and losses in sports, or moments such as the death of Mickey Mantle that left middle-aged men in tears for the first time since childhood?

## PLAY #11:
## COMPARING SPORTS TO LIFE

Let's get back to the Sportsaholism Recovery Playbook. This exercise is best done by writing your answers in your playbook. Then you may choose to share what you've written with your spouse or friend.

### Part I:
Compile a Top Five list of your all-time sports *thrills*. You might start with the most memorable moment from the previous exercise, then go on and add four more high watermarks in your life as a sports fan—pennants, championships,

meeting a favorite player, your team beating its main rival. Don't feel obliged to make your list correspond to how the sports media labeled the events you pick. If it was big for you, it belongs in your Top Five.

On the same page, compile a Top Five list of your all-time sports *disappointments,* those moments when you felt absolutely crushed by what happened to your team or player. These are the losses that stick, the stunning blows that threw you into a personal nosedive.

Pretty simple, right? If you're finding that a Top Five is just revving up your sports memory and you're thinking about other big moments that don't quite crack the Top Five, feel free to expand both lists to make each a Top Ten.

### PART II:

Next, on a separate page of your playbook, make a Top Five list of your all-time highs in your life completely *outside* of sports. These are your personal thrills, like that surprise job promotion or your first sexual experience. Again, if something pops up that may seem less than inspiring to the rest of the world but fits the Top Five for you, include it.

Now make the corresponding Top Five list of your all-time lows in life completely outside of sports. Try to stick with what really comes to mind, like the day your dog ran away when you were eight, rather than thinking about what *should* be in the Top Five by someone else's standards.

As with the Top Five sports lists, if you feel you really need to add on more highs and lows, you may choose to make Top Tens. But you may find that five do the job just fine.

### FOLLOW-UP:

Now place the two sets of lists (sports and nonsports) side-by-side in front of you. Which lists did you get more excited doing? Which came easier? If you honestly got more juiced up with your sports lists, that's natural for a passionate fan. Was it tougher to find those fourth or fifth moments on your lists of personal highs and lows from your own life outside of sports? That's also natural. Look more closely at the nonsports lists. Do you see many references to the people and circumstances around you in your life today? Many fans don't.

## Losing Off-the-Field Intimacy

How many of your sports thrills and disappointments are linked to the team you still follow every day, every season? If your relationship with the Yankees began when you were a kid, it's undoubtedly lasted longer than most relationships in your life. And maybe, just maybe, the bond between you and the Yankees runs deeper for you than your relationships with women, especially when the Yankees win the World Series. You can count on your relationship with your team. As many men say, *your team will never divorce you!*

Few relationships in life pack the same week-to-week excitement, intensity, and drama that you get from following your team —at least on the surface. As we discussed in Chapter 4, the drama of sports works like a drug, and its power can make any other potential drama in life pale in comparison. So the personal drama that may unfold more slowly in an intimate relationship with a woman simply may not keep our attention riveted the way it is when our team plays.

This is what really frustrates women living with a sportsaholic. They yearn for the closeness that builds moment by moment, night by night, conversation by conversation. The mystery, the depths of feeling, the simple acts of caring, the unshakable foundation of mutual trust and support—all these elements of a rewarding relationship take time. Building them requires digging under the surface. The joys of intimacy don't splash across the screen with the flair of a Steve Young pass to Jerry Rice, and they don't chalk up touchdowns as quickly and easily.

As men, we struggle with the conversion from intimate sports relationship to intimate *human* relationship. Our attention spans have been trained for a new play every thirty seconds, a finite result every two or three hours. We're used to clear-cut strategies and simple adjustments. In sports, we know how to try to make everything come out right, and when we're wrong we see it right away.

But it's all so much more subtle in an intimate relationship. And women expect us to recognize what we're feeling all the time, then identify it and share it. How do we do that? In sports, it's clear. When our running back makes a 70-yard touchdown run, we know we feel happy and satisfied. When our pitcher gives up three home runs in the first inning, we feel angry and upset. It's a direct cause-and-effect response. But in an intimate relationship with a woman, the action is seldom as clear. And we've got no play-by-play person or color commentator to offer clues to what we're seeing and experiencing.

Let's say we're sitting at dinner with our partner, talking about our plans for the summer. Suddenly, we zone out. Our partner sees us looking out the window and asks what's happening. Are we feeling angry, hurt, sad, anxious? Hard to tell. We don't have the same cues we get from a game. And through our socialization as men, we're even trained not to reveal our feelings—to be strong, to keep a lid on it.

Intimacy, then, is a tough game for any man who experiences his strongest feelings through sports. Sometimes when a woman asks what we're feeling or thinking at the dinner table, the truth is we might still be ticked off about the Knicks blowing that seven-point lead in the fourth quarter a few hours ago. We don't dare admit that to her. And maybe we're so emotionally spent from the 49ers-Dolphins overtime game that afternoon, we simply don't have any emotional energy left for a serious talk with our wives. We're spent!

For many men, when a woman sighs in frustration and temporarily gives up trying to communicate with us, we sigh in relief. We can go back to the game, where intimacy is far less complicated. It's like being a kid and having our mother declare, after a brief tussle, that we don't have to finish all our brussels sprouts—it's OK to leave the table and go watch TV. We're off the hook. We go back to the sports den, where we find our intimate bond with our team more comfortable and understandable. We're connecting with our Atlanta Braves, having fun and expressing ourselves.

But we may be falling further from richer communication and deeper intimacy with our spouse or partner in a couple of ways. One, we're allowing sports to serve as a haven, where we're hiding from the tougher tasks of real-life intimacy; and two, we're getting so wired from that black-and-white, high-stakes drama of sports, that we find it harder and harder to tune in to the subtler rhythms of an intimate relationship. We're vicariously fulfilling our needs for intimacy through our relationship with our team.

## Getting Our Feelings "Fix"

As men, we do require intimacy in our lives. We need to feel and express emotions as part of being alive. But because most of us were socialized as small boys to cut off our feelings, we don't usually feel safe or confident in letting them out at home, at work, and in most social situations. Those old gender stereotypes may be crumbling here and there, but for every movement to help free men from emotional prison, there's an equally strong backlash that pressures them to stick to the stoic ways of the past. That's why we get pulled so strongly toward sports. With sports, it's OK to express nervousness, excitement, frustration, anger, and elation. When it comes to emotional expression over sports, anything goes.

I had to laugh when a woman in the national survey said that men love sports because it gives them a place to let out their emotions without "touchy-feely crap" getting in the way. The truth is, I've taught and participated in a lot of personal-growth classes, and I haven't found many as "touchy" as the average football huddle. Players routinely hold hands, hug one another, pat one another on the rear end, rub each other's heads, slap palms and fists, dance together, and topple onto one another in celebratory piggy-piles.

As for the "feely" part, all you have to do is follow the cameras during a major playoff or championship moment. After we take in the winners celebrating, we zoom in on the losers' bench. There we witness the tears, the pain, the frustration. And in post-game interviews, we experience the gamut of feelings expressed by both winners and losers.

During my sportswriting days, when I went into a locker room after a game to interview players, the one question I asked most was, *"How did it feel?"* How did it feel when you fumbled one yard short of the goal line on the final drive? How did it feel when you sank the game-winning jump shot in the final seconds? How did it feel when your fastball got knocked over the fence for a grand slam that cost your team the game? How did it feel when you rolled in that thirty-foot putt with the tournament on the line?

**SURVEY RESULT: Who are your favorite sportscasters or sportswriters?**

1. John Madden
2. Bob Costas
3. Chris Berman
4. Al Michaels
5. Dick Vitale
6. Frank Gifford
7. Marv Albert
8. Keith Jackson
9. Vin Scully
10. Pat Summerall

**SURVEY RESULT: Who are your *least* favorite sportscasters or sportswriters?**

1. Brent Musburger
2. Dan Dierdorf
3. Dick Vitale
4. Frank Gifford
5. John Madden
6. Howard Cosell (deceased)
7. Billy Packer
8. Harry Caray
9. Joe Theismann
10. Bill Walton

Feelings are central to the appeal of sports. As fans, we expect to know the deepest feelings of anyone who plays a critical role in our games. When Michael Jordan is lying on the court cradling the basketball and sobbing as his team finishes its '96 NBA championship, we want to know about his feelings for his late father just as much as we want to know about his dunks. By sharing such emotional displays, players bring us emotionally closer to the experience of the game. And by their own behavior, they show us that it's totally acceptable to express intense feelings of joy and pain toward sports. They give us the permission we seek to act out our feelings in the stands or in our living rooms.

*Sports become the place where we get our feelings fix!* All the emotions that we might be contacting and expressing in response to the everyday events of our own lives, we live vicariously through our team's wins and losses. Of course, if our team is going to give us our emotions, we want only the goodies—joy, happiness, jubilation. We don't want any of that pain, sorrow, frustration. As men, our socialized training is especially weak on what to do with difficult feelings. To avoid them, we want our team to win, win, win! When they lose, as women will attest, we become a bear.

Over time, however, the vicarious emotional experiences begin to numb us to our own feelings about real life. If we're depressed about our own lives, we're too engulfed by the feelings we get from latching onto our teams to notice. We simply don't feel as deeply about the people, events, and situations in our own lives as we do about our Cleveland Indians. We lose touch with some of our own winning and losing—not just the big stuff, but the little peaks and valleys of ordinary life. We don't work as hard at setting our own goals and how we might achieve them. We're not as well tuned in to our own natural life setbacks and how to rebuild from them. We live out all these experiences through our Cowboys.

If the Cowboys beat the Packers in the big game on Sunday, we're not as concerned about the poor report card our daughter brought home Friday. When the Cowboys begin their postseason drive just after Christmas, we don't have much interest in making New Year's resolutions for ourselves. We just want that Super Bowl championship. When the Cowboys stumble in the playoffs, we're more invested in how they're going to shore up their weak spots on defense than how we're going to improve our unsatisfying work or career status. Our "job" as a sports fan is something we can count on more solidly, anyway. As many men say, *you can't get fired by your team!*

We may also feel dissatisfied in our relationships, but can't harness the emotional strength to delve more deeply inside them. We may feel cut off from the community where we live, but as long as we have our sports buddies, who needs others? We may get angry and depressed at the state of American politics or education, but instead of getting directly involved in efforts to change them, we skip over everything in the newspaper in our rush to get to the sports section. We learn how to get by on our jobs and at home, to do our necessary chores, to pass the hours between games. But we simply don't have the same juice available to build our own lives into the kind of champion we want our Cowboys to be.

Granted, we're talking about degrees of sportsaholism. My own experiences as a former sportsaholic, as well as what I've seen and heard from hundreds of other men who love sports, prove that sportsaholism, like many other addictions, manifests itself individually. Whether any of these effects of vicarious living through sports are true for *you,* only you can know. But it pays to keep your eyes open, and to listen to the observations of others. It may be that the best of you is being poured into your devotion to your team, and everyone and everything else is getting short shrift.

# ELEVEN

# When Sports Become Our God

*When I was ten or eleven, my mom and my grandma said
to me, "Football is your God!" So I went to the room to
watch the game and I figured, Well, it must be everyone's
God, because football is all that's on TV.*

—Ricky, a devout Pittsburgh Steelers fan

As men who love sports, we look to them to fulfill many of our
most basic needs. As we explored in the previous chapter, our
intense involvement with our favorite team can serve as our primary relationship in life. In Chapter 9, we saw how sports form
the bridge between many a father and son. We often treat our
commitment to our teams as our real job, to which we devote
more concentrated attention and energy than the work we get
paid for.

Sports also can become our drug, our companion, our passion,
our entertainment, our hobby, our emotional source, our escape,
our news, our community, our love, and our focus. And as many
sportsaholics admit, sports may even become our God. Let's consider how:

- Our devotion to our teams may run deeper than our devotion to anything else in life, including religion or spirituality.

- Sports, especially during football season, often become our Sunday focal point, rated higher in our minds and hearts than any religious service we attend.
- We've turned entire rooms of our homes into sports shrines, filled with posters, banners, flags, and all the other symbols of our team's exalted status, arranged with the care of an altar.
- We glorify our sports heroes by wearing their uniform jerseys, paying fees for their autographs, and buying the shoes and food they endorse.
- Attending live sporting events can feel to many of us like going to a worship service, where we sing our praise and shout our devotion to our team in the crowd's common passion.
- Through sports, we gain a feeling of connectedness to life all around us, especially those in the same "congregation" of fans who follow our team.
- Sports satisfy our spiritual thirst to be part of something larger than ourselves, where we experience a sense of mystery or awe.
- We turn to sports as a source of comfort or security when we feel troubled or lost.
- We use sports as a means to give our life clear direction and purpose, something we can always look forward to and can share our enthusiasm for with others.

In our nation, we've always treasured our religious freedom. We are a diverse people with many different religions and spiritual beliefs. We hold many varying definitions of God, religion, and spirituality, and although some groups have tried to declare their particular beliefs as a common standard, it's our rich diversity that makes us who we are. I've been reminded of this often in my own studies in spirituality. My beliefs have changed, expanded, evolved. Along the way, I was surprised to discover the role sports had been playing in my spiritual life.

It happened several years ago during a class on spirituality called "Quiet Mind, Open Heart" at the Omega Institute in

Rhinebeck, New York. Instructor Elizabeth Lesser invited us to answer this question: What did you consider "spiritual" when you were nine years old?

When I thought back to that time in my life, I recalled that I was still a practicing Catholic, but my parents were about to leave the church and its belief system behind. Catholicism was no longer what I considered "spiritual." I kept thinking, What else in my life at age nine did I feel devoted to, with a sense of connectedness, mystery, pleasure, sustenance, and a faith that I had something to count on, a love that would endure?

The answer came back simply and directly: sports. For the rest of my childhood and much of my adult life, sports served as my religion, my spiritual outlet and practice. That role changed only as I slowly began to let go of sports and allow new spiritual ways in. As I think back over those sports-worshiping years, I certainly didn't feel as if I were alone.

I remember one particular symbol of the common attitudes around me. When I was in my early teens, I had just begun to follow pro hockey's Boston Bruins, who were then Stanley Cup contenders with Phil Esposito their main goal scorer. One of the more popular bumper stickers around Boston at that time read, JESUS SAVES, BUT ESPO SCORES ON THE REBOUND! A joke? Sure, but like many jokes we laugh in part because of the truth at the core of it.

Everyone is different. Many passionate sports fans also hold deep and passionate religious and spiritual beliefs, and follow them at least as devotedly as they do sports—or more so. But in studying the results of my national survey, I was struck by the many references to sports assuming a greater role in men's lives than any religion or spiritual belief.

Let's look at the survey answers to Question #15 of the Sportsaholism Questionnaire, which asks what else in life grips sports fans with the same passion and intensity as sports. Religion ranked eleventh, right after food and well behind music, movies, and politics. Religion came in eighth in response to Question #29, which asks what else in life can fans talk about as enthusiastically as sports. And when asked in Question #59 what they would do more of, if they spent less time with sports, fans did not vote religion into the Top Twenty.

**SURVEY RESULT: What else other than sports grips you with the same passion and intensity?**

1. family/spouse
2. *nothing*
3. work
4. music
5. sex
6. politics
7. movies
8. outdoor activities
9. reading
10. food
11. religion
12. national/world events

**SURVEY RESULT: What else other than sports can you talk about with as much enthusiasm?**

1. family/spouse
2. work
3. politics
4. *nothing*
5. music
6. national/world events
7. movies
8. religion/spirituality
9. books
10. sex
11. travel
12. history

Gordon, the married sportsaholic who used to sell sports merchandise in a store near the Houston Astrodome, grew up in a household where sports ranked ahead of religion. "We didn't go to church at all," he explains. "Sports were my passion, totally. My dad was a big Oilers fan, and I idolized my dad. So on Sundays we were either at the game, or if the Oilers were out of town we had a party at the house to watch them on TV."

As Gordon grew up, religion became more important. He attended Bible college in Texas, where he met his wife, Jenny. But today Gordon confesses that the more that sports drive his adult life, the more religion takes a backseat. In answer to the question about any comparable passion or interest to sports in his life, he responds, "I would say God, but recently sports has consumed more of my interest. That's a sad testament. I put my relationship with God aside because I'm too busy. I'm tired from long hours at work, and when I come home I want to watch the game on TV."

## Ricky's Reverence for Sports

Ricky is the devout Pittsburgh Steelers fan quoted at the start of this chapter. He grew up in the small Pennsylvania town of Apollo, about a half hour east of Pittsburgh, as one of six boys in a family of eight children. Not surprisingly, he was molded into the male fraternity of sports with his father and five brothers. Ricky played wide receiver on his high school football team, and when he wasn't rooting for the Steelers in pro football on Sunday, he pulled for Notre Dame in college ball on Saturday. Like many sportsaholics, he credits sports with providing him with the emotional thrills he needs in life. But more than that, sports have served as a rock, an anchor, during some very troubling childhood times.

"My parents were constantly fighting and screaming," explains Ricky. "It seemed like the only stability I had was sports. Regardless of what was going on at my house, I knew that every September the Steelers and Notre Dame would play. I know that I was escaping from my shaky home life through sports, but maybe the enjoyment I got from sports kept me from turning to drugs or alcohol."

Because sports served him so well growing up, Ricky, a recent graduate of West Virginia University, wants to make them his life work. As part of his childhood escape into sports, he often would pretend he was a sportscaster. When he watched a game on TV, he'd supply the play-by-play in his room. Living on a farm in an isolated area, he would invent numerous backyard sports games with his brothers, and describe every detail in his emerging sportscaster voice. Even as a player on his high school football team, Ricky would assume mock play-by-play duties from the sidelines to chronicle what his teammates were doing on the field.

At college, Ricky got to be a real sportscaster for his school radio station's broadcasts of baseball and hockey games, along with filing halftime reports on women's basketball games. He's out in the job market now, seeking the first step toward becoming the next Bob Costas. When asked how he would spend his time if he ever cut down his sports devotion, Ricky replied, "I might get more religious."

It's not only as troubled children that we may turn to sports as a crutch, a trusted friend to lean on in times of stress or need. As adult sports fans, we also find that sports can be a safe island when turmoil threatens to engulf us.

Stewart, whose heartache from the Los Angeles Rams' playoff losses in the 1970s was chronicled in the previous chapter, recently experienced the end of his five-and-a-half-year marriage. His ex-wife hated sports and often expressed her anger over his sports-watching habits. To appease her, Stewart greatly minimized his sports involvement. That took a major effort for someone who admits that as a child, he looked up to his favorite players as God. Now that his ex-wife has left, sports may move back in. As he explains, "I anticipate that I will revive my interest in sports, more or less as a diversion and something to keep me company."

Many of us as men turn to sports news as a way of avoiding the impact of the depressing news of the real world. Sports *become* our real world, our true world. In that way, we find sports a comfort or a buffer against the darkness around us. Rather than turn to the Bible or other spiritual inspiration for reminders of what really matters in life, we turn to our sports statistics, newspaper sports sections, and sports magazines to keep us on track.

## How Women Worship

If you're a woman living with a sportsaholic, you may find yourself especially frustrated and confused by the high degree of reverence with which men regard sports. Not many women hold up sports as God. Women may like to play sports, and they may cheer wildly for their favorite gymnasts or swimmers during the Olympics, and even for some of the same major-college and pro sports men follow. But few women worship at the altar of sports.

When the game's over, women let it go. If they feel badly after a team they care about loses, they're more likely to feel sad for the players involved than sad for themselves as fans of a loser. They get on with life. They don't glorify the teams or players the way men do. Women don't carry the full scope of history that elevates each game and each season's result to worldly heights. They say to men, "It's just a game, remember?" But men continue to defend sports as fervently as any passionate religious believer defends his faith against the questioning or criticism of others.

That intense devotion begins when we're boys, as we grow up worshiping the latest Michael Jordans and Troy Aikmans. We get so mesmerized by their talent, their heroic feats, their charisma, and their authoritative presence telling us what foods to eat and what clothes to wear, that we see them in a Godlike image. We go to school dressed in authentic uniform jerseys with their names and numbers, and we defend their honor and supremacy against any other kid who brags about *his* hero. Even when our heroes' human mistakes and frailties remind us of their earthly roots, or when Jordan himself cautions us not to look upon him with such idolatry, we worship them all the more.

As men, we pick up additional cues about a religious dimension to sports right down there on the playing field. In the NFL playoffs several years ago, the New York Giants watched all their hopes for a playoff victory over San Francisco come down to a field-goal attempt in the final seconds. As the Giants kicker prepared to make his attempt, the cameras focused on most of the Giants players on the sideline. They were holding hands in a long chain, many of them kneeling. At home, we interpreted this scene as praying for the field-goal attempt to go through the uprights so the Giants would win and go on to the Super Bowl. And that's just what happened.

In the Super Bowl against Buffalo, the Giants again had their hopes for victory pinned to a final-second field-goal attempt. This time, it was the Bills lining up a kick that, if successful, would win the Super Bowl championship for Buffalo and send the Giants home losers. Again, the cameras found the Giants players holding hands and kneeling on their sideline—this time praying for the kick to *miss*. Across the field, cameras found the Bills players similarly holding hands and kneeling, praying for the kick to *succeed*.

The Bills kicker missed the field goal. The Giants won the game. Fans and media launched curious debates about whether God really cares who wins football games or picks which side to favor. Through all the confusing messages, those of us tuned in as fans took in one clear signal: Who wins the game is important enough to merit serious prayer and devotion.

As we know well, it's not just fun and games. Sports, to many, are vitally important endeavors. In looking for evidence, we can point all the way back to the November 1963 weekend when President Kennedy was assassinated in Dallas. As most business of the nation stopped on that Sunday, two days after the tragedy, the NFL football games went on as scheduled. No matter what else may be happening on any Sunday, sports go on.

## Worshiping a False Idol?

Some men do recognize that sports have become their God and decide to rearrange their priorities. Sometimes, this reordering can be part of major life changes, as it was for Elliott. A retail manager in his thirties, Elliott lives in Lawrence, Kansas, home of the University of Kansas Jayhawks. He's naturally drawn to the school's football and basketball teams, as well as pro football's Kansas City Chiefs. For years, he held season tickets to Kansas basketball games, and his weekly hours of sports devotion were well up in double figures.

"When I'd come home from a Kansas game, I'd watch it again

on tape before I went to bed," recalls Elliott. "Or, if that game wasn't televised, I'd pull out a tape of a big game from a previous season and stay up until one A.M. watching it. I'd get pretty upset when they lost. Once Kansas lost a game at Missouri on a shot in the final seconds, and I punched a hole in my living-room wall."

Today, Elliott still gets excited during games on TV. Like many fans, he will talk to the players and coaches on the screen. But after losses, he insists that he's able to forget it and move on, just take it in stride. He savors his team's success but finds that he no longer depends on a ball game for his peace and joy in life.

What changed? Elliott points to his conversion to fundamentalist Christian principles in the mid-1980s and a deep devotion to following them. In his life priorities, God passed sports as Number One. He realized that he needed to spend less time with sports, and he now reports watching NFL games only when Kansas City plays, and pro basketball only in the playoffs. He watches no baseball whatsoever. Sometimes when he watches a game on TV, he turns the sound down and does other things at the same time. He's even bypassed some important TV games to attend church-related activities. And those Kansas basketball season tickets? Voluntarily sacrificed. Elliott explains:

"God said to me, 'Hey, this is an idol. You have to give these up.' So I did."

Now Elliott is training to become a minister. If he winds up leading a ministry in the Lawrence area, he knows he'll have some serious Kansas sports fans in his congregation. He imagines what he might say in a sermon one Sunday morning in April, perhaps when Kansas has reached the Final Four and is preparing to play the next night with the national championship on the line, their fans gripped by that intense excitement and anticipation.

"That would be a great opportunity to talk about idolatry—how anything that comes between you and your relationship with your God is an idol, a false god," he says. "I believe anything in our lives can become an idol: TV, the stock market, our work, a hobby, a new house. God allows me to follow sports—the God I follow does not want to deny us pleasures in life—but He tells me that no other God can come between us. We need to keep sports in perspective."

Keeping it all in perspective—as an idea, it sounds simple. But when it comes to letting go of sports as our God, "simple" does not necessarily mean easy. If sports supply our sense of connectedness to other people and life around us, where's the drive to become a seeker of God, however we may define God? If sports serve as our life's rudder, offering us clear purpose and direction, what need do we feel to find a "higher" focus? If walking into Camden Yards or Wrigley Field fills our being with deep mystery or awe, why search nature or the cosmos for the answers to burning spiritual questions about our life on earth? And if sports appear to fulfill so many of our outer needs, why work to cultivate an inner life, a life of the spirit?

Religious conversion or a spiritual yearning may inspire some to curb their sports fanaticism, but that's a personal choice and not likely a prime motivator for a typical sportsaholic. When sports become our God, we're more likely to want to spread the word about the greatness of sports to others. We're not inclined to want to sacrifice what we most love and cherish. Even to consider such a thing, we need to be convinced that letting go of sports is right in a way that makes sense to us, a way that we can hear.

## Listen: A Passionate Plea from Women

As men who love sports, we've told our stories in these last three chapters. Women have tuned in to us, and they've undoubtedly learned a great deal about the roots of our sportsaholism and its intense hold on us. Sure, women may never be able to *understand* fully what it means to be a man who has loved sports all his life. It's not their experience. What they *can* do is begin to see how sports look from our eyes, and perhaps get a sense for how it feels from our hearts.

If you've been reading Part III as a couple, you may have already been talking about some of the new ideas and information she has learned, or some way in which she's been touched by one or more of the men's stories. If you're a woman living with a sportsaholic, this is an excellent opportunity to share with him anything that opened your eyes or particularly moved you about the role of sports in men's lives. Maybe you "get" something now that you didn't see before. Letting him know it could ease some of the old tensions.

You may find that Play #5 ("Vin Scully Playback") from your Sportsaholism Recovery Playbook in Chapter 5 will provide you with helpful structure to communicate what you learned. And you may want to call upon the same exercise to speak to anything that disturbed you while you listened to men tell their stories about sports.

And men, now that she's patiently listened to you explain more about the role of sports in your life, it's time for *you* to listen to her. One way or another, women have been trying to make a point, to get your attention. Beyond the blame, the judgments, the threats, the sarcasm, the arguments—there's something women really need to communicate to you about sports and you. Tune in to the heart of their message, and perhaps you'll hear a plea that sounds something like this:

"Guys, we want you in our lives. We want your attention, your energy, your time, your interest, your passion. Don't get us wrong. We don't expect a hundred percent of those qualities, only enough so we may feel like full and equal partners with you in a strong, healthy relationship. We love you, respect you, value you. You're important to us.

"We're not looking to replace sports in your life, and we certainly don't expect you to give them up entirely. We can see how important they've been to you and how deeply they reach you. We're asking you to make room for changes and adjustments, to be open to developing a new attitude. We're hoping you can find ways to make the rest of your life a little bigger, while sports become a little smaller.

"We come to you with this plea not out of selfishness, but out of a sense of commitment to what our relationship could become. We come with a willingness to be supportive of you in any changes you agree to try. We want to be your allies.

"It's not just for ourselves that we look to you for a different attitude toward sports and their place in your life. You, and all your unique abilities and gifts, are needed in our families. You're needed in our communities. You're needed in our society, and in our world. We're all living in a time of great change and upheaval, and the problems and challenges require us all to tune in and offer our ideas, our efforts, our inspiration. Come join in."

## PART FOUR

# Mapping Out a New Game Plan

# TWELVE

# Rediscovering Life

*I have always felt that I balanced my love of sports with everything else in my life. I have seen friends who haven't done that, and it has cost them a wife or a girlfriend. I will not let that happen to me.*
—Simon, age thirty, single, a banker from Odell, Nebraska

Men like a good challenge. Give them a project and a goal, and they love to plunge in and figure out how to accomplish it. They'll study the situation, brainstorm ideas, consider options, map out a strategy, and immerse themselves in carrying it out.

This is part of the appeal of sports, and why men enjoy watching them so much. They see a home-run hitter facing a challenge when he steps into the batter's box against the pitcher with the nasty curveball. They see a basketball scorer trying to overpower a double-team defense. They see the quarterback studying the opponent's secondary, seeking out that one potential weak spot.

For you or the sportsaholic in your life, these are challenges that are easily understood and deeply appreciated every day in your role as sports fan. But when *you're* asked to take on an important challenge yourself—perhaps a bigger challenge than anything you could imagine on the playing field—it can seem like an overwhelming task. Suppose it sounds something like this: **How can you begin to break your dependence on sports so you can build stronger intimate relationships and get more involved in the drama of your everyday life?**

If you're ready to take on this challenge, here's an important starting point: *Women are not the enemy!* Maybe there have been times when it was easy to see her as the opponent, the team you need to beat to get to the Super Bowl. You want to make her the Miami Dolphins, lined up against your Pittsburgh Steelers. So when she charges toward you with complaints and criticisms about your sports habits, naturally you want to thwart her at the line of scrimmage. And when she makes like Dan Marino and throws a bomb in the form of an ultimatum (i.e., what she needs from you to stick around) you want to intercept that pass and discourage her from trying another one.

Life is all about competition, right? Why should your arguments about sports be any different? The goal is to win. And if you just find the right answer or winning rebuttal to every one of her complaints, you can hold out. You can beat her at this game and keep things the way they've been, right?

Wrong. As you probably know by now, facing your differences about sports with the woman in your life is not like a Steelers-Dolphins playoff game. Her desire for change in your relationship is not an attempt to beat you or to win the game. This isn't about competition for her, it's about cooperation. Even if you approach things differently, you're on the same side. Remember the passionate plea from women at the end of the previous chapter.

The goal is understanding and compromise, rather than attack and counterattack. Toward this goal, it helps to call upon that "both/and" perspective that we talked about in our discussion about the addictive nature of sports in Chapter 4. She may continue to annoy you with sarcastic comments about sports *and* you may see that there's some truth to what she says. She may have her own obsessions and excesses, *and* you may find that letting go of part of your sports obsession may open new doors for you that you'd truly enjoy stepping inside.

For now, let's put aside your differences in relating to women over sports. We'll return to that realm in the next chapter, where you two can focus on your efforts together. First, let's see what you can begin doing yourself to meet the challenge of breaking your dependence on sports and allowing more of your own life in.

You, or the sportsaholic in your life, may be finding you're already making positive changes in your lives based on the suggestions in Parts I–III of this book. Or at least you may be feeling more inclined to loosen the grip sports hold on your life. That's really the biggest step any man consumed by sports can take—recognizing the need to make at least *some* changes. That's the gut check. Once you drop your defensive armor and admit that it's time to make some changes in your life with sports, the rest is much easier.

**SURVEY RESULT: How do sports hurt your life in any way?**

1. does not hurt in any way
2. less balanced in life interests
3. less time with spouse/family
4. anger/depression after big losses
5. spend too much money
6. get too competitive
7. less time working around house
8. less energy for job
9. lose sleep
10. gamble too much

You'll find that it *is* possible to meet this new challenge. It *is* possible to develop a new way of relating to sports so that they no longer chew up the major share of your time, energy, and attention. Not only is it possible, but many men have already done it. Men just like you have found a new direction in a life once dominated by sports—and they're doing just fine. Their relationships are stronger. They've developed new interests. They still enjoy the fun and excitement of sports, but they look at them differently now. They point to many different motivations and circumstances that got them moving. Here are a few:

- They decided they *had* to change in order to find and keep a relationship with a woman.
- They did something so extreme as a fan that they were convinced that they were taking it all too seriously.

- They discovered a new interest that became bigger for them, and sports suddenly got smaller.
- They suffered a major illness or injury that prompted them to reevaluate their priorities, forcing sports to drop a notch or two.
- The older they got, the younger the players looked—so they just didn't relate to the whole sports scene in the same way.
- They got fed up with the big business of sports and simply didn't enjoy it the way they did before player strikes, free agency, and outrageous multimillion-dollar salaries.

You may have glimpsed some of your own circumstances or attitudes from this list. You may be thinking of new ideas for personal changes you might try. Later in this chapter, we'll return to the Sportsaholism Recovery Playbook for a few more exercises to help get you focused. First, let's hear from other men who have taken bold steps to achieving a more fulfilling life beyond sports.

## What He Did for Love

Simon, the banker from Nebraska quoted at the start of this chapter, lived for several years in Lincoln. He's one of those Cornhuskers football fans who wears red wherever he goes. He also follows the Minnesota Vikings in pro football, and enjoys checking in on the Chicago Cubs and Baltimore Orioles in baseball. Obviously, he's surrounded by sports temptations.

Simon also has a girlfriend, Cindy. They met as fellow employees at a bank in Lincoln before Simon got a better job in Odell, an hour away. They've been going together for about six months. Cindy, not an altogether avid sports fan, will attend a Nebraska game with Simon once in a while, on those rare autumn Saturdays in Lincoln when the temperature holds above sixty-five degrees. Otherwise, she doesn't much care for sports. Because Simon and Cindy now live an hour apart, they can only get together during the weekend and occasionally during the week at night. That, of course, is prime sports time.

In considering his own choice point here, Simon remembered two things. First, his last girlfriend hated sports and—guess what —the relationship didn't work. Second, he's seen friends from his Fantasy Leagues whose sports obsessions got them in even bigger messes.

"One guy is on his second divorce, the other guy has had one. I figured sports were part of the reason," Simon points out. "Every time I went over to their homes, they always had a game on TV with their satellite dish and fifty-two-inch screen."

So Simon made a decision. As his relationship with Cindy heated up, he cooled it on sports. He chose to spend most of his free time with her, doing many of the things she liked. That meant more movies, more social outings with friends, more family events. Sports still occasionally come into play between them, but not often. A guy they both know told them that he was having problems with *his* girlfriend over the time he spent watching base-ball. This led Cindy to ask Simon, "Why don't you ever ask to watch baseball when we're together?"

"I told her that since we don't spend that much time together, I want to spend it with her, not watching a game on TV. When I'm with her, I don't even watch *SportsCenter,*" boasts Simon. "She says I can turn the TV over to that sports stuff, but I tell her that I don't have to. This relationship has potential. It's tough enough these days to find someone you can live with, without messing it up with something like too much sports."

## Going Too Far for Your Team

William is an avid Ohio State football fan in Lexington, Ohio. When the Buckeyes play well and win, he remembers exactly what he did. Then, for the next game, he does everything the same way: He gets his newspaper from the same spot, takes exactly the same change for his pocket (two quarters, one dime, two nickels, one penny), wears the same school-color clothes, sits in the exact same spot.

He followed all these rituals throughout much of the '95 season as Ohio State won several games in a row. This success raised hopes of winning the Big Ten, making the Rose Bowl, and even winning the national championship. In anticipation, William made reservations for a New Year's trip to the Rose Bowl. For his team's major showdown with Michigan, William tried to follow his same ritual. But the Buckeyes lost the game, and all hopes for a trip to the Rose Bowl and any national honors vanished.

"I felt like I was partially to blame for their loss," William confesses. "Maybe I didn't wear the right clothes, sit in the right seat or whatever. I was absolutely despondent and felt like I had lost a part of myself, or even like I had just experienced a death in the family. But after a few weeks, I got over those feelings. Then I looked back and said to myself, Oh God, how could you have been that morose over this thing? My behavior was silly. I haven't followed that ritual since. I've really changed how I look at sports now. While I continue to support my teams, I temper my reactions to losses."

## Growing Up

Stan used to love collecting baseball and football cards. By age ten or eleven, he had the best collection in his neighborhood. Life was great, and sports were everything. That was his attitude through his college years at the University of Virginia, where the football team once rose unexpectedly to number one in the polls for a brief period one season. Stan soaked it all up, living as a true sportsaholic.

Today, about five years down the road, he's got a managerial job for an environmental-outreach firm in Washington. He works fifty-hour weeks, and he's begun to dabble in the stock market on the side. He's more apt to read *Money* magazine than *Sports Illustrated*. When he's not working, he finds a need simply to relax, to take a long bike ride or watch a movie. He doesn't watch nearly as many games as in the old days. The wins and losses of teams he loves, like the Cowboys, just don't seem as important as planning for work, or focusing on something else to help him grow personally and professionally. He lives with three other guys who still throw their passion into sports. They try to lure Stan back, to be a big fan again, but he resists.

"They tried to get me into their Fantasy League, but I said, 'I can't touch you guys. You *live* this stuff.' It takes effort to keep up with all the stats and trades in those leagues," explains Stan. "They also invited me to go with them on vacation—they were going to see five ballparks in five days. At first I told them I didn't have the time. It was hard to admit to them that as valuable as my vacation time is, that's not how I wanted to spend it. I went with my brother on a canoeing and camping trip in Canada instead."

During his last significant relationship, Stan noticed a major change in his approach toward sports and women. If she wanted to do something, chances are he would want to do it too. He didn't think to himself, Darn, the Cowboys are on TV, I can't go out. One of Stan's roommates has a girlfriend now, and she knows she can't plan anything on weekends because of sports.

"If she was my sister," Stan asserts, "I'd tell her to forget him."

## The Game's Just Not the Same

Bud is a realtor who lives in Kill Devil Hills, part of the Outer Banks of North Carolina. He still spends about twenty hours per week with sports, and he loves basketball's North Carolina Tar Heels. But at age forty-five, he finds that he just doesn't have the same drive for sports he had when he was younger.

"At age fifteen, twenty, twenty-five, even thirty-five, sports were my primary interest in life," he recalls. "Since then, I've watched less, fished more. I've become more involved in my community. When my teams lose, I don't feel nearly as badly as I once did. Those feelings don't last more than half an hour now."

Tommy, a twenty-two-year-old college student in Chicago, is already cutting loose from the solid hold sports once had on his life. He was only seven when he watched his Dallas Cowboys lose a playoff game in the final seconds to San Francisco, on the famous Joe Montana touchdown pass to Dwight Clark, still known as "The Catch." Tommy couldn't bear to see his team lose like that. He cried all night long. But now that he's preparing to graduate, he's got more worldly matters on his mind. Seeing his Cowboys make the Super Bowl hardly even gets him worked up into a sweat.

"When the Cowboys reached the Super Bowl in '92, I would stay up late all week watching all those ridiculous pregame shows. I used to love watching what Jimmy Johnson did in his free time, or how many bowls of Wheaties that Nate Newton could eat in a day," Tommy admits. "But now, I just see them as overpaid professionals doing a job. The emotional attachment, where I felt that my life would be as successful as the Dallas Cowboys, that's gone now. I look back at how I used to feel and act toward sports, and I laugh."

## Walking Away from Sports

I was addicted to sports from the time I was nine years old. I went on to make sports my work life, as a sportswriter for the *Charlotte Observer*. But after twelve years in that business, I knew it was time for a change, especially when I got so bored covering college football that I'd read entire novels in the press box. So I left sportswriting about ten years ago, and after briefly hanging on to some lingering sports habits like my baseball rotisserie league, I gave up sports completely.

That's right, cold turkey. For nearly three years, I didn't watch a single sporting event in person or on TV, never checked in on *SportsCenter*, never surfed the radio for baseball games. I barely peeked at sports sections of newspapers, never picked up a *Sports Illustrated*, couldn't even tell you the names of the new superstars. And in many ways, this was the period of greatest learning in my life.

Instead of spending all my time trying to figure out what made the sports stars tick, I focused on what made *me* tick. I explored my own life and the life around me, first through fiction writing, then through the study of psychology, spirituality, and holistic lifestyles. For the first time since I was a kid, I actually got to know people who never paid any attention to sports. I got excited about what *they* followed. I studied with theologian Matthew Fox in a graduate program that integrated spirituality and psychology, and I joined exciting organizations and communities devoted to personal and societal change, such as the Omega Institute in New York.

I also discovered an entire outdoor world that I had shut out all those Saturday and Sunday afternoons. While living in Northern California, my treks into the redwood forest offered a deeper mystery than any baseball park. From my current home in Charlottesville, Virginia, I find great peace in the nearby Blue Ridge Mountains.

I did finally break my sports "fast" a few years ago when I heard that Duke's basketball team had reached another Final Four. Since I had always enjoyed spending time around Duke and coach Mike Krzyzewski in my sportswriting days, I decided to watch out of curiosity—sort of like checking in on an old friend. Today, I'll sit in on a basketball game two or three times during winter, and perhaps a bit more during March Madness or the NBA playoffs. I might also catch a few innings of a World Series game. And that's it. Sports are no longer front and center on the stage of my life. My life is pretty full without them.

What changed? I can't say it was any grand awakening. I never woke up one morning vowing to break free from sportsaholism. Ten years ago, you couldn't have told me I was addicted to sports. I wouldn't have bought it for a minute. For me it was a feeling inside of being pulled toward something else, and the more I followed that pull, the less interest I had in sports. The rest of life around me got bigger, and sports got smaller. And the longer I was away from sports, the more I could begin to see how my addiction had been holding me back.

That's my story, and everyone has their own reasons for leaving sports behind, or at least cutting down on the influence of sports on their lives. Sportsaholism, fortunately, is one addiction in which you don't have to stop the practice completely to break your dependence and create a more balanced life. You don't need to join a new twelve-step recovery program for sports to get moving. You can find room to develop a different kind of relationship to sports, one that still allows you to enjoy the fun and excitement without having sports interfere or limit you in other realms of life. You can make sports more of a casual pal than a best and only friend.

For most sportsaholics, renegotiating your relationship with sports is not a matter of *getting* a life. Rather, it's finding the path to *rediscovering* your life. And that path will lead you toward broadening your awareness of other subjects and interests, and freeing up more of your time and energy for intimate relationships. Ironically, here's where being such a great sports fan really does help. In considering the qualities and characteristics you most admire in your favorite players, you may find what you need to put more energy into the rest of your life.

## PLAY #12:
## HOW TO BE MORE LIKE MIKE

Open up your Sportsaholism Recovery Playbook. Review your answer to Question #23 of the Sportsaholism Questionnaire in Chapter 2, **"What are the abilities or qualities of your favorite players that you admire most?"** For each ability or quality of your favorite player, consider how that same ability or quality may show through in your own life today—and how you might develop more of it.

Let's say Cal Ripken is one of your favorite players, and dedication is the quality you most admire in him. Write down *dedication* in your playbook. Take a moment to consider how dedicated you are in your own life—to your spouse, your family, your work, your community, etc. Jot down in your playbook just how you demonstrate your dedication.

Now think about how you might become *more* dedicated in these same areas. Perhaps someone in your family could benefit from your dedicating a few more hours of your time each week helping them with a project. Or maybe there's a new volunteer organization that could benefit from your time and energy. Again, write down these ideas in your playbook under the "dedication" section.

If you regard Michael Jordan as your favorite player and point to his "discipline" as something you especially admire, look at how your own discipline gets exercised in your daily habits and endeavors. Give yourself credit for getting up at seven A.M. every day, or working out at the fitness club three times a week, or whatever you do that shows discipline. Record those forms of discipline in your playbook. Then consider how you might cultivate discipline in a new endeavor. Perhaps you want to take up photography, learn to play the guitar, or begin a meditation practice—all activities that will require the utmost discipline. Jot down these ideas to help you remember to follow up on them later.

You can do this for any quality or ability you relate to your favorite players. Do you appreciate their ability to come through in the clutch? If so, validate yourself for those times when you've come through in an important time for someone in your life. And think about how you might become more of a clutch player in your relationship—being there when you're most needed with your best effort. Maybe you like the way your favorite sports stars fit in as team players. Where are you a good team player already, and what can you do to become a stronger team player in your family, workplace, and community?

You may be thinking of additional qualities you admire in your favorite players that didn't make your answer to Question #23. Think about how those qualities relate to your everyday life. You may find that you have more in common with your heroes than you imagined, and that the very qualities you most appreciate on the field are those that already are the most important ones in your life. Use your playbook to list as many qualities as you wish, along with how you can manifest more of them today.

Of course, as a passionate sports fan you may often display your best qualities when you're *watching* sports. You're "dedicated" to the cause of the 49ers. You're "disciplined" about watching every Knicks game. You're a "clutch player" because your Fantasy-League trade on the trading deadline gave your team the home-run hitter you needed to win the Fantasy-League pennant.

If that's what you're discovering about yourself, it's good news! It means you're becoming more aware of how your "work" as a sportsaholic has been teaching you qualities that you can apply to almost any endeavor—*to put new life into your life*. And, as you know, you're already doing it much of the time. Let's look at some of those qualities that a true sportsaholic cultivates just by being a big fan:

### Focusing

The ability to tune out all outside distractions and zero in exclusively on the game and everything about it.

### Devotion

The willingness to study everything about the players and teams you follow (and their rivals), devour statistics, master the rules and strategy, and become an expert on the history of the game.

### Intuition

The knack for knowing exactly what's going to happen next in a game or predicting the best play for your team to call—and seeing it pan out as you would have diagrammed it!

### Perseverance

The character it takes to stick with a losing team for several years while waiting for them to become winners. This experience also cultivates patience and loyalty.

### Community

The camaraderie you create with like-minded sports fans by connecting with them at games, at sports bars, through Fantasy Leagues, the internet, or just talking sports at work or social gatherings.

### Celebration

The freedom involved in letting loose your joy and happiness over your team's championship or big victory.

### Heartbreak

The experience of feeling totally crushed by your team's major losses—and getting through it.

### Playfulness

The silly, almost childlike behavior you sometimes engage in while watching sports with the guys—telling stories, bragging, kidding, arguing, tossing pillows as if they were footballs.

### Understanding

Using your knowledge of the game and players to decide why your team wins or loses at any time, so you have an explanation that makes sense to you and allows you to accept and forgive your guys.

You may recognize other qualities you've been perfecting through your devotion to sports, such as prioritizing—deciding which of three simultaneous games to watch live, which to tape, and how often to check in on the others. Or discernment—choosing which announcers bother you so much that you have to turn the sound down when they come on. Or individual expression—cultivating your own unique fan style, from wearing face paint of your team's color to stand out at the stadium, to curling up on the sofa with your good-luck pennant. Or a sense of humor—laughing at Dennis Rodman's antics, or Chris Berman's nicknames, or those sports blooper videos.

## PLAY #13:
## YOUR DAILY POWER WORD

Here's another exercise for your Sportsaholism Recovery Playbook. Make a list of those qualities that you recognize in yourself as a sports fan. If you're reading this with the woman in your life, she may have additional suggestions. You can include the items just outlined, or any other quality you see yourself building when you follow sports. Write them down in your playbook, then copy each one on small, separate slips of paper. Fold them over so you can't see your writing, and place them all in an empty bowl, shoe box, or perhaps your team's souvenir basket.

Each day when you get up, select a slip of paper and read which quality you selected. This is your Power Word for the day. Focus on it and watch how it comes out naturally in the course of your daily interactions and activities. Experiment with how and where you can bring more of it to light.

Let's say you selected *intuition* as your Power Word. You might notice in driving to work that you intuitively knew the light was going to turn red just before you reached the intersection. Or your intuition told you exactly what a coworker would say to you five seconds before he or she said it. Now you can experiment with your expanding intuition. You might intuitively recognize that one thing to do or say when you get home that will bring the warmest smile from your spouse or partner.

Maybe you pulled out *community* as your Power Word. During the course of the day, pay attention to friends you may meet or hear from, and remember how and when they first became part of your community. Look at your schedule for the week and see how it reflects your participation with different groups, organizations, or social circles that form your community. And because this is your Power Word, take the opportunity to consider how you might add to your community. Is there a new friendship waiting to be made? Or maybe a church or social group to check out for yourself or as a couple?

### FOR THE WOMEN:

If you're the woman living with a sportsaholic, you may want to borrow from his list or make a list of qualities yourself, then use them as Power Words in the same way. This will give you something important to share together. Try this exercise as an experiment for a week. Then you'll know whether you want to end the experiment, or perhaps make it part of your daily routine.

If you're a man feeling a bit self-conscious about using Power Words, think about how, if you ever played organized sports as a kid, your coaches employed similar exercises to help you build certain qualities. Do you recall your football coach saying things like, "OK, men, today we're going to work on toughness"? You knew what *that* meant! Or you'd be informed that you'd be focusing on courage, or consistency, or listening, or sacrifice.

Maybe the coach would tell you directly what the emphasis of the day would be, or maybe he'd keep it to himself. But even if he didn't officially announce "the word of the day," if you think back to any given practice day, you're bound to see a common theme running through it. Your coach undoubtedly knew the

Power Word you were working on, but chose not to share it with you—perhaps so he could maintain greater control.

The characteristics emphasized by your coaches were not meant for sports use only, nor did the exercises apply solely to that team or that time in your life. Remember hearing things like, "These lessons you're learning now on this team are lessons you can apply later in life to any time or situation," or "Playing sports builds character"? It stands to reason, then, that if athletes develop character and abilities from playing sports that they can apply later in life, then you as a sports fan develop positive, constructive qualities from *watching* sports that can help you in whatever you do.

Best of all, you don't have to wait until your "watching days" are over before you can apply what you've learned! You can take what you're learning as a sports fan and use it to make changes or begin new ventures in your life now—as long as you're willing to get up out of your viewing chair and do it. Your perseverance in sticking with the Chicago Cubs for thirty years can be transferred to developing the perseverance to earn a graduate degree and launch a new career. Your patience and understanding toward the rookie wide receiver who runs the wrong pass route can be translated into patience and understanding toward your children's mistakes. Your playfulness in doing silly things with the guys during the game can be brought into your relationship with your wife, and can lighten up how you relate to each other every day.

We all learn by example. But when we cocoon ourselves in our sportsaholic world, it's easy to miss how we can take our sports behavior and use it to make us feel more alive and become more present in our day-to-day lives. We may feel a little protective of our sports world, believing it's the only haven in which we can celebrate and get loose and wild. Or we may feel self-conscious about how focused and intense we get over sports and don't want others to see us that way outside, where we've always been known for our calm, laid-back manner. And sometimes it's just a matter of practice, learning how to transform our sportsaholic behavior into constructive action in our life beyond sports.

## PLAY #14:
## IF I WERE A SUPERSTAR...

Open up your Sportsaholism Recovery Playbook again, and see how you answered Question #24 of the Sportsaholism Questionnaire, **"If you were a millionaire sports superstar, how would you live your life?"** If you're like most respondents to the national survey, you probably feel outraged by the exorbitant salaries of real sports superstars today. You may be critical of how those millionaires behave, and believe that if *you* were making that kind of money playing sports, you'd carry yourself very differently. Sure, maybe you'd use some of the big bucks to buy new cars and homes, but beyond that you'd represent your sport better than most of those guys out there.

For this exercise, copy your answer to the question about how you'd live your life as a millionaire sports star. For each item you mentioned, ask yourself, or have the woman reading with you ask, How can I do that more in my own life today?

Let's say you wrote down that as a sports superstar, you'd give back to the community or to worthy causes. Are there places and causes in your community where you can give more of yourself today, if not in the extra millions you'd be making if you were Troy Aikman, then perhaps in your time, effort, and energy? If you believe that as a sports superstar you would travel more, maybe that's a reminder of how you could do more traveling today, as your money and resources permit.

Perhaps you said that if you were a highly paid athlete, you'd be a good role model for children. So how can you be a better role model toward your own children and others you know through your lifestyle and attitudes of respect, caring, and compassion? If you claim you'd take care of your family if you got paid all that money, how might you take better care of your family today? Not by taking them on expensive cruises, but by giving them more of your undivided attention at home.

It's true that many sports superstars don't lead exemplary lives. Rather than berate them for their failings, you can use that realization as a reminder of how *you* want to be in your own more simple life. Of course, you probably do that now. Many respondents to the national survey told me they hoped they would still live the same way as a superstar that they live today. So doing this exercise may simply reinforce your best intentions, and it may also offer you clues of something new you may want to take on. Take a few moments to jot down any other ideas that come to you, and keep your playbook open for one last exercise in this chapter.

## PLAY #15:
## A TWO-HOUR BREAK FROM SPORTS

Here's something tangible that you can do today to begin breaking your dependence on sports. Look back to how you answered Question #59 in the Sports-aholism Questionnaire. Let's put your answer in motion.

**SURVEY RESULT: If you didn't spend so much time and energy as a sports fan, how might you spend it?**

1. reading
2. time with spouse/family
3. don't know
4. work
5. chores around the house
6. movies
7. other TV programs
8. outdoor activities
9. music
10. exercise

If your answer matched the most frequent response in the national survey, you mentioned that you'd spend more time reading. So this week select one two-hour time period that you had penciled in for sports-watching and spend that time reading instead. No, *Sports Illustrated* won't count for this exercise. Nor will your *Dallas Cowboys Weekly,* or the latest book about the Yankees' World Series championship. Use the time to start a novel, or a nonfiction book about history or travel or movies. It can be something you enjoy reading already, or you can take this opportunity to browse through your bookstore or library and select something in a new area that draws your interest or curiosity.

Similarly, if you answered "hiking" in response to Question #59, take an extra two-hour hiking break this week—or go to a movie, or listen to music, or exercise, or catch up on household chores, or whatever you mentioned. If you responded that you'd spend more time with your spouse or partner, by all means include her in this two-hour break. Just be sure you select the two hours from time you actually would have spent with sports. Yes, you can exclude your team's big game from consideration, but be honest about finding a time you really *wanted* to devote to sports so that you make the exercise meaningful.

As many sports fans have learned during pro sports strikes, it can be amazing what you find yourself doing during time you'd normally devote to sports, and how easily you can live without sports—at least for the length of time of an average basketball game. You may begin to see that you really have been missing out on something valuable during all those hours holed up with sports! After taking your two-hour break from sports, use your playbook to write down what you did, how it went, and any new ideas for the next time you try this exercise.

Now, close your Sportsaholism Recovery Playbook. You deserve a breather!

## Furthering the Process of Discovery

Way back in the introduction to this book, I invited you along on a process of discovery. I suggested that you look upon the Sportsaholism Questionnaire, the stories that emerged from the national survey, and all the playbook exercises as the means to explore the role of sports in your life along with the woman who may be reading this with you. By now, you've probably made lots of discoveries. Some you may feel you could have done without.

You may also feel that some of these exercises caused you to overanalyze your life situation. Maybe you decided not to try them all right now. That's fine. Not all the exercises are right for every person who lives with sports. You may find that three or four work best for you—in which case, stick with them until you feel comfortable moving on. You'll know what's right. But if you find yourself dismissing overanalysis again and again, try to remember this: When you immerse yourself in the rules, strategies, statistics, and debates about sports, you're overanalyzing sports. Or, at least, that's how women view you.

And yet, it really may be simple for you to make new agreements about sports, to steer them more into balance in your day-to-day life. In relationships, you may find it's natural to take the sharp focus and unbridled emotions you display as a sports fan and bring them into your relationship with a woman. You may see how you can still enjoy the world of sports *and* appreciate and engage more in her world, and the real world around you.

When you cut down your sports time even just a little, as you did in the last exercise, you may find you're becoming more curious, more attentive, and more interested in new ideas, subjects, and people. Without needing to break your sports habit, letting go a little can open up new perspectives for you and give you a new lens through which to look at what's around you. You may see that you're now putting more energy into your own life goals than riding with your team's goals. You may even notice that you're comfortable expressing yourself emotionally without using sports as an excuse, and you don't get quite so angry and distraught when your team loses.

**SURVEY RESULT: If you spent less time with sports, what would you gain?**

1. knowledge of other things in life/balance
2. nothing
3. time with spouse/family
4. more money
5. don't know
6. free time
7. better home maintenance
8. boredom
9. advancement at work
10. more sleep

In reading this book, you've shown a great deal of patience and openness in looking more closely at the role of sports in your life. Whether you've been making this journey by your own initiative or whether a woman urged you to come along, you've displayed the heart and guts of a quarterback standing firm in the pocket against an all-out blitz. You've hung in there. You've faced some very tough questions about your love of sports and your life's priorities. And you have the answers that are right for you.

This isn't time to take another exercise. It's not even time for another man-woman talk. We'll be doing that a few last times in the next chapter. This may simply be a good opportunity to sit back and allow your true answers, your own direction, to come to you. Sometimes, you don't have to *do* anything.

Even people who have wrestled with serious physical addictions, such as alcoholism, often say that it wasn't necessarily the support of a twelve-step recovery program or a brush with death while drunk or stoned that got their lives moving in a new direction. Sometimes it's something much simpler, with no clear explanation or motivation behind it. There may come a moment where you find yourself thinking, It's time to make some changes, and I'm going to do it. I'm not kidding myself, either. I *know*.

And change really happens.

# THIRTEEN

# Tuning Out Sports, Tuning In to *Her*

> *If he spent less time with sports, our relationship would be
> better. We would have a lot more time to spend together,
> time to get to know each other much better.*
>
> —Joanne, a woman involved with a sportsaholic in Vine
> Grove, Kentucky

That's the wish, isn't it? As a woman living with a sportsaholic, you
imagine him clicking off the remote just as a good game begins,
turning to you, and declaring once and for all, "OK, honey, that's
it. I've been wrapped up in sports for too long. Let's start doing
more things together. I want to get to know *you.*"

It could happen that way, especially if he's been doing his own
thinking about how much he's missing out on while he's wedged
behind the great wall of sports. But, as you probably realize better
than anyone, such a dramatic change is not likely to happen—
even if it did, it might be scary coming all at once. As one woman
in the national survey put it, "If he suddenly stopped spending
most of his time with sports, I'd have to entertain him all the time.
I don't know if I could handle the pressure."

For a typical sportsaholic, weaning himself off his sports obsession is a gradual process of tuning in to sports a little less, and
tuning in to you and the rest of his life a little more. And he's not
going to take this on all by himself in the corner, either. You
should expect to keep playing an active role, as you have been in
reading this book and doing the exercises in the Sportsaholism

Recovery Playbook. Change, you'll remember, seldom occurs in a vacuum. As the woman involved seeking change together with him, here are several points to keep in mind about what it will take on your end.

First, remember this: *Men are not the enemy!* When we explore how women and men act and see things differently, it's easy to get stuck at the point of focusing on differences. We look at each other as polar opposites and say, "That's the way men are," or, "That's the way women are." This black-or-white message is pervasive in our culture, especially in movies and on TV. Men and women characters poke fun at each other, get exasperated, move further apart, then reluctantly conclude that the best you can hope for is to make do with them as they are.

But this perspective tends to keep us in our corners, and doesn't account for our commonality. Though we may act differently, men and women want many of the same things: love, respect, understanding, fulfillment, enjoyment. And when we look more closely at the world around us, we see signs of significant changes in the ways of the sexes. Look at how powerful and invaluable women have shown themselves to be in the workplace, and how much more nurturing men have become with their children at home. We may not be as stuck as it sometimes appears.

We can use our differences to learn from each other—not to be *like* the other but to become more balanced and whole in who we are as men or women. With sports, when women let go of seeing men as the enemy and regard them more as allies, men become open to learning more of what women know from their unique experiences and life choices. And it works both ways. As a woman, you may learn a few things from the example of how he acts around sports that will help you become more balanced in your own life. Sure, he may look silly to you sometimes. But might there be places in your life where you'd benefit from showing as much passion toward some interest or hobby? Couldn't you learn from his sports behavior how to let go and get a little wild and uninhibited at times?

Also, when you see him more as your ally than your enemy, you'll have more room to validate what you *do* like and appreciate about him. Even for a man who loves sports to an extreme, being a sportsaholic is seldom the full definition of who he is or how he relates to you. Don't forget to remind him of what you like and appreciate. Helen still finds a great deal to appreciate in her husband, Scott, the Washington-area sportsaholic with the hundred-hour weekly sports habit we visited in Chapter 5. He does all the food shopping, laundry, vacuuming, and even cooks. He helps their two daughters with their homework. And when Helen chose to get a graduate degree to pursue her career as an accountant, she found Scott fully supportive. Helen's women friends have been duly impressed by Scott's household contributions. Helen explains, "They ask me if I can clone him."

So even if he's got the game on in the background or on his headset as he does the chores, if he's helping out, it's a good idea to let him know it. Here are some other useful reminders of what to focus on as you relate to a sportsaholic:

### *Clarity*

Continue to tell him what you want in your relationship in direct, specific terms. A request just to spend more time together is vague, and there's no standard by which to measure whether or not he's honored it. Choose a specific goal. If you want to spend all day and night together either Saturday or Sunday every weekend, that's what you should ask for.

To help communicate clearly what it is that you want, review your answer to Question #24 in the Women Who Know a Sportsaholic Survey, **"If the role of sports in your relationship with him *did* change, what is the one way that you would most clearly see the difference?"** Share your answer with him again, so that he understands exactly what you're looking for, and how you both will know when it's happened. If your answer to this question was not specific enough when you first wrote it, sharpen it now.

Also, anytime you have a complaint about how you feel hurt, let down, or left out because of sports, let him know about it in specific terms. Avoid generalizing. *Don't* say: "You never help out around the house because you're always watching sports." *Do* say: "I spent five hours cleaning the house this weekend while you watched sports. Next weekend, I need you to clean the house while I go out with friends." If he refused to give up a big game to join you at your friend's wedding, don't say: "You never give up sports to do anything with me." Do say: "I really missed you at this wedding and really would have appreciated you going with me."

### Persistence

Many women in the national survey admitted that they stopped trying to share their feelings about the excessive role of sports in their relationships because he just got angry, defensive, or simply ignored her. Yet half the women taking the survey said that if he spent less time with sports, they believed that their relationship would significantly improve! If you give up going after what you want, nothing's apt to change. And you'd end up feeling pretty miserable much of the time.

It's hard, I know. It may seem that he doesn't want to listen to you, and that the media's got the deck stacked against you with its sports bombardment and their glorification of sports. It's frustrating, too, because in the words of Judy, whose wish to see sports banned from TV opened Chapter 5, "It's not as much of a man's world out there as it used to be. Some things are changing. But it's still a man's world in *sports*, where nothing changes." But your voice can be heard if you keep speaking it. And the stronger your message becomes, the more other women and couples will want to join in with you.

### Respect

When you bring up what you don't like about sports and the degree of your sportsaholic's obsession, you need to do so with respect. You don't want to come to him with anger, blame, judgment, or criticism. You want to show that you respect his feelings and his desires. By treating him with respect, you're also demonstrating that you respect yourself and what *you* feel, want, and need. Remember to approach him when the game is off, not when it's on. The goal is communication, not confrontation.

## *Understanding*

For you to play an active part in changing the role of sports in your household, you need to keep expanding your understanding of the terrain. You need to know as much as you can about why he loves sports so much, how they work for him, and how strong a hold sportsaholism really has on him. If you read Part III carefully and have done many of the exercises with him, you should have a better understanding already. But keep your eyes, ears, and heart open for more clues, so that you'll know what you're dealing with and can make sense of his response. Keep asking him to help you understand!

Recognize, too, that real change in the role of sports in his life is likely to emerge more from changes in his *attitude* than from anything he does. He has to believe that sportsaholism has a hold on him, and that he wants to begin to break free. Again, it may be a gradual process. As you continue to tell him about the change you wish to see, he may also find it helpful to reread sections of this book for reminders of sportsaholism's damaging effects on relationships, and how other guys have forged a new way. Give him room to do that.

It's also important to remember that if he begins to let go of sports, he's going to experience real withdrawal symptoms. This is no joke. He has a powerful craving for that drama, the drug of sports. Remember, that drama is intense, clear-cut, exciting, and never-ending. Changing the role of sports in his life is not simply a matter of reducing the time he spends with them. At some point he's going to be searching for a substitute, something else to satisfy his craving.

Your understanding can help him see how simple, day-to-day life and intimacy offer a different kind of drama. It just takes more time to discover. Try to devote some of your free time together doing fun and exciting things, so he can get some of that rush he's been getting vicariously from sports. And yes, no matter what you do together, he may still feel sometimes that it pales in comparison to sports. Don't get discouraged. You're not aiming for a quick, overwhelming victory. You're in this for the long haul.

If he's trying, let him have his moments of frustration along the way and try to understand their origins.

### Flexibility

Keep in mind that he believes he's demonstrating heroic flexibility in trying not to obsess over sports. He's looking for comparable flexibility on your part, and the more you can respond, the better off you'll both be. Sometimes that flexibility may take the form of compromise over new agreements related to his sports time. You ask for one sports-free weekend every month and no more Fantasy Leagues. He may be more willing to sign on to dropping three of his four Fantasy Leagues and spending one sports-free weekend every month except January.

You may be surprised to learn that there's a greater gift of flexibility you can offer your sportsaholic, which will demonstrate your clear commitment to meet him halfway in this effort you're making together. I'm referring to sports talk—and your willingness to play with it. You may be as tired of hearing sports metaphors here in this book as you are when you encounter them at home, at work, and in the media. But he's stretching already, so you need to stretch, too, and if you make the effort to talk a language he understands, he may be able to hear you more clearly and communicate more accurately.

More important, he'll become a better listener, particularly when you speak about other matters that are critical to you. Agreeing to use sports metaphors does not mean you are giving yourself over to sports, or letting him win while you lose. Think of it more as a temporary building bridge between your two worlds.

## PLAY #16:
## DAILY CHECK-INS, *SPORTSCENTER* STYLE

Here's an exercise for the Sportsaholism Recovery Playbook, where a woman can display her flexibility and you both can perform a few sports-related antics. It can also be a lot of fun!

As anyone in a sportsaholic household knows, ESPN's *SportsCenter* begins with a light, snappy, theme-oriented preview of what will follow on the program. It may include snippets of great plays, but the emphasis is on those silly little things people in sports do, say, or look like. The goal is to make us laugh, relax, and welcome the sports-news report to follow.

As a couple, try the same format for your check-ins when you first greet each other after time apart. Take turns on alternate days. Begin your check-in with a snappy opening pegged along a common theme. So when he comes home, she may act out an opening like this:

"Ever have one of those days when everything seemed a little upside down [holds portable phone bottom side up]? A day when what's down is up [lifts up rug and places on top of cabinet], and what's up is down [takes picture hanging over bed and places it underneath bed]? A day when nothing seemed to stick [pulls off refrigerator magnet and drops on floor] and the light refused to shine [drapes a dark sheet over lamp shade]? Well, sit down and get comfortable as you prepare for *Cindy's Center,* next . . ."

Of course, you wouldn't use this format when something serious happens. But on those run-of-the-mill days of routine work and minor annoyances, this exercise can liven things up and tap into your creativity. The memory of his check-in yesterday can make today look brighter, and the fun you have can inspire you to find other new ways of enjoying each other's company.

You're not apt to do this exercise often. But a woman who's willing to try it once in a while as a lark shows that she's not making a demon of sports. Here's one more characteristic to remember as you pursue your goals of improving your relationship:

## *Openness*

If the sportsaholic in your life has been reading this book with you, or at least sharing much of it, he's been opening himself to some new and tough places. He's been more vulnerable with you, and since most men didn't get adequate training in how to reveal themselves, he's out on the edge of his learning (a growing edge) and apt to be going even further out in the months ahead.

In seeking greater intimacy together, you as the woman also need to be willing to open to new places in yourself. You're challenged to become more open about your own life—your hopes and dreams, your obsessions, your walls. Consider the word *intimacy* for a moment by breaking down the different parts you hear in the word:

*Intimacy* = *"Into me, see."*

In other words, in a growing intimate relationship he's allowing you to see into more of him, and you're allowing him to see into more of you. Women make a mistake when they criticize any man as being emotionally closed and unavailable, then believe the only way to change that is to change *him*. A woman stands a better chance of succeeding when she agrees to a goal of both parties changing and becoming more open about themselves, with each person supporting and encouraging the other along at their own comfortable pace.

You may assume that as a woman you're much more open about yourself than the sportsaholic in your life is about himself. But while he's actively trying to reveal more of his thoughts and feelings, it will help if *you* do some of the same exercises yourself, so he can see how things look in your life. Toward this goal of greater openness on your part, turn back to a couple of the exercises that he's already taken on in the Sportsaholism Recovery Playbook in Part III.

## A New Spin for the Playbook

Look back at Play #9 in Chapter 9, when he shared the story of the first sporting event he ever attended as a boy. Think about a comparable first-time experience you had as a girl. What childhood event left a lasting impression on you? Was it your first kiss? Your first time riding a bicycle? Your first memorable teacher? Your first role in a school play?

Once you've decided what first-time moment you want to share, invite the sportsaholic in your life to ask you some of the same questions you asked him about his first sporting event. Bring back all the details as vividly as possible, and share your real feelings from that period of your life and how you look at it today. This will help him understand what shaped you early in life, just as you understand better how his sports initiation shaped him.

Next, look at Play #11 ("Comparing Sports to Life") in Chapter 10, where your sportsaholic listed the Top Five highs and lows in his experience as a sports fan—the Yankees winning the World Series, etc.—with separate Top Five lists of the highs and lows in his personal life outside of sports. Unless you consider yourself a big sports fan, you won't get much from the first part of this exercise. But you can certainly take on the second part. So go ahead and list the Top Five thrills or high moments, and the Top Five disappointments or low points of *your* personal life. Then share your lists with him.

You may come up with something that he didn't even know about. But even if he's heard these stories before, you can present them now in a new context and help him see more of what's influenced you. You'll be sharing something that puts you on equal footing. Not only that, but reliving wonderful moments and painful times may also add a little perspective to your old arguments over sports.

For example, if a few of your Top Five highs in life involve shared moments with your sportsaholic, you may remember that his sports time has not ruined *all* your opportunities for intimacy. And when he hears you pay tribute to a special moment in your relationship when sports were not part of the scenery, he may be motivated to pursue more of those times with you. On the flip side, if your life's lowest moments include a serious illness or injury, you may see his sports obsession in a broader context, where it doesn't seem quite as serious.

Both of your perspectives are broadening by now. These next few exercises for the playbook will help you understand one another further, and guide you to a common wavelength.

## PLAY #17: WOMAN AS TEACHER

This exercise is especially useful for any woman who has ever played the role of pupil to her man as sports teacher, or a woman who intends to take a few sports lessons from him to show her flexibility. For this exercise, you and the sportsaholic in your life agree to one specific area of study that you, as the woman, can teach him. It should be something you know well from your own experience, and that you would enjoy teaching. For the man, it needs to be something that he feels willing to take on and practice himself.

Maybe you'll agree on cooking, gardening, learning a foreign language, reading mystery novels, or unraveling the inner workings of the PTA in your child's school. Perhaps it will be something related to your job—points about the law or accounting that he's never grasped. Once you've agreed on the subject to teach, set aside regular time for lessons.

You may want to structure your lessons to correspond to the amount of time he plays sports teacher. Give yourselves room to play and have fun. Maybe he'll enjoy learning from you how to cook ethnic dishes. Or you both may laugh when he gets mixed up trying to learn the names of the different plants and flowers in your garden, just as she could never remember all the names in the Baltimore Orioles' starting lineup.

You can discover again how you both have much to learn from each other, and alternating the role of teacher and pupil brings more balance and harmony to your relationship. You may even decide to expand on it. If he has another major interest outside of sports that he's willing to teach you (and you're willing to learn), you can experiment with assuming the role of pupil in that realm. Maybe you're game to learn how to play the guitar. He might teach you enough so you can play yourself. Then you might give him lessons on how to draw, sculpt, or paint.

We learn from each other in the natural course of sharing life's simple activities and responsibilities. But when sportsaholism is involved, we can get stuck in those polarized positions in which he knows everything about sports, and she knows very little. And because his time is so consumed by sports, he has little opportunity or desire to learn much about her interests and endeavors. If she begins to learn a little about sports, it places him in a one-up role that can remain unbalanced in the relationship. By making it a point to swap the teacher/pupil role, you're both recognized as experts.

## PLAY #18: FINE-TUNING YOUR NEW SPORTS PICTURE

Even as he's making changes in his sports habits and attitudes, you know he's still going to watch *some* sports. But you may find that fiddling around with the *way* he watches sports can satisfy some of your desire for greater intimacy. Here are two suggestions:

**Silent telecasts**—Some women say that if he agrees to watch the game with just the picture on but the sound turned all the way down, she can join him in the room and appreciate his company, while she reads, does a crossword puzzle, or knits. Without the hype of the sportscasters and the reaction of the crowd at the stadium as stimuli, he may not get as emotional about the game. There may be room for conversation during lulls in the action. Many discriminating sportsaholics turn the sound down sometimes, anyway, when they can't stomach a certain sportscaster. So agreeing to a silent telecast for the purpose of enhanced intimacy is not an unreasonable expectation.

**Postgame cooldown**—After reading this book, he's going to be approaching sports with a more levelheaded perspective—sometimes. But when he does still get worked up in the aftermath of a tense game, you know how difficult he can be to talk to or just be around. Maybe he wants to talk about all the big plays, critique every controversial call by the officials—or maybe he doesn't want to talk at all. Scheduling a ten-minute cooldown period after the game can help you both avoid that familiar collision.

During those ten minutes, your role as the woman is simply to let him be. Even if you're upset about the time he's frittered away or the ranting and raving you heard from him in the past three hours, give him this space to unwind. You know that his emotions over the game do not end when the final whistle blows, so allowing a postgame cooldown simply signals that you're going with it, not against it.

As the sports fan, your role during the cooldown is to experience your full response to whatever happened. Your hopeless Jets blow another one? Get angry, curse, assess blame, bemoan your fate in riding with them. But do it for five minutes, then start letting it go. Then spend the next five minutes focusing on what's ahead in the rest of your day or night. Do some prep work for time with your wife, or dinner, or whatever it is, just as you prepared yourself for the game. And recognize that in a few minutes, you'll be called upon to step fully into those events, with the same focused attention and energy you devoted to the game.

## PLAY #19:
## CULTIVATING NONSPORTS FRIENDSHIPS

Between games, here's another suggestion for expanding the framework of intimacy: If you've followed a pattern typical of most sportsaholic households, you socialize with other couples *only* if the other man is another sports lover. Your man may say that he gets bored or uncomfortable spending an entire evening in which sports not only are off the TV but off the conversation table. So he agrees to go out with other couples only if he knows he can hang out with the other guy watching or talking about the Cowboys and the 49ers.

By now, you're ready to branch out. Seek out a couple you've recently met through work, church, or maybe that new shared activity you took up together from Play #8 of the Sportsaholism Recovery Playbook in Chapter 6. Only make sure neither the man nor woman in this new couple follows sports. Get together with them for dinner, a movie, a hike, or anything else not involving sports that all four of you agree on. When you're with the other couple, ask them about their main interests in their lives and what they enjoy together. How do they fill up all their hours without sports? Inquire about why they enjoy their particular passions—and, just out of curiosity, check out their attitudes toward sports.

You both might find this a revealing and refreshing experience. And if the two guys hit it off, the sportsaholic in your life may form a nonsports-based male friendship, which is a critical component of life beyond sports.

## PLAY #20:
## IS HE READY FOR THE ULTIMATE CHALLENGE?

As we know, men like a challenge. By now, you or the sportsaholic in your life may be ready for the ultimate challenge concerning sports. No, I don't mean giving them up entirely, though if your man is one of the few whose life is leading him in that direction, there's no need to discourage him. More likely, an ultimate challenge by his definition might take the form of a voluntary three-week sports blackout. Or maybe he'll agree to watch only his two or three main teams all year, and not spend any time on all those "filler" games that get hyped up by TV and quickly balloon a four-hour weekly diversion into a twenty-hour sports obsession. Maybe he'll agree that he can live without Fantasy Leagues and sports-talk radio. Or he'll commit to limiting his weekend sports consumption to one game on either Saturday or Sunday, or his total hours devoted to sports from twenty hours per week to ten.

Take a moment to discuss the ultimate challenge he wants to take on. Write it down in specific terms in your Sportsaholism Recovery Playbook. Decide when he's going to put himself to this new test.

But if you're the guy all revved up about trying this ultimate challenge to prove how tough you are, or how willing you are to sacrifice for her, be careful about changing too much too fast. Do it on a short-term, experimental basis. If you wind up feeling a bit lost or resentful, be ready to compromise on a new agreement. Don't forget, it's an addiction!

## Forging Your Way As Pioneers

That's the final exercise for the playbook. If you've been doing several of the exercises as a couple, take a moment to stop and simply appreciate each other for what you've done. You've taken some important steps toward establishing a more cooperative relationship with sports in your lives!

This is a great opportunity for each of you to give the other person three specific expressions of appreciation about something you learned or saw in them while reading this book together. Maybe he appreciates how she listened to him tell the story of his first game as a boy. Maybe she appreciates how he took the results from his Sports Time Log and immediately cut his sports consumption by 25 percent. Appreciations of any kind can play a powerful role in building intimacy. After reading this book, those appreciations relating to the compromises you've made around sports become even more special.

You also should take credit for what you're giving to others. You two are true pioneers! In doing these exercises, and throughout your exploration into the role of sports in your relationship, you're covering new ground. You're taking the lead on the trail to a broader understanding between women and men.

Think of the books you've seen and the discussions you've

heard about the differences between the genders, and how to handle them while living together. How many times do you see sportsaholism addressed as part of the picture? Probably never, except maybe in one of those passing jokes about football widows or in a TV episode of *Men Behaving Badly*. By agreeing to take a real look at the impact of sportsaholism in your household, you're following a path of discovery that will prompt others to want to learn from you. So you're not only teachers to each other, you're teachers to other couples facing the same frustrations over how to deal with Sports Glut USA.

Thousands of couples want to know how to talk more openly, and what to do, when sports come between them. They want to make sense of their different attitudes and perspectives and find some common ground. You're finding those keys for yourselves now. You may also discover a bonus—*as you learn how to talk openly about sports, you open the door to be able to talk about anything!* Any other difference or stuck point now becomes easier to see and face. You're cracking the code of how to relate more fully and openly as men and women. You're also providing examples of how to move beyond those socialized gender roles.

As women, you can show that sports need not be a private man's world that women simply can't enter. You can help break down the gender barrier with men simply through your genuine understanding of his obsession with sports. And the compassion toward him you practice along the way will be something you can call upon as you seek new changes and challenges together.

As a woman socialized to stifle your needs, you can develop greater assertiveness through this exploration into sports. You are challenged to claim your own passionate interests in life. You're learning to communicate more directly with him about what you want in your relationship. You're speaking up where other women may be stewing in silence.

As a man, you can practice empathy and improved listening skills as you tune in to her frustration about missing you. As you learn to become more open and emotionally expressive in your relationship, you can show that it's OK for men to focus on how they feel, even when the game's not on. And you can both challenge those old stereotypes that say, "Men watch the game, women shop and cook." You're both discovering that each person can take on several roles, many ways of being. It doesn't have to be the way it's always been.

As pioneers, you also know that there's no one way to go in seeking new directions. As a woman living with a sportsaholic, you may find that as you better understand how and why he loves sports so much—and he becomes better able to express his feelings, listen to you, and make changes—the actual amount of time he spends with sports may not matter so much. You may recognize that you're developing a more loving relationship and a deeper commitment to each other. Many of your most important goals may already have been met!

Or perhaps you can acknowledge that he's at least made a start. One woman in the national survey told me she didn't even think her boyfriend would want to participate, but after he filled out the questionnaire she expressed how happy she was that he considered how sports impact his life and the lives of people who love him.

But for millions of other women fed up with the effects of living in Sports Glut USA, small compromises and piecemeal efforts simply don't get to the heart of the matter. She wants the sportsaholic in her life to make substantive changes. She wants him *really* to understand how completely sports consume him, how sports have become a substitute life and love for him, how much she misses him. She hopes he can take what he's learning and use it to set new life intentions and new priorities—to embark on a new direction.

If this perspective describes how you look at your sportsaholic, take heart. Even if he wouldn't read this book with you right now, he may be like many of the men I've talked to through my national survey—men who do feel strongly that sportsaholism gets in the way of greater intimacy and a more well-rounded lifestyle, even if they may not have found a way to let the women in their lives know about it. I'll offer one final illustration, from a caller on a sports-talk show on KKAR radio in Omaha, Nebraska.

"I was on vacation with my wife in South Dakota," the caller began. "We spent a night in a cabin in the woods. When we woke up, we could see that it was a beautiful morning. We could see deer and other animals right near the cabin. My wife wanted to stay there all day and walk in the woods. But I remembered that it was Saturday, and Nebraska's football game was on TV.

"I convinced her to leave early. I told her that I wouldn't go somewhere to see the game on TV, I'd just listen to part of it on radio while we were driving, so she could still enjoy the scenery. But I felt bad about doing that. I really felt sick all day. As it turned out, I couldn't even get the game on radio. Even so, I knew I was betraying my wife and the spirit of our vacation. That's not how I want to be."

Many men really aren't content with the way things are. They do want to change. They do ache for greater intimacy. Many men today say they measure their success in life much more by how well they do as husbands and fathers than by how much money they make. With sports, as in relationships, men who draw the old gender lines are increasingly out of step with our changing environment. To say that men can watch sports anytime they want and women will just have to make do—that's an old line that now sounds harsh and extreme not just to women. Many *men* feel the same way.

As a man changes his attitude toward sports and their place in his life, he can learn much from the woman who loves him. She can offer support and encouragement, understanding and acceptance. By speaking to what she likes and wants, and how much she values his time and presence, she can serve as a reminder of what else may await him as he begins to tune out sports. She can work with him in cultivating a relationship in which he no longer needs to say:

"Not now, honey, I'm watching the game."

# IN CLOSING

I offer my support and encouragement as you continue your challenging journey of recovery from sportsaholism. Keep me posted on how it's going! Let me know what you're learning and experiencing as you seek new directions in living with sports. Send your notes or letters to:

*Sportsaholism Recovery Circle*
*P.O. Box 4782*
*Charlottesville, VA 22905*

# BIBLIOGRAPHY

Andelman, Bob. *Why Men Watch Football.* Lafayette, Louisiana: Acadian House, 1993.

Beckwith, Sandra L. *Why Can't a Man Be More Like a Woman?* New York: Kensington Publishing Corp., 1995.

Coakley, Jay, Ph.D. *Sports in Society: Issues and Controversies.* St. Louis: Times Mirror/Mosby, 1986.

Eitzen, D. Stanley and George H. Sage. *Sociology of North American Sport,* 5th ed. Dubuque, Iowa: Wm. C. Brown Communications, 1993.

Eitzen, D. Stanley. *Sport in Contemporary Society: An Anthology.* New York: St. Martin's Press, 1984.

Glass, Lillian. *He Says, She Says: Closing the Communication Gap Between the Sexes.* New York: G. P. Putnam's Sons, 1992.

Goldstein, Jeffrey H., ed. *Sports, Games, and Play: Social and Psychological Viewpoints.* Hillsdale, N.J.: Lawrence Erlbaum Associates, 1989.

Gray, John, Ph.D. *Men Are from Mars, Women Are from Venus: A Practical Guide for Improving Communication and Getting What You Want in Relationships.* New York: HarperCollins, 1992.

Guttmann, Allen. *Sports Spectators.* New York: Columbia University Press, 1986.

Hendricks, Gay, Ph.D., and Kathlyn Hendricks, Ph.D. *Conscious Loving: The Journey to Co-Commitment.* New York: Bantam, 1990.

Hendrix, Harville, Ph.D. *Keeping the Love You Find: A Personal Guide.* New York: Pocket Books, 1992.

May, Gerald G., M.D. *Addiction & Grace: Love and Spirituality in the Healing of Addictions.* New York: HarperCollins, 1988.

Messner, Michael A., Ph.D., and Donald F. Sabo, Ph.D., eds. *Sport, Men, and the Gender Order: Critical Feminist Perspectives.* Champaign, Ill.: Human Kinetics, 1990.

Mooney, Al J., M.D., et al. *The Recovery Book.* New York: Workman, 1992.

Nelson, Mariah Burton. *The Stronger Women Get, the More Men Love Football: Sexism and the American Culture of Sports*. New York: Avon Books, 1994.

Phelps, Janice Keller, M.D., and Alan E. Nourse, M.D. *The Hidden Addiction and How to Get Free: Recognizing and Breaking the Habits That Control Your Life*. Boston: Little, Brown, 1986.

Roberts, Michael. *Fans! How We Go Crazy Over Sports*. Washington, D.C.: The New Republic Book Co., 1976.

Schaef, Anne Wilson. *When Society Becomes an Addict*. New York: HarperCollins, 1987.

Scher, Barbara, with Barbara Smith. *I Could Do Anything If I Only Knew What It Was: How to Discover What You Really Want and How to Get It*. New York: Dell, 1994.

Small, Jacquelyn. *Transformers: The Therapists of the Future. Personal Transformation: The Way Through*. Marina del Ray, Cal.: DeVorss & Company, 1982.

Welwood, John, Ph.D. *Journey of the Heart: Intimate Relationship and the Path of Love*. New York: HarperCollins, 1990.

# INDEX